C000226565

Broken Ra

Christian Wolmar is a writer and broadcaster specialising in transport and other social policy issues. He writes a fortnightly column in *Rail* magazine and contributes regularly to a wide variety of other publications, including the *Independent*, the *Independent on Sunday*, the *Evening Standard*, the *New Statesman* and *Public Finance*. He also appears regularly on both television and radio and has a weekly spot on LBC.

His books include *The Great British Railway Disaster*, *Stagecoach* and, most recently, *Forgotten Children*, an investigation into the abuse scandals in children's homes, which was published by Vision in 2000.

Broken Rails

HOW PRIVATISATION WRECKED
BRITAIN'S RAILWAYS

CHRISTIAN WOLMAR

AURUM PRESS

First published 2001 by Aurum Press Limited,
25 Bedford Avenue, London WC1B 3AT

Copyright © 2001 by Christian Wolmar

The moral right of Christian Wolmar to be identified as the author
of this work has been asserted by him in accordance with the
Copyright Designs and Patents Act 1988.

All rights reserved.
No part of this book may be reproduced or utilised in form
or by any means, electronic or mechanical, including photocopying,
recording or by any information storage and retrieval system without
permission in writing from Aurum Press Ltd.

A catalogue record for this book
is available from the British Library.

ISBN 1 85410 823 9

Designed by Geoff Green Book Design
Typeset in Stone Print
by M Rules
Printed and bound in Great Britain
by MPG Books Ltd, Bodmin

Contents

To Scarlett MccGwire for all her support and love

Acknowledgements

There are far more anonymous quotes in this book than I would have liked. The railway is a paranoid industry. It is a reflection of the fact that few people, even those still working in it, believe that the current structure is viable that they are prepared to talk about it so frankly off the record. It is quite common for them to agree wholeheartedly with what I say in my regular column in *Rail* magazine, but then argue the opposite point publicly. As the early Gay Liberationists used to say, 'It is time to come out of the closet lads' (there are precious few lasses involved). The privatised railway is like the emperor with no clothes. If they all started arguing publicly for its reform, then they would get it. This is not to criticise the people who have helped anonymously to whom I owe my deepest thanks. Without them I would be as ignorant of the industry as many of the politicians and civil servants who have helped contribute to its unfortunate state.

Several people read the manuscript or parts of it. These include Jon Shaw, who has been extremely supportive and helped keep me going, and John Fowler, whose detailed knowledge of the railways prevented several mistakes, and several others who must remain anonymous, and I am deeply grateful for all their suggestions.

I am always struck by the enormous generosity of fellow writers and journalists who are always willing to share stories that they might have spent weeks or months digging out and their knowledge that has taken years to accumulate.

I would like to thank: Howard Johnston, who researched and helped draft chapters two and three; Nigel Harris, my editor at *Rail*, who gives me the space every two weeks to vent my prejudices and opinions and who is ever full of good ideas; Roger Ford, who knows far more about the railways than I ever will and is a real informed source; Juliette Jowit of the *Financial Times*, who always seems to have the exclusives; Barry Doe, who has unsurpassed knowledge of the timetable and train services; my fellow journalists at *Rail*, Pip Dunn, Phil Haigh, Lynne Best and Mel Holley, all of whom have been very helpful; Terry Gourvish, Stan Hall, John Ware, Richard Hope, Brendan Martin, Richard Macqueen and anyone else whom I may have forgotten.

I hesitate to mention anyone currently working in the rail industry, as they probably will not thank me for it, given the controversial nature of parts of this book. They know who they are and I hope they feel this book will help bring about an improvement to Britain's railways. However, the following bear absolutely no responsibility for any views expressed in this book but have been kind enough to help me: Alan Nichols, Professor Roderick Smith, Richard Malins, Adrian Shooter, Chris Garnett, Chris Green, Malcolm Tunley, David Smith, Tony Berkeley, Peter Rayner, Donal McCabe at Railtrack, Jay Merritt at ATOC, Alan Bevan of Rail-future, M A Mc, and, many, many more.

My agent, Andrew Lownie, has been extremely supportive and I would like to thank the people at Aurum Press for rescuing this project so quickly.

Thanks, most of all, to my wonderful family – Scarlett, Molly, Pascoe and Misha – for putting up with my obsessions.

CHAPTER 1

The man who stopped the trains

Disasters always have their roots in trivial incidents. In March 2000, when wagons carrying new rails to replace a cracked section of track arrived at the site near Hatfield, the workers on the line found they could not unload them because it was the wrong type of train. They would have had to turn off the overhead line electrification, a process that would have taken too long and caused a delay to the reopening of the line. So the new rails went back to the depot and the cracked rail remained in place with dozens of trains thundering over the faulty section of track at 115mph every day. Three more attempts to deliver the rails were made and, when they eventually arrived, it was too late because the busy summer timetable did not allow for the lengthy line closure such a major job required. So, for a further six months the line was left unrepaired until, on 17 October 2000, it gave up the ghost. As the 12.10 London to Leeds express passed over the damaged rail, it shattered into 300 pieces causing seven of the nine coaches to jump off the tracks. Most seriously, the buffet car smashed into a stanchion holding the overhead wiring and four of its occupants were killed.

In the long history of rail disasters Hatfield was a relatively minor accident. Certainly, four people were killed, but further up the A1 in Yorkshire six people were killed in a road crash three weeks later and there was barely a mention in the national press. But the incident on 17 October 2000 will be remembered in the annals of transport and, indeed, political, history for much longer than many other, far more deadly, disasters. It was the accident which nearly brought Britain's railways to a halt and, even more important, exposed the, quite literally, disastrous way in which they had been privatised. The two other major accidents after privatisation, Southall and Ladbroke Grove, had been more serious in terms of loss of life but it is Hatfield that will be remembered as a watershed for the railways. After Hatfield, it was impossible for anyone, even the Tories, to defend what had been done to one of Britain's most vital industries in the name of liberalisation and competition.

In a neat irony, the way that Hatfield was allowed to wreck the railways mirrors the manner in which the system that allowed the disruption to occur was created – both were the result of hubris which led to vital decisions being taken by ill-informed people. Just as the railway system was carved up by politicians, abetted by some equally Thatcherite civil servants, none of whom had any in-depth knowledge of the industry, the decision which resulted in the imposition of hundreds of speed limits across the rail network was effectively taken by a man with just a few weeks' experience of working in the railways and with no engineering qualifications.

Jonson Cox is not a household name, but he will go on to be remembered in railway folklore as the man who stopped the trains. He had joined Railtrack in September 2000, just seven weeks before the Hatfield crash, as director of operations. The forty-three year old was a management high flyer who had previously been managing director of Kelda Group (formerly Yorkshire Water), having started his career with Shell, and he was to play an absolutely crucial role in turning a relatively minor accident on the railways into a disaster which crippled the industry, its finances and, ironically, his own company.

On the day of the Hatfield crash it quickly became apparent that a broken rail was the cause of the disaster. The events leading up to the accident are examined in depth in chapter 9; here we look at its consequences for the railway system as a whole. In the weeks following Hatfield the rail network suffered a catastrophic breakdown. Within a few days over a hundred 20mph speed restrictions were imposed at sites throughout the network and, one of the major routes, the West Coast Main Line, was even closed completely for a day. Months later, train services were still in a state of semi-paralysis, Railtrack had been brought to the verge of bankruptcy, train operators were drawing up £100m law suits, the prime minister was exasperated and the very structure of the railways was in question. All because of one relatively minor train crash.

The key question is whether Railtrack overreacted, causing unnecessary chaos to millions of travellers because of the company's lack of confidence in its own ability to handle the engineering task which was its basic function, or whether the network had so deteriorated that these extreme precautions were essential to preserve the life and limb of rail passengers. Either way – and the issue is considered below – Railtrack and the process of privatisation have a lot to answer for, but what is most extraordinary is that the decision to impose these speed restrictions should have landed in the lap of a man who had worked for the railways for just forty-eight days.

Cox had been brought in by Railtrack to help the chief executive, Gerald Corbett, who was struggling under the weight of running a diffi-cult company in the face of tremendous political, media and operational pressures. The structure of Railtrack was so badly designed that Corbett had twenty people reporting directly to him. Moreover, Corbett's job had been made more difficult because the chairman, Sir Philip Beck, who had been approximately tenth choice for the job when his prede-cessor, Bob Horton, departed in July 1999, was weak and ineffectual, giving no support to the executives. A search for a new chairman had proved fruitless and instead it was agreed to help Corbett 'from under-neath', as an insider put it. Cox had a reputation as a doer, a man who would make a difference, and Corbett gave him the role of director, operations even though Cox had never worked in the railway industry. His title was significant and misleading. The word 'operations' really referred to operating the company, as with the commonly used title 'chief operating officer' in American firms, but in the railways the oper-ating director is the executive who runs the railways, something Cox knew absolutely nothing about. And it was to prove his and his com-pany's undoing.

Under Railtrack's safety case – the vital strategy which outlines how the company manages risk – the director, operations was the person responsible for the overall safety of the railway. Somehow, no one in Rail-track had noticed that this key role was being given to a rookie. It was Corbett's worst mistake and one which ultimately cost him his job.

Within a few hours of the crash, speed restrictions, mostly of 20mph, were placed on eighty-one sites across the network. These were the parts of the network where there was evidence of gauge corner cracking and where, as at Hatfield, a decision had been taken to rerail, though this may have been scheduled for up to two years ahead. 'Gauge corner cracking' was the name given to the phenomenon which, it was assumed, had caused the Hatfield rail to break. The gauge corner is the top inner corner of the rail which is in contact with the wheel flange and it is subject to the most stress, as it must absorb lateral forces as well as bearing the weight of the train. At Hatfield these cracks had been spotted back in November 1999 but due to a series of blunders by Railtrack and its maintenance contractors, Balfour Beatty, the rail was not replaced. Moreover, this mistake was compounded by the failure to impose a speed restriction on the damaged stretch of rail. The absence of that single speed restriction was to lead to over a thousand being imposed around the network.

Although Railtrack had known about gauge corner cracking before Hatfield, the company lacked the engineering knowledge to understand how fast the cracks could propagate through a rail and even the extent of the phenomenon on the network. In the hasty privatisation of 1996/7, key railway skills such as engineering were lost as a result of the fragmentation of British Rail into nearly a hundred companies. Moreover, the company at the heart of the network, Railtrack, did not even have a register of its assets or their condition, a lacuna it inherited from BR, and, after fragmentation, it had no method of recording defects centrally.

Another remarkable result of the upheavals of privatisation is that Railtrack, a company whose primary function is supposed to be organising the maintenance of one of the nation's primary engineering resources, is largely run by people with no relevant technical background. There were just two engineers on the board, and the most senior, Richard Middleton, the commercial director, was responsible for dealing with the train operating companies and therefore not in a position to exercise influence over engineering decisions.

There was another gap in Railtrack's structure. The company did not have a research department or undertake any R&D. All of it was left to outsiders. Whereas BR had been one of the world leaders in railway research, that expertise was lost at privatisation when BR Research was effectively disbanded. A highly experienced engineer, responsible for many engineering research projects for the railways, describes what happened when he approached Railtrack soon after it took over from BR in 1994 and asked whether the new company would be needing his expertise: 'Get yourself a proper job. This is the real world now', he was told by a Railtrack executive. 'We will contact you if we need your services.'[1] That call would come after the Hatfield disaster.

Without in-house expertise, Railtrack was at the mercy of outside consultants who, as one insider put it, 'always have their own agenda, which is often to ensure that as much work as possible is needed'.[2] The real value of in-house researchers is not so much that they will make the key discovery that will save their company millions of pounds, but that they develop expertise in the field which is invaluable in a crisis. Railtrack, created at the height of the outsourcing craze of the mid-1990s, was supposed to be a 'lean and mean' organisation, pared to the bone, with as many functions as possible sub-contracted to outside 'experts' and it therefore had no access to impartial advisers. Instead, the Railtrack managers were at the mercy of consultants, many of whom had their own interests at heart and lacked the ability to assess the situation dispassionately.

Moreover, Railtrack had no idea of the extent of the problem with the track. Under the contracts set up at privatisation, it is the maintenance contractors who are supposed to be aware of the condition of the network. The contracts give Railtrack only a loose form of control and it is therefore hardly surprising that Hatfield caused panic among Railtrack's executives who lacked the knowledge to assess the situation with regards to gauge corner cracking on the rest of the network. They were feeling their way in the dark and they therefore became extremely cautious, terrified that there would be another, similar disaster. They did not even know where to look. Inspections of the hundreds of sites known to contractors to have evidence of gauge corner cracking were immediately ordered and, in the meantime, dozens of speed restrictions were imposed based on criteria drawn up by Railtrack's head of track, David Ventry. No one at that time seems to have realised that the cumulative effect of the restrictions would cripple the whole network.

Claiming that it cannot comment because of legal constraints, Railtrack has refused to explain precisely what happened in the next few days and the following account has, therefore, had to be pieced together from various industry sources. The man responsible for the track was Ventry and he reported to the head of asset management – there was no chief engineer – Andy Doherty. Formally, under the safety case, Ventry, a relatively junior manager, was responsible for preparing the guidelines for imposing speed restrictions but it was Cox who was responsible for endorsing or rejecting that advice. Cox as director, operations was put in charge of Operation Response, the team quickly set up to deal with the implications of the gauge corner cracking issue. Because Cox was new, Chris Leah, Railtrack's previous operations director, and John Curley, the performance director, both veteran career railwaymen, were in the group which met daily and conferred by conference call with the seven zone directors, all experienced railway managers. A senior engineer, Andrew McNaughton, at the time head of the Great Western zone, was quickly summoned to head office to help deal with the crisis. But it was Cox, as the senior manager, who had the final say on decisions.

The task of Operation Response was a difficult one. Was Hatfield a one-off or had rails begun deteriorating around the whole network to such an extent that further disasters were likely? There was little information to go on, given Railtrack's failure, in its six years of existence, to draw up an asset register, and the dispersal of information among the thirty main contractors.

Here Cox's lack of experience and his character came into play. Cox is an extremely ambitious man and 'arrogant' is a term that quickly comes up in any conversation about him. By all accounts he is a man who likes making decisions and is not given to self-doubt or easily influenced by his subordinates. Moreover, he had been scarred by the experience of Yorkshire Water and the drought of the mid-1990s. Although at the time he was working for a different part of the company, he saw at first-hand how a relatively minor problem could quickly degenerate into a PR disaster. The situation he faced was exacerbated by the tendency of John Prescott, the politician in charge of transport, to attack the industry in the aftermath of rail accidents, as he had done after the Ladbroke Grove accident the previous year.

Faced with the rail break, which was clearly his company's responsibility, Cox's number one priority was to ensure that it did not happen again. That would have been the PR disaster to end them all.

Given Cox's management style and his ignorance of railway engineering and the political context, it was inevitable that Cox and Operation Response would take a very cautious view, imposing speed restrictions across the network. Because of the dissipation of engineering knowledge, Cox and his team did not know that the decisions they were making would wreck the railway for several months and result in a cost to

Railtrack of well over £1bn, partly in compensation claims and partly in much unnecessary engineering work.

After the imposition of speed restrictions on the initial eighty-one sites, Ventry recommended that restrictions should also be placed on all other sections of tracks where there was evidence of gauge corner cracking. McNaughton argued that the restrictions should be at two-thirds of line speed, whereas Ventry suggested 20mph for all of them. The difference was crucial. There were several hundred sites involved and the imposition of 20mph limits on all of them would cause a virtual breakdown of the rail system. Over the weekend after the crash, Ventry prepared a memo recommending universal 20mph restrictions and Cox, stressing that there should be 'no risk', accepted the advice, despite the fact that McNaughton continued to argue for two-thirds of line speed.

At this stage the lack of Railtrack's in-house expert advisers was felt particularly acutely. Had there been some well-informed research staff, the probable result would have been the imposition of a few speed restrictions at the worst affected sites and a rapid increase in the rail replacement programme. Instead, there was panic that there would be further similar incidents. The Railtrack executives were particularly frightened by the fact that the rail had shattered into so many pieces. There was no Corporal Jones to say 'don't panic'. Although, in fact, the rail had probably disintegrated because the first break had occurred some time, possibly days, before the accident and the rest of the rail had been weakened by the cantilever effect of the trains going over it. As a result, when there was a second break on another part of the rail which had also been affected by cracks, the train, travelling at such a high speed, got caught up with sections of rail flying about and broke them up into hundreds of bits.

Cox was responsible for Railtrack's seven zone directors and it was inevitable that, in a crisis like this, managers at the zone level were looking to head office to make the tough decisions. Therefore, when Cox was rung up by zone directors in response to Ventry's recommendation, he took a very conservative line, fearing the possibility of another rail break. His gung-ho approach in making such vital pronouncements on the hoof reached its zenith with the decision to close the West Coast Main Line a week after the accident. The Scottish zone director, Jeanette Anderson, phoned Cox warning him that she had so many suspect areas of rail with cracks on her section of the line that his approach would mean the West Coast had to be closed immediately. She requested a different approach. Cox responded that he could not understand why she had phoned to query his instructions and that if the line had to close, than so be it. The decision was taken at 4 p.m. and the line closed a few hours later, much to the fury of the Post Office whose mail trains were stuck either side of the closure between Gretna Green and Law Junction, just south of Glasgow. Sleeper train passengers found themselves forced to spend the night in stationary coaches at Euston, Glasgow and Edinburgh.

An amazing aspect of this crisis was that Cox failed to keep Gerald Corbett, the chief executive, and his other board colleagues such as Middleton informed during this decision-making process. While Cox was happily sanctioning the closure of the West Coast Line, causing delays to thousands of passengers, Corbett was working in a nearby office on the thirteenth floor of Railtrack House, dubbed the Black Tower in the industry, preparing for his forthcoming appearance at the Cullen inquiry into the Ladbroke Grove disaster, and went home that evening unaware of what was happening. He only heard about it the next morning over breakfast from the *Today* programme. Corbett later told the House of Commons Transport sub-Committee that he went 'ballistic' when he found out what Cox had done. As the Committee reported,

> The way in which [the decision to close the West Coast Main Line] was reached was indicative of poor communication between layers of management in Railtrack, an inability on the part of the company to see its activities and responsibilities in a wider context, and shows scant regard for the public interest.[3]

The line was reopened a day after its closure.

By the Thursday after the crash 150 speed restrictions had already been imposed on track with gauge corner cracking and, owing to the rigid criteria, almost all were 20mph. At a meeting of Project Response a week after the crash, Cox, having sought advice from outside engineers, decided to endorse the guidance from Ventry that any site with cracks longer than 30mm (just over an inch) should have an immediate emergency temporary speed restriction of 20mph. He did not, however, consult with Middleton, a permanent way engineer and the one person on the board who knew anything about rails. They were barely on speaking terms because Cox had tried to bar the more experienced man from his operational meetings with zone directors and other senior HQ staff.

Cox effectively set the rules without anyone knowing how many such sites would be affected. The best early guess had been that around 300 sites were showing signs of gauge corner cracking but ultimately there turned out to be 6,821. Not all resulted in the imposition of speed limits but temporary restrictions, mostly of 20mph (because that is the speed at which it is thought a train will not topple over if derailed), were suddenly popping up around the network like mushrooms on a rotting tree. At the peak, around a month later, there were 574 restrictions imposed as a result of the Hatfield crash (in addition to the 500 or so routine restrictions placed on sections awaiting repair) and overall, by 21 May 2001, there were 1,286 sites where post-Hatfield restrictions had been imposed at some point following the accident. Given that many of these were on busy parts of the network, the result was the worst set of delays to the trains in the history of the railways, except those caused by industrial action.

Under BR the person in Cox's position would have been an experienced engineer. He would have taken the advice, which he would have realised came from people busy covering their backs, considered it and then made a decision based on his knowledge of the railway. Cox's overreaction had spread through the organisation. The board, chaired by the feeble non-executive Sir Philip Beck, far from standing up to Cox's conservative assessment was equally risk-averse, chanting the impossible mantra of having a 100 per cent safe railway. As one insider put it, 'Crassly conservative engineering decisions were being made as everybody was arse-covering and these decisions were made far too low a level in the organisation.' Moreover, 'The maintenance engineers began to use this as an excuse to chuck all their dodgy rails into the pot because they saw it as an opportunity to get things done more quickly.'[4] Cox did not command any respect from the seasoned zone directors, who may well have been content to see him dig his own grave by imposing these unnecessary restrictions.

Cox was to pay for his errors. Within a month of the arrival, in July 2001, of John Robinson as the new chairman at Railtrack, Cox was shown the door (although he continued to receive his £300,000 annual salary until he got another job) because of the continuing poor performance of the company. By then, ironically, Cox had learned a bit about the industry and begun to understand the nature of the mistakes he had made. In one of his last memos, which was subsequently leaked[5] to the press, he suggesting reorganising the company into eighteen divisions, to fit in better with the geography of the train operating companies. The plan was rejected, and in sacking him Mr Robinson clearly placed the blame on the departing executive for the company's failure to reduce delays: 'We are determined to improve Railtrack's operational perform-ance,' something which Cox had signally failed to do in his ten months in the job.

With hindsight, clearly Cox should never have allowed himself to get to a position where he had to make such important decisions given his inexperience of both engineering and the railways. Moreover, as we see later in the book (chapters 5 and 9) the privatisation of the railways had created the situation in which a Hatfield-type debacle was almost inevitable. Perhaps a man of different character, unscarred by the experience of Yorkshire Water and the drought, would not have embarked on the disastrous policy of endorsing the decision to impose 20mph speed restrictions across much of the network without a proper assessment of the situation. Cox, who has been barred from speaking to me by Railtrack's legal advisers, would claim that he had no option but to take the 'no risk' option. However, running railways can never be a risk-free business. Furthermore, if Cox had been aware that his actions would bring the company almost to bankruptcy, he too would have chosen another option.

Railtrack justified the decision to impose so many temporary speed limits on the basis that it had no alternative – it was, according to a press release,[6] 'an appropriate and necessary response to the phenom-ena [sic] of gauge corner cracking'. The official line was that Railtrack could not risk the possibility of another rail break, which would have drastic repercussions for the company (possibly not, however, quite as dramatic as those that followed anyway). The vast majority of people in the industry felt that Railtrack had been far too cautious, citing the fact that no rail in the same poor condition as the one at Hatfield was ever found in the course of the thousands of inspections prompted by the accident. For example, Sir Alastair Morton, the chairman of the Strate-gic Rail Authority, told ITN that the closure of the West Coast Main Line was an 'overreaction'. Many engineers concurred. The drastic reaction was, it was felt, a result of the company's lack of engineering expertise. Arthur Grose, a BR former civil engineer, argued in *Modern Railways*[7] that the widespread application of 20mph limits was because Railtrack was 'out of its depth on the technical front'. He said that there was a well-known formula cited in literature on managing the railways' permanent way[8] which would have allowed Railtrack to determine the optimum speed – in terms of spreading forces onto both rails – for each curve where there were cracks. As Grose put it, 'The blanket imposition of 20mph restrictions was a cavalier, irresponsible, deeply unscientific and colossally incompetent act', caused, he felt, by the lack of engineering expertise at the head of the organisation. Another engineer, Clive Bonnett, a former operations director for London Underground, was unequivocal: 'Neither I nor any of the former BR regional civil engineers would ever have suggested wholesale imposition of so many 30kph speed restrictions.'[9] He suggested that reducing speeds to around 60mph would have been perfectly adequate given the forces involved.

Mr Bonnett's use of the word 'suggested' is key. Under British Rail there would have been a team of directors running a region or sector of the railway covering such disciplines as civil engineering, rolling stock, operations, marketing and personnel. They would have reported to the director or general manager who made the ultimate decisions. Therefore, civil engineers would probably never have even dared to suggest blanket 20mph speed restrictions and had they done so, they would have been given short shrift. The general manager would have balanced the needs of the engineers with those of the other directors and the requirement to keep the railway running.

The study of gauge corner cracking – or rather the wider concept of rolling contact fatigue – commissioned by Railtrack from Professor Roderick Smith after the disaster, has turned into the largest ever investigation of the problem as all the rails taken out under the repair programme have been examined. According to Professor Smith, not only has no rail as bad as the one at Hatfield been discovered, but 'reassuringly, the cracks have not travelled as deeply into the rail as may be thought from the surface cracks'. In other words, many of the rails taken out were not in any danger of breaking.

A Railtrack source privately accepts that these experienced engineers were right:

If we had more engineering experience, this would never have happened in the first place because we would have picked up the issue earlier. The maintenance was based on different guidelines by the contractors and there were no consistent standards. Railtrack did not have enough engineers. We should never have imposed so many 20mph limits. Having 20mph everywhere was stupid. Good quality engineers should have the confidence to make the right decisions.

But once the process unleashed by Cox was underway, it was impossible to rein back. The quaintly named Her Majesty's Railway Inspectorate, part of the Health and Safety Executive, became involved. Although the imposition of a speed restriction did not need the sanction of HMRI, removing it did. The inspectors – again taking a very conservative view because the recent spate of accidents has made them very, probably too, risk-averse – ruled that before any restriction could be lifted, Railtrack had to carry out a risk assessment of that particular site. Moreover, Railtrack had to produce more detailed guidance on the criteria it was using to impose and remove speed restrictions before being allowed to lift any restrictions. In other words, Railtrack, through its 'cavalier' approach, had entered a legal quagmire. Railtrack was remarkably slow in changing its guidelines on speed restrictions. Eventually, it slipped out in May 2001[10] that the company had 'changed the guidelines based on the extra information about causes and risks of the problem, and how to deal with it, accumulated since Hatfield'. Railtrack insiders have admitted that they could and should have lifted many restrictions more quickly.[11]

Whatever the rights or wrongs of the decisions on speed restrictions, the result for the train operators was chaos. On the second weekend after the accident, as the number of restrictions spiralled out of control, the trains literally ground to a halt. A 20mph limit even for a small stretch easily adds ten minutes on to a journey as the train has to slow down and pick up speed again. Several such restrictions on a journey can add hours. One train driver reported having to go for 22 miles at 20mph after an emergency restriction was imposed between Grantham and Newark on the East Coast Main Line. The rail companies resorted to advising their customers not to use their services. A Midland Mainline spokesman, Kevin Johnson, told a Sunday newspaper: 'We have been told the disruption is going to last for at least two weeks but on Sunday I would suggest people do not travel at all.'[12] The suggestion of two weeks was, of course, to prove ridiculously optimistic. By Easter 2001 there would still be 163 speed restrictions and there were predictions that the delays caused by gauge corner cracking would last well into 2002.[13]

The railways quickly became the subject of despair for many passengers. Journey times were doubling or worse, forcing many people used to taking a day trip from, say, London to Manchester, to travel overnight and stay in a hotel. The GNER line remained closed for twenty-four days, forcing trains to be diverted and delaying all the main-line services along the route. Horrendous journey times became commonplace. The Inter-City services were particularly affected. It was frequently taking five hours to reach Manchester or Liverpool from London, and journeys between provincial towns were equally affected: Birmingham to Bristol, for example, routinely took three hours, rather than the normal ninety minutes. Longer distance journeys almost became too protracted to bear. Bristol to Glasgow became a nine-hour marathon.

Then the skies opened, ensuring that 2000 would become the railways' *annus horribilis*. Within a couple of weeks of Hatfield, the persistent autumn downpours created widespread flooding, the worst for many years. The GNER line north of York was closed for several days and many lines in outlying areas such as Wales, the West Country and Scotland were shut for days or even weeks. One branch line, between Exeter and Barnstaple, remained closed for five months, not reopening until April 2001. The train companies were so overwhelmed that on some routes they did not even offer replacement bus services. Public transport, was, in effect, suspended, a poor advertisement for the rail industry's wares which was to have a long-term effect.

It was, though, the speed restrictions that caused the most persistent problems. The travelling public was prepared to put up with floods because they understood that the railway companies cannot control the weather, but the speed restrictions which made trains crawl through large sections of the British countryside seemed inexplicable. Because trains were taking so much longer, neither rolling stock nor crew were available to run the full timetable. Chris Garnett, the chief executive of GNER, explained:

> At first, we tried to keep as much of the service running as possible but we soon realised it was impossible. We realised we were getting unsafe ourselves because of the length of time that crews were having to drive. The drivers would get off the train shattered. And it affected our equipment, too – our use of disc brakes went up threefold.[14]

Therefore operators began drawing up temporary timetables, a process which would normally takes six months but was now being done on a weekly or fortnightly basis. New restrictions were being added every week, as new hairline cracks were discovered, which meant these new timetables were unworkable as soon as they were produced. Conveying this new information to passengers proved hard, even with the use of the internet. For example, it took three days for a new timetable to be loaded into Railtrack's public timetable and therefore website visitors would get misleading information. People ringing up the National Rail Enquiry Service would frequently turn up at the station to find no trace of the service they had been advised to take. Even platform staff often found themselves unaware of the train timetable, and sophisticated computerised 'real time' information schemes were made redundant as they could not cope with the frequency of changes.

Gradually, Railtrack began to realise that the basis on which it was making decisions was too conservative, but it had embarked on an unstoppable process. After two weeks, gauge corner cracking was reclassified into severe, medium and mild, though severe was still reckoned to be anything 30mm long or more, and yet the number of temporary speed restrictions continued to rise. This was because both Railtrack and maintenance contract people on the ground had, by now, got in the habit of taking very conservative decisions about the potential danger of cracks. The whole of Railtrack was now focused on avoiding another catastrophe caused by a broken rail, rather than trying to run a railway. In fact, there were a couple of minor incidents which ensured that safety fears remained uppermost on the Railtrack agenda.

A couple of weeks after Hatfield, a mail train apparently went through a red light and crashed into a stationary goods train, causing extensive damage and another blockage on the line. Then on 26 November a Virgin train near Glasgow was derailed at slow speed due to the very poor condition of the track – because of poor maintenance the rails had separated, enlarging the gauge sufficiently for the wheels to come off the track. None of the 400 passengers was injured but, unaccountably, as a result of police bungling and concern from Railtrack about walking alongside track (albeit closed), they were not allowed off the train for several hours.

Professor David Begg, the chairman of the Commission for Integrated

Transport, summed up Railtrack's attitude in the aftermath of Hatfield and these minor incidents:

> There is a real culture of fear at present. Rail managers are very scared of corporate manslaughter and there is growing evidence that Railtrack have if anything overreacted to the broken rail at Hatfield. No one can be complacent on safety but if we reacted the same way on our roads as we did to minor rail derailments, we would be closing our motorways today.[15]

Sir Alastair Morton, head of the Strategic Rail Authority, argued that Railtrack, in its panic, had 'exported' the risk to train operators and rail passengers through speed restrictions and that the industry was having 'a nervous breakdown'.[16]

The sense of chaos within the industry in general, and Railtrack in particular, was not helped by the sacking of Corbett a month after the Hatfield accident. He tendered his resignation on the day of the crash, but the board, influenced by the surprising amount of public support for Corbett, rejected it, only to change its mind when the non-executives, supported by Sir Philip Beck, the chairman, staged a coup and demanded that Corbett be given the bullet. Corbett had tried to stand up to Prescott and his fellow politicians, arguing that their statements about absolute safety on the railways were placing an impossible burden on the industry and had contributed to the climate in which the post-Hatfield chaos occurred. Bernard Jenkin, the Tory spokesman on transport, backs up this point:

> After Ladbroke Grove, Prescott went round saying that there would be a safe railway whatever the cost. It is nonsense to talk like that. There is always the chance that there will be accidents and it is crazy to spend millions on schemes that are simply not worthwhile in terms of the number of lives saved.[17]

The apotheosis of delays was reached on 27 November when passengers on the 10 p.m. from London to Nottingham took nine hours to reach their destination. Things started to go wrong forty minutes into the journey when there was a signal failure, but the train seems then to have been forgotten by Railtrack staff who only gave it permission to move at 3.50 a.m. When the train reached Kettering the passengers were told to get off because of maintenance work and a very slow bus ride eventually got them to Nottingham at 7 a.m. Even then, the passengers

were only offered free taxis after a bitter argument with officials of Midland Mainline.

The publicity for incidents like this compounded the problems for the
railways, which are ever the Aunt Sally for the media. The hostile coverage meant that people were even put off using lines where trains were
running relatively normally, such as some (but by no means all) of the
major London commuter routes. Inspired by the media's distorted pre-
occupations with safety – which mean the 3,500 road deaths each year
are ignored while even minor rail incidents are given blanket coverage –
there were even tales of people driving from London to Scotland because
they thought it was safer, though statistically this is a nonsense.[18] The
government was put in a difficult situation. While John Prescott was
quick to criticise the rail companies, his own government's failure to do
anything for the railway in its first three years of office (see chapter 6)
opened the way for criticism of Labour. Tony Blair began to take a strong
personal interest in the railways and he summed up the situation perfectly during an ITV interview[19] with members of the public, when he
said that rail travel had become 'absolute hell' and that it was 'my
responsibility' to turn it around.

Road congestion also increased. Trafficmaster, which monitors transport volumes on motorways and A roads, reported that congestion (in
other words, traffic jams, not the number of cars) increased by 40 per
cent in the two weeks after Hatfield and remained 20 per cent higher
even five weeks later.[20] The big beneficiaries of the rail crisis were the
domestic airlines whose passenger loadings soared to record levels. BAA,
which operates most of Britain's major airports, saw domestic traffic rise
by 14 per cent in the last three months of the year. The London–Manchester route saw loadings up by more than 40 per cent and British Air-
ways responded by putting on larger planes. The cheap airlines like Go
and easyJet also enjoyed massive increases in load factors for their
domestic flights. Even transport gurus like Professor David Begg confessed to abandoning rail travel between London and Scotland and
taking to the air.[21]

Figures for punctuality and reliability problems had gone off the scale.
Several companies such as Great Eastern (normally one of the best in the
country), West Anglia, Great Northern, Virgin West Coast and Cross-
Country and GNER had fewer than one in four trains running on time[22]
in the month after Hatfield, whereas in normal times punctuality

hovered around the 90 per cent mark. According to the Strategic Rail Authority's figures,[23] just under half of long-distance trains arrived on time during the last three months of 2000. Even those figures underestimate the number of delays, as many of them were calculated against temporary timetables which already incorporated considerable extra time added on to the normal journey schedules. Complaints reached record levels.

By early December, according to Railtrack, there were still 553 speed restrictions, of which 401 were 20mph. Around 10,000 trains out of 18,000 each day (55 per cent) were running late. Temporary timetables meant that many journey times were still taking twice the normal time and a quarter of passengers had abandoned the system to use other means of transport or not to travel at all.

Not surprisingly, while airline ticket sales soared, train companies' revenues shrunk commensurately. Some companies, particularly those operating long-distance services such as GNER, lost half their revenue for a couple of months. Railtrack suffered even worse, having to go cap in hand to the government to be bailed out after announcing that the Hatfield disaster and its aftermath had cost the company £600m, which turned out to be a gross underestimate (see chapter 10 for details of the financial mess after Hatfield).

Hatfield ensured that the railways would never be the same again. There were predictions that they would take up to five years to recover their market and, although these were rejected by the operators, it is clear that it will take a long time for people to trust the trains again. Indeed, the very way that people think of the railways changed. Inter-City's hard won reputation as a reliable, quick, comfortable and safe way of getting to important meetings or events was lost forever. This was epitomised by Virgin's admission that it could not provide any extra services for London football fans going to the semi-final game between Arsenal and Tottenham at Old Trafford in April 2001. In the event, a charter firm provided five trains but the vast majority of people had to use the overcrowded motorways. One relatively small crash had changed the railways from being a buoyant growth industry into a financial disaster area with a near-bankrupt company at its heart. As a financial analysis put it, Hatfield had made 'everyone [wake] up to the fact that a single event had almost brought the whole industry to a standstill. Train operators, in particular, despite being at the sharp end of the customer and financial interface had no control over the situation.'[24] It was not a recipe that was likely to appeal to private investors.

How had the railways been allowed to get into a state of such vulnerability and weakness? This book is an attempt to explain that process and to identify some of the villains who brought a vital and reasonably well functioning industry to its knees at the cost of billions of pounds of taxpayers' money in the name of ideology and narrow political and commercial interest. It is a tale that has lessons for other parts of the economy and which should sound a warning to all politicians who see privatisation as a panacea for all the faults of public services.

CHAPTER 2

Government and the railways:
a terrible dependency

The relationship between government and the railways has always
been fraught. Although this is not intended to be a historical book, it
is essential for an understanding of the present predicament to take a
brief look at the development of the railways and in particular the complex interface between the public and private roles in the industry. The
railways were, of course, built by private enterprise and on the cheap,
which is the root cause of many of today's problems, such as the large
number of unnecessary curves which reduce speeds. They were, with few
exceptions, barely profitable or even loss-making right from the start and
therefore continually suffered from under-investment. Yet the construction of the railways could, arguably, be considered as the finest achievement of the Victorians, and while the development of the whole network
took some seventy-five years, the core of today's system was already in
place by the end of the 'railway mania' in 1852. By then there were 6,600
miles of railway route open compared with just 100 in 1830.[1]

It was inevitable that even Victorian governments with their *laissez-
faire* ethos should become involved in what became the country's largest
industry and one which had all kinds of social, political and economic
ramifications. They were, however, usually one step behind; legislating
too late in order to remedy past ills, rather than addressing the future,
not least because the railways were as new and bewildering to Victorian
legislators as the internet is to western politicians today.

In the quarter century following the first run of the train hauled by
George Stephenson's *Locomotion* along the Stockton & Darlington railway in 1825, the map of Britain was transformed by the creation of a railway network stretching from Aberdeen to Plymouth and from Holyhead
to Lowestoft. The Stephensons were to dominate the development of

new lines and technical innovation for the next twenty-five years. It was George's son Robert who was the force behind the opening of the Liverpool & Manchester Railway in 1830, which demonstrated railway's potential for carrying passengers as well as cargo. The Liverpool & Manchester was effectively the first 'modern' railway, linking two major towns with a double track line throughout and, unlike its smaller predecessors, eschewing the use of horses for any traction. It was partly in response to the power of people like the Stephensons, who wielded an influence in Victorian Britain comparable to that exercised in the contemporary US by Bill Gates, that the government began to respond, perceiving the need for economic regulation, safety requirements and technological innovation and standardisation.

The legislature, as opposed to the government, had, of course, been involved in the railway industry right from the outset because the planning process for building railway lines involved getting a private bill through Parliament. It was, though, a haphazard process. Although many bills were rejected, there were no clear criteria and success was dependent on the ability of a strong and partisan local MP to argue for a particular scheme. Most MPs knew nothing about the railways and those that did often had a vested interest, either as a supporter of the scheme under debate or of a rival one.

The government of the day did not control this parliamentary process and there was no central planning of the rapidly growing rail network as happened, for example, in Belgium where the state took an active part in the design of the network. Because of the vagaries of the private bill system many patently uneconomic lines, often duplicating existing routes, were approved and built. Far from having a strategic overview, the government was soon left behind by the explosion in new railway construction and found itself impotent in major decision-making, having little influence over the formation or management of the first major companies. The railways can be seen as a battleground, with the *nouveau riche*, principally northern, entrepreneurs seeking, through the compulsory procedures granted to them in the railway bills, to take land from the old propertied classes. Because of the government's failure to take an active role in the planning process (which, as we shall see, has much resonance with events of the past few years), the railways were dependent upon an inefficient and expensive mechanism for their development. As one writer put it, 'In the absence of centralised state planning, the country's railway capitalists had no choice but to engage in a prolonged parliamentary free-for-all for complete incorporation, commercial territory and the power to expropriate land.'[2] As with today's fragmented, privatised railway, lawyers enjoyed a bonanza – one estimate suggests that by 1862 the railway industry had spent £30m on parliamentary business, much of it going to lawyers.

After a few years of watching from the sidelines, the government was first gently stirred from its slumbers in 1838 when the state-owned Post Office demanded a universally fair price for the carriage of its mail, instead of being selectively overcharged on certain routes. The Railways (Conveyance of Mails) Act was therefore one of the very first pieces of railway legislation. The first significant act, the Regulation of Railways Act 1840, which was followed by eight similarly named acts in the subsequent half-century, created the embryonic railway inspectorate; but safety was not the main impetus behind the legislation, as the inspectorate's principal task, initially, was the assessment of the validity of schemes coming up before it. However, the safety role of the new body, the railway department of the Board of Trade, was important and gradually increased. It included the inspection and approval of new lines for passenger use and the investigation of accidents; it also provided a means of putting pressure on the railway companies to adopt technological improvements, particularly for safety reasons. The *laissez-faire* approach of the first few years was abandoned forever.

Apart from war, famine, disease and free trade, railways were the most controversial issue on the parliamentary agenda of the middle years of the nineteenth century. It was hardly surprising that there was not a clear government attitude to the railways, as the two main political groupings, Tory (Conservative) and Whig, did not have coherent policies, but rather pursued the private agendas of their more influential MPs. There was, nevertheless, a fundamental division, with much resonance still today, between those seeking increased regulation of an industry that, at times, appeared out of control, and the free marketeers who felt it best left alone. In truth, that was even less possible then than it is now.

The railways were such a fundamental part of Victorian Britain that it is almost impossible to exaggerate their importance. They affected every facet of life. Agriculture prospered because of the better links between town and country, and farmers were able to reach markets more quickly and cheaply with everything from fruit and milk to chickens and cattle; areas of the country which could not be reached easily before were suddenly opened up; labour became much more mobile; tourism became possible; and even the fish and chip shop owes its existence to the faster transit of fish inland.[3]

The growing importance of the railways ensured that the government was forced to react in 1844 when the infamous 'railway mania' began threatening not only the finances of existing railways but those of many hapless investors in new railway schemes. With the main lines already largely mapped out, the railway mania saw an explosion of speculative and ill-devised railway projects. Between 1844 and 1847, plans laid before Parliament envisaged 20,000 miles of railway, many in direct competition with each other. (In fact, the whole network peaked in the Edwardian age at around 23,000 miles.) Some of the schemes had no hope of delivering a dividend to innocent investors and others were just plain frauds like those of the 'Railway King', George Hudson, who exploited legal loopholes to gain control of a collection of companies owning some 1,000 miles of route. He then became an MP, apparently with the sole aim of defeating rival schemes, but it emerged that he had been fiddling the books, paying his investors £200,000-worth of dividends out of the capital of their own company, Eastern Counties, and he disappeared, leaving hundreds of bankrupted shareholders.

Gladstone's government tried to impose some order upon the industry and drew up a powerful bill which would have imposed strict controls, including the compulsory purchase by the state of strategic lines. The bill was also prompted by fears that the railway companies would establish themselves as monopolies whose charges would have to be controlled. However, predictably, the free marketeers, including the large number of railway directors sitting in Parliament,[4] objected and the bill was weakened during its passage, although it did include a right for the government to buy lines built subsequently if they made excess profits, but this was never used and was formally abandoned on the recommendations of a Royal Commission in 1867. The Act also required railways to permit the electric telegraph to be installed beside their lines and provided for troops and police to be carried at times of unrest but, overall, the legislation was, as one commentator put it, 'in tune with the deregulatory spirit of the age'.[5]

The early mention of nationalisation in the Bill was not the first. In the late 1830s the Duke of Wellington, a member of Lord Melbourne's government, had publicly expressed his concern over 'monopoly and mismanagement' and suggested state ownership. As one historian put it, 'The issue of public ownership versus private enterprise for the railways was as old as the industry itself.'[6] Indeed, some European networks, such as the Belgian system, were developed by the state rather than private enterprise, and even privately founded systems, like the Swiss railways, were soon nationalised, while those which continued to develop privately had government involvement in their management. In many European countries there was an additional factor in that railways were considered a vital strategic asset and the military took a close interest in their development. But in free-enterprise Britain, government meddling, whatever the motive, would have been anathema. The developers thought that great fortunes could be made out of the railways, though, in practice, with a few exceptions, most turned out to be mildly profitable at best or, in the case of most rural services, uneconomic from the outset.

Gladstone did, however, introduce a key measure, the Parliamentary Train, which was to greatly widen the market for railway travel that had hitherto been confined to the relatively affluent. Third-class travellers, who often endured appalling conditions, had to be offered at least one train a day, stopping at all stations and averaging no less than 12mph with fares not exceeding one (old) penny per mile. While some of the railway companies realised the potential of providing such cheap services, others responded as private enterprise does so often to regulation – in a surly, minimalist way. Their Parliamentary Trains were poorly timed in a way that deterred passengers rather than attracting them to the railway.[7] Others continued to force their cheaper paying customers to travel in conditions that would have been cruel to livestock. The Great Western, for example, did not offer their third-class passengers the opportunity of looking at the countryside since they were 'encased in a box without windows, only permitting such light to penetrate as could find its way through the top Venetians'.[8]

The plethora of applications for railway projects also prompted a Royal Commission on the gauge, the width of separation of the two rails. In a decision which was to affect railways across the world, the Commission decided to support the 4ft 8½ ins used by the Great Northern Railway between London and York and this size was widely adopted in a majority of countries, even those like France which used the metric system of measurements. By the end of the railway mania, during which Parliament approved schemes for 9,000 new route miles, not all of which were constructed, virtually all the current main lines in England had been built or approved.

The railway network created by this haphazard process was, inevitably, not as good as one that would have been designed by a more rational allocation of resources with the involvement of the state. The duplication of lines created by the emphasis on competition rather than cooperation dogs the network to this day and, indeed, this same mistake was to undermine the Tories' 1990s privatisation. Writing in 1846, Macaulay lamented the failure of the government to exert its influence in the face of the dominant commercial interests of the day. Indeed, the whole development of the railways can be seen as the product of government's failure to put the interests of the public above those of the railway companies. Questions affecting the convenience, prosperity and security of the public had been subordinated to the narrow interests of the railway companies: 'That the whole country was interested in having a good system of internal communication seemed to be forgotten,'[9] he said, and while the interests of speculators and landowners had received careful attention, 'nobody appeared to be heard on behalf of the community'.

The lack of a visionary government response to the railways is well illustrated by its failure to encourage amalgamations and mergers. Several companies did grow through acquisition, as promoters of rural lines, often independent landowners, were happy to allow main-line operators to handle day-to-day operations and indeed most allowed their lines to be absorbed completely to escape insolvency when traffic volumes failed to live up to expectations. However, far from encouraging major amalgamations, the government actively frowned upon them, partly because self-interested railway MPs were worried that a conglomerate could gain an unfair advantage over their own companies, but also through fear of the railways establishing themselves as monopolies. Thus, when two substantial companies, the London & North Western Railway and Lancashire & Yorkshire, proposed merging in 1871 because they had similar interests in the North West, both houses of Parliament expressed strong opposition. The companies' plans went on ice for another fifty years and they did not merge until the great consolidation of 1922. Nevertheless, the rail companies were impressively large by the standards of the day. By 1874 the four largest companies owned 39 per cent of the track mileage and claimed 47 per cent of the gross receipts,[10] but their dominance did not grow after that because of the government's reluctance to allow further mergers. Nevertheless, the largest railway company, the London & North Western Railway, had a capital value of £117m by the end of the century, bigger than that of any other domestic company.[11]

To some extent the railways did enjoy a monopoly. With road transport as yet undeveloped, and the canals so slow, the railways could determine the prices for the carriage of goods, particularly small parcels. The railway companies tried to secure regional monopolies through amalgamations. As Michael Freeman recounts, 'The problem was compounded by the very limited influence that Parliament exercised over railway freight rates.'[12] The issue, as he puts it, 'developed into an epic struggle', particularly over the railways' habit of quoting a preferential rate for particular places, districts or even individual clients which discriminated unfairly against others. This 'remained a constant irritant in the relationship between companies and their customers right up until 1914' when the state took over the running of the railways and established clear rates for carriage (which was to cause a host of other problems).

While government kept out of such commercial issues as much as possible, its big success was the improvement of safety, but only after a series of accidents which allowed it to override the powerful 'railway interest' in Parliament. The government was also able to impose improved standards because, on this issue, it had the support of the public after a succession of gruesome accidents whose toll was often increased as a result of the use of wooden carriages, gas lighting and even such bad railway habits as locking passengers into their compartments. Illustrious lobbyists for rail safety, such as Charles Dickens, who was deeply affected by his lucky escape in an accident at Staplehurst in Kent, helped the rapid progress on accident rates. Stanley Hall, a former railway manager and the author of a number of books on rail accidents,[13] argues that major improvements rarely resulted from a single accident but rather from a series with a similar cause over a period of several years. During the Victorian era, the key improvements involved what were known as lock, block, and brake, all of which were codified in the momentous Regulation of Railways Act 1889 that was hastily introduced following the Armagh disaster earlier that year.

'Lock' involved connecting – interlocking, as it is called on the railway – the levers in a signal box in such a way that the signaller could

not set the signals for a train to proceed unless the points were set cor-
rectly. The key accident was at Warrington in 1867 when a signaller
cleared a train to go ahead along a route which was already occupied by
another train. 'Block' meant the adoption of a signalling system in which
lines are divided into a series of blocks or sections on the principle that
no two trains are allowed simultaneously into the same section. Prior to
the adoption of this system, trains had been allowed to proceed a set
time after the previous one, which often led to accidents when a train
stopped unexpectedly because of a breakdown or an obstacle. As early as
1869, the Board of Trade had asked the railway companies to notify it of
the proportion of their lines using the block system, a request that was
received with 'explosive indignation'[14] by the railway companies who
had become increasingly unpopular as a result of their perceived disregard for safety.

The key improvement to the brake system was to introduce automatic
continuous brakes throughout the train, which ensured that, if the train
split through some mishap, the brake would automatically be applied on
both halves. It was the Armagh disaster on 12 June 1889, one of the worst
ever on the railways, which prompted this change. A Sunday School
excursion overloaded with almost 1,000 passengers stalled on a steep
gradient and the train crew decided to split the train to allow the engine
to take half the carriages up the hill and return for the others. Unfortunately, the brake system on the rear section of the train, which did not
have continuous brakes, was not strong enough to prevent it sliding
down the hill and smashing into another train on the way up, killing
eighty people and injuring three times that number.

The public outcry which followed the Armagh disaster ensured that
the government had to act quickly on all these three key safety features,
despite the protests of the less enlightened rail companies which had
been reluctant to introduce these expensive measures. Armagh brought
to a head a series of issues over safety which had been brewing for many
years, and the speed with which the legislation was introduced – it came
into force on 30 August, just seventy-nine days after the disaster –
showed what could be done by a government acting decisively with
public support. As a result of this legislation, the accident rate on the railways fell dramatically, and for the first time, in the early twentieth century, there were two years, 1901 and 1908, when no rail passengers were
killed in a train accident.

The great railway age, when the railways were at the height of their power, stretched from 1850 to the outbreak of the First World War. If anything, the importance of the railways later in the Victorian age was even greater than in the early days of the industry. The railways employed a staggering 648,000 people, a figure which did not include those who worked for manufacturers of railway equipment both for domestic use and for export. There were a myriad other ways in which the railways influenced the development of modern society. As Andrew Dow points out, 'The extent to which, for example, railway practices prompted the growth of professions such as accountancy and mechanical engineering may not yet have been documented in full.'[15]

The beginning of the decline of the railways coincided with much greater government involvement as the state took over the running of the system in 1914 after the outbreak of the Great War, using powers under the Regulation of the Forces Act 1871. The war was to change the management of the railways forever. The railways, which had reached their peak size of 23,000 route miles, were expected to shoulder the overwhelming burden of transporting materials, munitions and people, and this could only happen with government control. While it would be simplistic to argue that it was the government's greater role which damaged the railways, the state that the network was left in after the war was to cause insuperable problems for the industry in the ensuing decades. The railways were sweated and over-used, with very little compensating investment since resources were concentrated on the war effort. The railways had been run into the ground, with a major backlog of maintenance of equipment, and administrative chaos.

When hostilities ended, the government, aware of the political benefits of running the railways, relinquished control only slowly. The government's wartime controls were not lifted until 1921, by which time it was evident that the businesses – 120 individual railway companies lumbered with Victorian business values and equipment – stood no chance of recovering their former exalted position. A mass duplication of facilities – towns sometimes had two or three stations with competing services as a result of the lack of central control and the Victorians' fear of monopoly – was clearly nonsensical when none of them could deliver a quality service. And for the first time, road transport became a viable alternative with the motor bus, the ultimate predator, beginning to become sufficiently reliable to pose a threat.

Company amalgamations – many of them discussed well before the war – were on the agenda again, but this time the government forced the railways' hand with the 1921 Railways Act whose principal aim was to increase national efficiency by the elimination of wasteful rivalry. War had meant that there was less interest in promoting competition, the obsession which had so dominated the Victorians' policies in relation to the railways. Even nationalisation, supported by the Labour Party and the National Union of Railwaymen, was in the air in 1919 and publicly discussed by ministers, but ultimately it was rejected because of public opinion, which was concerned, as *The Economist* put it, about putting themselves at the mercy of 'bureaucratic bunglers'[16] and 'the fact that state owned railways overseas had frequently proved disappointing'.[17] It was decided, instead, to create the 'Big Four' large administrative groups on a geographical basis: the London & North Eastern Railway (LNER), London Midland & Scottish (LMS), Southern (SR), and Great Western (GWR), the last broadly unchanged apart from the absorption of a large collection of small independent South Wales systems. The Act also gave the government power to fund major investment schemes for the railways, a recognition not only of their strategic role but also of the impossibility of making such investment profitable without at least an initial subsidy.

Government regulation of freight charging policies was also introduced, which was designed to deliver the same overall rate of return as companies would have expected in 1913, a year before hostilities began. In return, the railways became 'common carriers' who were obliged to offer a range of carriage facilities on demand, whether or not they made a profit on that service.

It was a great theory but was, in fact, a recipe for disaster. No one had seen the warning signs that the railways were no longer in the same kind of dominant situation as before. Both passenger and freight traffic first stagnated in the immediate aftermath of the war and then slumped. Freight suffered particularly badly in areas when a traditional industry went into decline, like coal in South Wales. There were external threats, too, such as the lorry, which scarcely featured in early twentieth-century railway planning. In the 1920s road hauliers, who had bought cheap surplus army lorries, started to cream off local short-journey freight business, particularly agricultural produce. The rural branch line which ran from nowhere in particular to a remote main-line junction was already becoming a redundant asset. For the first time ever, closures began to outnumber openings, of which there were very few as the days of railway expansion were over.

The period between the two world wars is seen by many as the golden age of the railways. That is a credit to the public relations departments of the Big Four who created the image of prestige streamlined expresses that still lives with us seven decades later. The elegant posters commissioned by the railway companies survive on many living room walls today to perpetuate this romantic image which, indeed, persuaded John Major, briefly and unsuccessfully, to back a return to the Big Four as the route to privatisation in the 1990s. Lynda Lee-Potter, present-day *Daily Mail* columnist, still longs for the return of the Great Western Railway buffet car with pressed linen tablecloths and silver cutlery, and there were many other features on offer, such as the renting out of headsets for radio reception, hairdressing salons and secretarial services, but few passengers could afford these luxuries. There was a sharp contrast between the elite services of fast expresses between large cities and the shoddy conditions on minor and branch lines where services were often slow and dirty.

The Big Four's twenty-five year existence can be characterised as an unsuccessful struggle to achieve profitability which, in turn, meant that the system suffered badly from under-investment. The government's promise, when it forced through the grouping of the Big Four, to maintain the companies' net receipts at 1913 levels through the regulation of charging rates proved impossible to fulfil, given the fast-growing competition from other forms of transport which meant that the 1913 targets were hardly ever met. Eventually the government paid £60m to the Big Four to discharge this obligation. Freight was the key market to maintain profits, and while core industries – collieries, steelworks, quarries – still relied on railways for the bulk movement of raw and finished products, they were mostly in decline while the new industries that were replacing them, such as motor manufacturing, electrical engineering and consumer goods, shunned the railways, with many establishing themselves on peripheral industrial estates far from any railhead. Passengers, too, were no longer prepared to put up with shoddy service away from the main lines with corridorless trains that provided neither toilets nor refreshments.

The Great Depression which started in 1929 further worsened the financial situation of the railway companies and depressed morale since staff were compelled to accept pay cuts. Employment levels were threatened and the government had to intervene by making funds available for building new locomotives, stations and freight depots, and modernising equipment which the companies simply could not afford to do themselves. The increased involvement of the government led to the recurring problems suffered by all industries that get embroiled with government. They became tools of overall macro-economic policy and subject to political whims, neither of which necessarily served their short- or long-term interests. The railway companies were distracted by a blinkered government which urged them to press on with often misplaced investment that protected jobs. Little effort went into achieving basic economies – such as the abandonment of duplicated routes – which had been precisely the purpose of the 1921 Act in the first place. Even the largest of the Big Four, the LMS, which was described as the biggest joint-stock company in the world in the 1920s, with a capital of almost £400m, did little to improve its productivity because government was reluctant to endorse the socially unacceptable issue of reducing capacity. It was certainly not a commercial decision, for example, that left the company, twenty years after the grouping, still owning three major rolling stock manufacturing and repair factories with a combined staff of 100,000. The expected closures of duplicated lines did not happen either, as the companies were reluctant to retrench, despite the growth of road transport, and no one, least of all the government, which feared increasing unemployment, was taking a strategic view of the railways.

The lack of profitability as a result of the stagnation of traffic, both passenger and freight, meant there was always a squeeze on the money available for investment. Though some impressive schemes were pushed through, such as the electrification of many heavily used commuter routes on the Southern and, with government help, the addition of extra track capacity on the East Coast Main Line, the railways did not modernise sufficiently under the grouping arrangement. By the end of this period the LMS, for example, had undertaken very little electrification (the Great Western did none, a legacy that remains today apart from the Heathrow Express trains), and its stations were 'infrequently cleaned, seldom painted and bore a generally shabby appearance',[18] a scene familiar to many of today's rail passengers.

As part of its Keynesian strategy of trying to boost employment through public works, the government made considerable funds available in the 1930s, but the money was not focused on schemes that addressed the railways' fundamental problem of retaining market share, but instead tended to be spent on locomotives which were not necessarily needed. The ability to invest was also hampered by the companies' prioritisation of dividend payments to shareholders rather than concentrating scarce resources on improvements, a decision that was echoed in 2001 when Railtrack insisted on paying a dividend to shareholders despite losing £534m. Even so, the dividends were meagre. In the late 1930s, the Great Western paid the highest dividends, 2.8 per cent, with LMS just behind at 2.7 per cent, while Southern shareholders received only 0.65 per cent and the LNER paid nothing. Indeed, the LNER was an exception, remaining 'determined to invest in its railway even in those years where the ordinary shareholder received nothing'.[19]

LNER's insistence on investment paid off and instigated something of a regional golden age in the run-up to the Second World War. The company had already shown a far-sighted interest in express travel with fewer stops and tighter schedules to bring the provinces closer to London, and its new streamlined Silver Jubilee high-speed trains between London and Newcastle, launched with much fanfare in 1935, gave the railways a modern image which has since characterised the interwar period in a way that it did not entirely merit. Overall, far from the grouping representing the heyday of the railways, the Big Four were hampered by historical constraints and the lack of governmental understanding of changes in the world of transport. As well as the inability to invest, they were constrained by common carrier obligations which were a leftover from Victorian times when the railways had a monopoly in the carriage of freight, and by antiquated and unimaginative fare structures. It was not all the railways' fault: as the railway historian Terry Gourvish, assessing the interwar years, puts it:

> The continued obligation to accept traffic, publish charges [which rivals could exploit], provide a reasonable level of service, avoid 'undue preference' in the treatment of customers and submit to government regulation of wages and conditions, left the railways vulnerable to their more flexible and less constrained competitors.[20]

In fact, the unfairness of the situation led the companies to launch a

'Square Deal' campaign in November 1938 demanding an end to the legal constraints under which the railways operated, such as the requirement to publish rates and treat all customers equally, but, although the government accepted the need for changes, the war intervened.

There is an odd feature of British railway history in that just as things were going swingingly, external factors intervened to put an end to it. Thus the Second World War ended a bronze, if not a golden, era, just as the First had, although it should be noted that revenues had started to plummet in 1938 because of a worsening depression in trade. As we shall see, privatisation occurred just as BR was getting its act together, and the arrival of the motorway did much to wreck the massive 1950s modernisation programme.

In 1939, as in 1914, the railways were taken under government control with charges being frozen and maintenance and renewal largely sacrificed to the war effort. This was done with extreme haste, the government assuming control on 31 August, a few hours before Germany attacked Poland, a recognition of the extreme importance of the railways. Indeed, this was also demonstrated by the fact that the railwaymen were not sent to war but kept at home in their 'reserved activity' which meant that they were expected to remain in their jobs, unlike twenty-five years previously when they were encouraged to enlist. The railways had to move troops, like the 319,000 rescued from Dunkirk in 1940 and taken from the ports in 620 trains, carry millions of tons of munitions, construction materials for aerodromes, and fuel and bombs for aircraft. At a time when petrol for road transport was severely rationed, the railways were utterly indispensable.

Perversely, the war was the rail companies' financial heyday, when they earned impressive profits, almost half of which were retained by the Treasury. However, costs were increasing rapidly while rates and fares were strictly controlled by the government, and this put the railway companies under severe pressure in the immediate aftermath of the war. Indeed, after six years of this intensive use, the railways were utterly exhausted. During the war, investment had been negligible, leaving the companies with old wagons and carriages, many locomotives that were life-expired, the track in terrible condition with two years of maintenance backlog that led to a series of major accidents with dozens of fatalities,[21] and a major Hatfield-type derailment (though not as fast) virtually every other week.

With petrol becoming more widely available (though still rationed) and the service offered by the clapped-out railway inadequate by modern standards, competition from road grew again. Revenues fell dramatically in the two years after the war as there was a return to more normal conditions and there was little money available for leisure travel to the seaside. Nevertheless, there was a naïve expectation that passengers and freight customers would stay with the railway even though the alternatives were becoming available again. As we shall see in the next chapter, this endearing and enduring optimism was to remain a feature of the early days of BR and result in much misallocated investment.

The actions of the Labour government which came to power in 1945 included bringing all the principal utilities under public ownership. Labour saw this as a crucial priority. It was also convenient – the government was spared the embarrassment of having to bail out a bankrupt railway industry. The decline of traditional industries was accelerating; the railways' lifeblood, coal, found itself in competition with alternative fuels, from gas to, later, nuclear power, neither of which was exactly suited for rail carriage. The more modern business practices of light industry, with its precise schedules and low-cost distribution systems, were in direct conflict with the working practices of the railways, whose staff still often believed they ruled the world and who consistently underestimated the threat of rival methods of transport.

Labour had long had a commitment to nationalisation of the railways, having first agreed the policy at its 1908 party conference. But it is worth noting, as the argument has contemporary resonance, that it was not only those on the left who advocated nationalisation. Industrialists and traders, keen to move their goods cheaply, saw the railways as a public service which should not be run as a profit-making business. After the First World War, there had been a fierce debate over the merits of nationalisation and, within the coalition government, Lloyd George had intimated that he supported the idea and, according to Terry Gourvish, 'Winston Churchill, electioneering in Scotland in December 1918, suggested, somewhat injudiciously, that the government had definitely decided to nationalise the railways.'[22] As we have seen, the nationalisation argument was lost, however, when the government decided on consolidation into the Big Four with relatively tight regulation. However, the Labour Party continued to press for nationalisation of the railways and, indeed, went further by advocating the creation of a national transport board to integrate all types of inland transport, an idea which eventually bore fruit with the 1948 nationalisation that brought virtually all public transport under a single British Transport Commission (BTC).

Integration was the buzz-word (as it was in Labour's 1997 manifesto).The Big Four, plus London Transport, were to be state-owned from 1 January 1948. A Railway Executive was set up, reporting to the BTC, to manage the day-to-day rail business with other executives charged with roads, inland waterways and London Transport.

In a scenario with powerful parallels in the 1990s, when the Tories rushed through privatisation without sufficient thought for the consequences, the Labour government used almost indecent haste to push through and implement their radical plan to nationalise not only railways but virtually all freight and public transport under the BTC. It was an unwieldy structure that would not help BR's genesis. Partly this was a result of the stroppiness of the railway boards who refused to participate in the preparation of the legislation – in sharp contrast to BR's executives who, in the 1990s, largely cooperated in their own demise. Instead, they ran a fierce anti-nationalisation campaign, which, although defeated, helped their shareholders receive rather more favourable terms for their stock than they might otherwise have done.

The refusal of the railway managers to cooperate in the nationalisation process was not only damaging because the scheme had to be drawn up without any input from industry expertise, but also because it meant that most of them did not join the new set-up. At a key time the railway industry lost focus: 'The railway company directors began to lose interest in the day to day operations of their companies and concentrated instead on fighting for favourable compensation.'[23]

The three-tiered structure controlling the railways, with the BTC overseeing a Railway Executive which in turn was responsible for the regions, was not a happy one. The Railway Executive was perceived to be a 'collection of prima donnas with no conductor'.[24] There was managerial friction all the way down the scale. It was decided to retain much of the former company management structure in the form of six virtually autonomous regions – London Midland, Eastern, North Eastern, Western, Southern and Scottish, each with its own general manager and board of directors. They were used to their own fiefdoms and believed their decisions should be final, without recourse to the Railway Executive or the BTC, and it was, in fact, to be another thirty-five years before the power of the regions was broken.

Apart from the last-ditch resistance from the companies and their directors, the fundamental reason for the flawed structure was political expediency. Labour was in a hurry to nationalise the railways – and many other industries – and, just as in the 1990s during privatisation, there was little discussion of the *transport* implications of what was being implemented – 'what mattered was political and administrative expediency',[25] a pattern repeated in the 1990s.

There was the inevitable parliamentary opposition from the Tories who, to a great extent, batted for the interests of the rail companies. The Tories were obstructive, tabling 800 amendments, and much of the resulting parliamentary debate centred on detail, such as the well-founded criticism that the administrative structure of the BTC was unwieldy and subject to too much ministerial patronage. While the government conceded that short-distance road freight should be excluded from the legislation, the biggest row on the railways was over the terms of compensation for shareholders and the directors themselves.[26] The eventual deal was very generous to the railway company shareholders. Their holdings were valued at a staggering £927m,[27] equivalent to over £20bn in today's money (contrast this with the £2.5bn received for Railtrack in 1996). The shareholders were given a fixed level of payment, irrespective of the performance of their company. Moreover, they still, in effect, retained a stake in the railways; their shares were exchanged for government bonds on which they were to receive a fixed rate of return, which was to be a charge on the nationalised industry, irrespective of its performance. Shareholders were thus given a generous risk-free investment. In the event, the financial performance of the railways deteriorated rapidly in the face of competition from the car and as a result of the lack of investment. This generous compensation package was to have a long and damaging effect on the future of the railways in public ownership because of the constant drain on the resources of British Railways (see next chapter).

While politicians, managers and workers jockeyed for position, they overlooked basic issues such as the state of the network. At its creation BR took on 632,000 staff (compared with a fifth of that total for the same number of passengers today), 20,000 miles of track to bring back up to standard, 20,000 steam locomotives (half of them worn out), 36,000 passenger coaches (21 per cent were over 35 years old, including a few gas-lit Victorian six-wheelers), 4,200 electric commuter train sets, and a staggering total of 1,223,634 low-capacity freight wagons (many of them made one journey a year, if they were lucky). And there were 7,000 horses used for traction in yards, with some still being used in 1964.

Right from the outset, BR had a host of worries ranging from the dreadful condition of its assets to the artificially low fares imposed by a socialist government, with wages now accounting for three-quarters of the fare revenue before any other bills were considered. BR, therefore, did not have an easy legacy or an auspicious start. Given these circum-stances, its future mixed record was something of a triumph, as the next chapter will show.

CHAPTER 3

Was BR as bad as its sandwiches?

The collapse of Railtrack in the aftermath of the Hatfield crash prompted so many calls for the renationalisation of Britain's railways that British Rail's performance has to be examined in some detail. As we have seen, BR was not nationalised in propitious circumstances. The First World War had left a legacy of under-investment and an exhausted rail network; the situation after the Second World War was equally bad.

The early years of BR – and, indeed, most of its history – were dominated by the struggle to stem the rising losses due to the fall in passenger numbers and freight carryings while bringing the network up to modern standards. In the early years freight traffic was transferring to the roads at an average of 5 per cent annually; many small branch-line passenger trains were running empty; losses were mounting; and the trades unions, at a time of labour shortage, were ever spoiling for a fight.

There was no easy, quick fix for these entrenched problems and, worse, there was the legacy of the way that the industry had been nationalised, which resulted in administrative disarray because of the complicated structure of the British Transport Commission, and financial problems due to the generous compensation terms. In its early days the BTC, which was also responsible for long-distance road haulage, paid insufficient attention to the railways, and decisions were confused by the three-tiered management structure that controlled the industry.

During the war, the executive consisted of the railway general managers, a system which had been felt to work well, while British Railways was perceived as a remote and formless body with its unresponsive bosses enjoying the splendour of the 222 Marylebone Road headquarters (now a luxury hotel) and the BTC even further away at 55 Broadway, St James's Park (later the London Transport HQ).

Therefore administrative reorganisation was always on the agenda, especially after the change of government in 1951 when the Conservatives were elected with the ageing Winston Churchill as prime minister. The experiment with widespread state control and an integrated transport policy through the British Transport Commission was to be short-lived. Road haulage had only just been dragged 'screaming and kicking into the public domain'[1] when, in the first of a seemingly perpetual series of reorganisations, the Conservatives partly dismantled the British Transport Commission through the 1953 Transport Act, which abolished the Railway Executive and appointed railway boards directly under the BTC. This was the first of 'several defective solutions'[2] for the organisational problems of the railways imposed on the industry in its fifty-year history of state ownership, all devised by outsiders with insufficient weight being given to the views of rail managers. The Act also denationalised road haulage, resulting in the sale of 24,000 lorries to small road hauliers who were able to compete, without any restriction on their charges, against BR which had its rates fixed by the government.

The investment programme was hampered by the large payments to the former shareholders, which increased losses. As David Henshaw notes in his ground-breaking analysis of the Beeching cuts, 'Whereas a private company would have paid little or no dividend in lean years, the return on British Transport Stock was guaranteed . . . the railways were obliged to pay a fixed sum of around £40 million per year – even when they were making substantial losses.'

That money would have been much better spent on improving the railways. According to a calculation by the Central Statistical Office,[3] the railways suffered a net disinvestment of £440m in the period 1938–1953 (about £9bn at today's prices) – in other words, their assets deteriorated faster than they were being renewed. The disappointingly low investment in BR's early years was also partly a result of the shortage of both labour and materials in the aftermath of the war and of several other factors: narrow-minded managers often more concerned with the short-term interests of their particular section of the railway, the layers of bureaucracy – there were thirteen management levels where five were reckoned to suffice[4] – and the plethora of government controls, in particular the constant Treasury interference that was to be the Achilles heel of the railway industry for the rest of the century. Moreover, with charges, both freight and passenger, strictly controlled by the government, the Railway Executive eschewed major projects such as electrification because they could not earn a rate of return through increasing fares.

Money was wasted, too, by the failure to understand the need for modernisation and, in particular, to replace steam. Although some thought was given to investigating other forms of motive power, the idea got clogged up in the bureaucracy and meanwhile new steam locomotives continued to be ordered. The Western Region added nearly 300 steam shunters to its stock in the first five years of nationalisation, even though diesels were known to be much more efficient for the task. The railways, therefore, missed a big opportunity. The failure to introduce diesels – which were more expensive to build but much cheaper to run and therefore more economical in the long term – and the railbuses used widely on the continent was to prove disastrous for branch lines once Richard Beeching became chairman of the BTC a decade later. Motorway construction, first mooted in the war, had been delayed as a result of lack of finance, and this should have afforded the railways the chance of retaining their market share. Instead, without investment or clear direction, they stagnated.

MODERNISATION PLAN

They were, however, to be given one last chance. The British Transport Commission, aware of the structural shortcomings of the network and desperate to stem losses, pressed the government to accept the case for a renewal of the railways. This was presented as the massive Modernisation Plan published in January 1955. By then, rising costs, road competition and frequent industrial action had pushed the railways into a £22m annual loss. The Conservative administration was faced with a stark choice – modernise the railways or see them die.

The scale of the plan was breathtaking, a wholesale re-organisation of railway activities. It envisaged spending £1.24bn (£20bn at today's prices) over fifteen years to revamp the railways, including £335m on diesel locomotives and electrification, £285m on coaches and station facilities and £210m on freight services. There was to be total replacement of steam power by 100mph diesels, mass electrification and conversion of branch lines to diesel unit operation, while the stations, with

facilities little changed in a century and patched-up after Hitler's bomb-
ings, would be replaced by airy structures of steel, glass and concrete.
(That neo-classical Euston was one of the stations to get this treatment
was possibly the greatest act of architectural vandalism of the 1960s, a
decade with several such outrages to its discredit.)

Freight, uneconomically packed into small wagons, which often went
missing for weeks or never arrived at all, would be speeded up with new
vehicles shunted into order in vast new mechanised marshalling yards.
Oddly, however, there was little concentration on improving the main
trunk network, even though, as we saw in the last chapter, as far back as
the 1930s the advantages of high speed trains had been demonstrated.
Although electrification of the West Coast Main Line was included in the
plan, it was not prioritised, and as a result of escalating costs and a lack
of commitment, the scheme – which was tremendously successful in
boosting passenger numbers – was not completed until the late 1960s.

The aim was to make the railways profitable. Instead of having to be
rescued by the government on an annual basis, British Railways would
deliver a permanent annual profit of £85m (£1.3bn in today's money)
within six years. This starry-eyed vision saw the 1955 Modernisation Plan
pushed through Parliament with little detailed debate. The Tory government was surprisingly receptive to the plan, seeing it as part of the post-
war modernisation programme for which funds had, at last, started to
become available. The Labour Party was more sceptical, suggesting that
the Modernisation Plan was a complete waste of money. However, the
party's line was not based on any cogent analysis of its shortcomings but
rather on the view that the railways were finished, road transport was the
way ahead, and it should be the minimum entitlement of every working
man to own a motor car.

The plan was to be a once-in-a-generation opportunity to revamp the
railways but it was based on a major misconception: that, given sufficient
investment, people would flock back to the railways. The opening sentence seems, with hindsight, stunning in its naivety: 'The Modernisation
Plan will win traffic back from the roads. Freight traffic will also return
and grow.' As one of the few dissenting voices, H.P. Barker, a part-time
member of the Commission put it, the plan was based on the false notion
that 'the present operational conceptions of the British Railways are
viable in the long run, given modern equipment', whereas, he said, 'a
substantial proportion of our movement operations, as carried today, are

grossly uneconomic'.[5] Indeed, it is difficult to comprehend how both politicians and railway managers persuaded themselves that there was a realistic prospect of a serious railway revival. Since entering the car ownership club was the ultimate ambition, and becoming feasible for the average family, there was little incentive to walk a mile to a scruffy BR station to wait an hour for the slow train that bore no resemblance to what the government was promising in its modernisation manifesto. The plan used a scattergun approach to fire investment at all parts of the railway with little sense of overall objectives or priorities. As well as the inherent misconceptions, the plan failed because of the BTC's inadequate appraisal of the value of the planned investments, technical problems, government interference and, ultimately, a shift in government policy.

The plan was a mixture of the sensible and the insane. The Eastern Region, for example, was quite right to seek to extend electrification to places such as Bishops Stortford, Ipswich and the Essex coastal towns and, later, parts of the East Coast Main Line to Newcastle. But then it gets silly. The Eastern also hatched a bizarre secondary scheme for a further 1,247 miles of electrification, which included the branches to Cleethorpes, Cromer, Hunstanton, Grimsby via Boston, and Skegness. Not only did this fail to happen by 1985 as planned, but many of the lines mentioned did not even stay open as long as that. In similarly eccentric fashion the Southern Region, predominantly a third-rail electric suburban railway, wanted to string up masts and electric wires over the 338 miles between Waterloo, Exeter, and Weymouth.

The inherent flaws in the plan were, with hindsight, pretty easy to spot. One obvious example was the tendency of rail managers, seeing that money was suddenly available, to put up the most ridiculous schemes. The London Midland Region, for example, seriously believed that it would need 660 electric locomotives for the West Coast Main Line (WCML). The Eastern Region advocated electrification of minor Norfolk branches. The Western demanded a vast fleet of diesel-hydraulic diesels straight off the drawing board, at the same time openly admitting that they might not even work. By 2001 even an extended WCML from Euston to Glasgow survives on far fewer than 100 locomotives; those minor Norfolk branches have been closed for nearly four decades and the Western's diesel-hydraulics were all scrapped by 1977, remembered as a maintenance headache and an operating irrelevance. In another case of wild over-optimism the Scottish Region's requests included an unbelievable eighty-five locomotives just for the sparsely used former Highland Railway system north of Perth.

The new freight marshalling yards were another disaster, not only because goods were moving to the roads, encouraged by motorway construction, but because the future for rail freight lay in running whole train loads rather than individual wagons shunted in huge yards. The government had approved £85m (£1.4bn in 2001) for 25–30 new or re-equipped yards of various sizes. All but four were built but within a few years it had become clear that freight would continue to haemorrhage to the roads. A massive 300,000 new wagons were ordered, but as basic products like farm produce, fish, horses, cattle and newspapers went over to road haulage, the freight business sank further into the red. BR had 1.14 million wagons in 1955 and it was discarding 8,000 each week by the early 1960s. Today there are fewer than 40,000. The new Perth yard was the earliest casualty. When it opened in 1962 it was handling 1,200 wagons per day for 58 scheduled train arrivals, with seed potato traffic providing a seasonal surge of an additional 250 consignments a day. Six years later the traffic had all gone and the yard was facing closure.

The plan's most visible white elephant was the Bletchley flyover, which can still be seen by passengers on the WCML. It was built for £1.6m (£30m today) but never used as it was part of a grand scheme to use the Oxford–Cambridge line as an east-west route avoiding London that never materialised. It took six years to build and was completed in January 1962 – by which time there was no traffic to feed it.

Some of the new technology did not work as expected or proved to be unreliable. The government's insistence on certain purchases, such as domestically produced locomotives as opposed to cheaper imports, did not help. Expensive technical mistakes were made, such as trying to fit all freight wagons with compatible braking systems at vast expense, and ordering unreliable locomotives designed in haste led to an overheated supply industry. A ridiculous number of prototype diesel designs, 171, were tried and, because of the sudden availability of cash, many were rushed into production without the usual three-year testing programme. The result was a loss of reliability – and even occasionally the temporary reintroduction of steam – which hardly reinforced public confidence in the new technology.

The finances of the plan had always looked shaky. There was no built-in increase for wages and yet it was clear that above-inflation rises were needed to tackle labour shortages. The plan was reviewed in 1956 and it quickly became apparent that there was nothing in it to justify the notion that the BTC could achieve profitability for BR in 1970, let alone 1962. Quite the opposite. Passenger numbers were rising, with 1956 seeing a post-nationalisation peak, but the extra income was not enough to stop losses increasing. Deficits went up, reaching £90m in 1958. The financial situation had been exacerbated by government control of electorally unpopular fare rises. Twice in the 1950s, agreed rises had been stopped by government intervention at the last minute and rail fares had risen by well under the rate of inflation since 1938.

In essence, the problem was that the plan was little more than a series of investment schemes put up by the regions with crudely worked out rates of return based on optimistic assumptions about growth. For example, as BR's official historian put it, 'Large sums of money were committed to freight modernisation without a clear and unanimous statement of future policy.'[6] The focus was on purchasing hardware, such as locomotives and massive marshalling yards, rather than boosting revenue through better services. Moreover, little attention was paid to reducing costs. Perhaps someone should have heeded the forthright comments of former Eastern Region chief general manager Gerard Fiennes, who later blew the lid off railway politics in a book: 'The BTC's simple error was that it bought the tools before it knew what job it wanted to be done.'[7]

The remarkable point about the great Modernisation Plan was that its overarching optimism did not arise out of some political fiat but was the result of proposals presented by the most senior figures in railway management from information collected from all tiers of technical, operating and management. That it all got past the most senior officials in the Treasury, and ultimately a fairly parsimonious government, seems all the more remarkable. Was it that none of them foresaw the decline of the railways in competition with the car, or did they simply stick their heads in the sand, refusing to acknowledge that the century-long heyday of the railways was over?

While it would be easy to blame the government entirely for the failure of the plan, that would be to ignore the crass errors of the BTC and BR's senior managers. Within just five years the plan, which managed to consume £1,000m of investment – worth ten times that today – was in ruins as the government turned off the cash tap. Instead of the hoped-for grand revival, passenger and freight revenues had fallen even faster than before. The government changed tack, dramatically.

In 1960, poring over the ever-worsening figures for the railways' finances, transport minister Ernest Marples decided that the railway spending roadshow had to be stopped. It had been pure fantasy that the railways could ever have made £85 million profit by 1962. The 1961 balance sheet (the last before Beeching) was a shocker. The business, affected by a mild recession, had recorded a loss for the year of £87m (almost £1.2bn in today's money), an increase of £19m in a single year and it would get much worse in 1962. Add to that a further £49m in interest and fixed charges, and it is easy to understand why politicians had got fed up with the railways.

Transport politicians can usually be characterised as either being pro-rail or pro-roads, and Marples was unequivocally a roads man, a keen advocate of the motorway (he had founded one of the construction companies that built the M1) and sceptical of the value of rail investment. The government had, in any case, already hedged its bets, having announced a £212m scheme to modernise the road network only days after the publication of the Modernisation Plan and the first motorway, the Preston by-pass, had opened in December 1958.

Using analysis from the United States which argued that the railway was obsolescent, Marples decided to freeze most UK railway investment. And he brought in a man in his own mould to wield the axe – Richard Beeching, a scientist with no experience of the railways whose previous job had been technical director of ICI. His brief, as the new chairman of the BTC (then as chairman of BR after the BTC was rapidly abolished), was simple: make the railways profitable, whatever it takes. There was to be no consideration of the social benefits of the railway: his instructions were that if any line were not profitable, it should be hacked out.

Beeching's report,[8] published in 1963, provided a trenchant picture of the state of the railways. His analysis showed that half of BR's 17,830 route miles were not worth modernising as they carried only 4 per cent of the traffic; 3,368 stations generated only 4 per cent of the parcels business; coal trucks made one trip on average every three days, and of the 5,000 coal depots, 4,000 received fewer than six loads per week. Stock utilisation was so poor that some 9,000 passenger coaches stood idle for three-quarters of the year, waiting for the summer seaside business, and 2,000 were used fewer than ten times per year. It was easy to understand why road haulage was stealing all the business when Beeching found that it took an average of two days for each wagon to deliver its consignment and that the average wagon would only be used twenty-five times a year on a journey of just sixty-seven miles. Some were lost for weeks on end. Freight locomotives spent half their time shunting in sidings and the other half hauling an average of a scant twenty wagons between marshalling yards. As Henshaw added, 'Someone had even proved that it was quicker to walk across London with a parcel than to send it by rail.'9

British Railways senior staff had, perhaps, been too preoccupied with the transition from steam traction to diesel and electric, and with devising a modern freight policy, to realise that one in nine families now owned a motor car, and that the other eight were saving to buy one. Now, for the first time, there was a recognition that given the increasing popularity of road transport, it was no longer socially necessary for the railways to cover the country comprehensively. Only 10 per cent of journeys were by train (interestingly, the figure now is 2 per cent, but the number of train journeys has remained remarkably stable since World War II while car journeys have increased massively).

Beeching's brutal fifteen-point solution to this situation was to put the railways into profit by 1970 by cutting swathes of lines, discontinuing most stopping services and transferring the displaced diesels to replace steam on the remainder. He proposed to shut some 2,363 small stations and 5,000 miles of track, and cut out duplicate lines. Beeching planned to damp down seasonal peaks by scrapping under-used coaching stock, coordinate suburban train and bus services and charges, and improve the parcels and postal service. Coal and other heavy traffic would be mechanised, and rates for loss-making freight increased to the point where much would go on to the roads.

The Tories lost the 1964 election before much of Beeching's work could be completed. The new prime minister, Harold Wilson, who on the hustings had promised a thorough review of the railway closures and denounced Beeching's report in powerful terms, showed his customary duplicity by executing a remarkable U-turn after he was elected. It took some time for rail campaigners to extract a clear statement of policy from

government but when they did, in March 1965, it was a great disappoint-
ment. Wilson claimed that he did not have the power to stop any of the
thirty-eight closures which were on the desks of incoming ministers at
the time of the election. (Of these, twenty-five had already been closed
but in the event some, like the Dumfries–Stranraer line, were saved and
remain in operation today.) Instead, the closure programme was speeded
up: while Ernest Marples authorised the closure of 991 miles of railway in
1964, Tom Fraser, his Labour successor was to authorise 1,071 before the
end of 1965.[10]

The confused state of railway policy in this crucial period is illustrated
by the fact that in 1965 the Labour government received a second report[11]
from Beeching which advocated a series of further reductions to the network but, while rejecting it and choosing not to renew Beeching's tenure
at the British Railways Board, still proceeded with a series of closures
which were to prove the most damaging to the railways in the long term.
The second report advocated concentrating investment on key major
routes but, as a *quid pro quo*, closing vast swathes of the network. Only
3,000 route miles out of the 7,500 advocated for retention in the first
report were to be actively developed, with the rest allowed to wither
away – though he avoided the word closure (in fact around 10,500 miles
survived). The railway would merely link a few major cities such as
London, Manchester and Glasgow; Newcastle would find itself at the end
of a single-track freight branch from Leeds;[12] while the London–Leicester, Newcastle–Edinburgh and Plymouth–Penzance routes were all to be
shut.

Closures advocated in the first Beeching Report, in fact, continued
throughout the 1960s but slowed to a trickle by the mid-1970s and then
dried up altogether by 1977, although the attempt by BR to close major
sections of the railway only ended in the 1980s with the unsuccessful and
highly dishonest attempt to shut the Carlisle to Settle railway, now
intensely used by freight and passenger trains and as a diversionary
route.

It was the closures after 1966 that seem inexplicable. Before then most
closures had been of structurally uneconomic lines, but the lines taken
out of the network after that date caused lasting damage to the coherence
of Britain's rail network[13] and reduced the system to a size which served
proportionately fewer of Britain's towns and cities than comparable
European systems. While at the time Labour had one of the ablest ever

transport ministers, Barbara Castle, the civil servants who had developed the Beeching strategy were very much in control at the ministry and their views were allowed to prevail. The chief casualties, which were either partially or wholly dismantled, were the Great Central (which a freight group is currently seeking to reinstate) that was an alternative route from London to the Midlands and North West, the Somerset & Dorset between Bath and Bournemouth, Oxford–Cambridge and the alternative Exeter–Plymouth line.

It was, indeed, the failure of those who carried out the Beeching cuts to consider the railway within a wider context that was the greatest mistake. For example, at the very time that the Oxford–Cambridge line was being axed, the government was busily drawing up plans to turn Milton Keynes, within easy reach of the line, into the nation's fastest growing city. The Great Central, heavily used, was an equally short-sighted closure as, at the same time, Harold Wilson was negotiating with the French to build the Channel Tunnel that would have linked in with the line which was built to European gauge standards. It was, too, a classic example of BR's tactics in closing lines by stealth. Run down the line over a period of years and after passengers have fled as a result of the poor services, it becomes uneconomic, justifying closure.

The anomalies resulting from the haphazard way in which Beeching's cuts were implemented, with some lines being cut while others survived, are legion. Cross-country routes were decimated, leaving many major towns without direct links to each other or to London, while isolated communities in Central and Mid-Wales, the wild moorlands of Scotland, and remote areas of Cumbria, Norfolk and East Lincolnshire still have stations that can never attract more than a couple of dozen passengers a day. For example, the sizeable Lincolnshire port town of Boston, once a 'main-line' station, was deprived of its direct London link and can only now be reached via the circuitous route of Sleaford and Grantham, just to save sixteen miles of track south to Spalding. Stratford-on-Avon has become an outpost of the West Midlands suburban system, which means a circuitous journey for all those tourists seeking to visit Shakespeare country from London. And so on.

The short-sightedness of the policy is demonstrated by the desire of the present-day Strategic Rail Authority to reinstate many of the gaps in the national network left by the post-Beeching butchery such as Oxford–Cambridge and the Manchester–Sheffield line via the Woodhead tunnel, which even Beeching had sought to retain for its heavy freight potential. Now Trans-Pennine franchise hopefuls are talking about reinstating the line with its long tunnel at a cost of £200m. There is talk, too, of reopening London's direct link with Lewes via Uckfield, cut to save a paltry amount of money but not safeguarded so that a road now crosses the old rail track, but the cost, estimated at £50m, may be prohibitive.

Labour allowed the Beeching plan to be rushed through with little attempt to exercise simple operational economies such as de-manning stations, simplifying signalling, and on-train ticket sales – which could all have played a part in seeing rural routes survive the tough 1970s and 1980s. Beeching's cuts were never going to save much money. He estimated annual savings from closures and cuts in stopping passenger services at around £30m, less than a third of the overall deficit. So little attention was paid to other possible cuts: as late as 1968, there were 7,000 freight guards, even though few trains still had a brake van and their role was 'not immediately obvious'.[14]

It is difficult from the standpoint of 2001 to realise just how strong the belief was that the car represented the future. There was no conception that high-speed trains, even on Britain's under-invested network, would be the preferred form of travel for journeys such as London–Manchester or London–Leeds rather than the car or the aeroplane. It was that faith in road transport which underpinned Beeching's thinking and led to the massive closures, even of lines that carried large numbers of people.

Beeching's logic for line closures was largely discredited by critics. While there was a case for some closures, with an anti-rail minister in power and aided by dubious use of figures, Beeching went much too far. He had thought of a solution and found figures to back up his case. There were well substantiated allegations that 'losses' were contrived in order to achieve the closure objective. Decisions on individual lines were based on a nationwide passenger survey conducted during the week ending 23 April 1961. This was an unfair date for lines with seasonal business, but the subsequent report dismissed this as an 'irrelevant objection'. Moreover, revenue was often misallocated. Seaside towns, where few people paid their fares, as most arrived with return tickets, were made to look uneconomic when, in fact, they could have been highly profitable. While it might have seemed to save money to scrap rolling stock used infrequently, the cost of retaining it to cater for such holiday traffic was, in fact, minimal.

Where Beeching so often went wrong was in his disregard for knock-on effects. Cut off the branches and the tree may die. Many local routes were slated for closure without much regard to their importance as feeders to main lines, which then landed in financial trouble. Beeching also created a climate in which the whole thrust of management was geared towards seeking closures, often by massaging figures rather than seeking new markets and business for their industry.

Instead of looking at cheaper ways of running services through the use of railbuses or diesel units, closures were made merely on the basis of existing costs. Moreover, social benefits were not taken into account. There was no attempt at cost-benefit analysis by, for example, considering the extra road accidents caused by people travelling in cars and all the other disbenefits of motoring. Logic, though, was not part of the Beeching process. As Henshaw argues, the whole sorry episode was about achieving a shift away from the railways to roads by a pro-roads administration.

Like the Modernisation Plan, Beeching's policy was based on a misconception, albeit a completely different one – that the railways could be made profitable if loss-making branches were closed leaving a core network that could earn money. The fallacy behind this argument was explicitly admitted in Beeching's second report, which stated that even a 3,000-mile railway would not necessarily guarantee profitability.[15] In other words, the only way to ensure there were no losses was to close the railway entirely. This was borne out by the figures for BR's deficit. As BR's official historian points out,[16] the accumulated losses for 1963–73 were £775m, much higher than those for the previous fourteen years which amounted to £560m at the same prices. The Beeching plan was a failure in its own terms.

Beeching also made the mistaken assumption that people displaced from trains would be happy to travel by bus. In fact, the many substitute bus services introduced to appease opponents of closures were quickly removed since patronage was low, even where trains had previously been full. People, particularly the middle classes who are heavy users of rail services, prefer trains.

The switch in policy which had seen the Modernisation Plan replaced rapidly by Beeching's swinging cuts left the railway in a terrible state: 'The new railway system, billed as compact, efficient and modern, was really demoralised, inefficient and chronically short of investment capital.'[17]

Things did get slightly better. Barbara Castle's 1968 Transport Act, which introduced the concept of a social railway, made explicit, at last, the idea that railways could no longer be judged on a narrow financial basis but existed to provide a service to the public which needed subsidy from the taxpayer. Specific grants were made available for loss-making services and although, inevitably, the amounts were insufficient and calculated by a bizarre formula, it was at least a recognition of the wider role of the railways. Integration, having been promoted in 1948, but dropped in 1962, was now back on the agenda. (It featured prominently in Labour's 1997 manifesto, too, but was barely mentioned in 2001.)

One of the great successes of the 1968 Act has been the creation of self-managing Passenger Transport Executives (PTEs) in the major cities of Manchester, Newcastle, Glasgow, Birmingham, Liverpool and Leeds; this has worked wonders in revitalising suburban rail systems. The creation of PTEs allowed metropolitan authorities to decide transport strategies for major centres of population and also transferred financial control of these services to councillors who were aware of local needs. They were given a large measure of control, including the power to specify fare structures, integrate bus and rail services and, from the mid-1980s, buy rolling stock.

MODERNISING BR

The 1968 Act gave BR a somewhat sounder financial footing by wiping out its historic £1,200m debt, and, boosted by the success of the West Coast Main Line electrification, the modernisation of the network, rather than its dismemberment, became the accepted aim. The Board, under the forward-looking Richard Marsh, began to develop a series of prestige projects to modernise the railways but also considered a series of closures, most of which proved politically unpalatable to implement because they were in rural areas controlled by the Tories who had won the 1970 election. The fuel crisis of 1973 ensured a renewed interest in rail as it was patently the most fuel-efficient form of transport – a two-car diesel multiple unit which can carry over 100 passengers, for example, manages four miles to the gallon.

The railways, however, had to be bailed out again when Labour returned to government. This was because there had still been no recognition that the railways needed continuing financial support, rather than just a one-off debt wipe-out. Therefore, when Harold Wilson returned to power in 1974 he was immediately faced with a financial crisis in the railways. He allocated £2.1bn to BR, including £1,500m for subsidising loss-making services over five years, a final recognition of the need to maintain a socially useful network. This was done through the Railways Act 1974 which created the Public Service Obligation, the grant payable annually to BR that was based, rather vaguely, on the provision of a service broadly comparable with the level of service pertaining that year. There was, however, still no clear resolution as to what the railways were for. The BR Board continued to argue that a profitable railway was around the corner but that goal was never achieved.

Beeching's prediction that air would be the favoured method of transport between major cities had failed to take into account the limitations of domestic airline services. Big aircraft were not economic on short-haul routes, and capacity problems of air traffic control, as well as the hassle of travelling on congested roads to out of town airports, gave rail a competitive advantage, provided BR could speed up services. This was the key project of the 1970s. The solution was to introduce fast diesels – the highly popular High Speed Trains (HSTs) – on some routes such as those out of Paddington and St Pancras, and to electrify others such as the East Coast Main Line out of King's Cross. Britain sadly eschewed the French solution of building dedicated high-speed lines, instead upgrading existing lines for higher speed travel.

It was a successful strategy. The introduction of the HSTs in 1976 and the adoption of the InterCity name boosted passenger usage and radically improved railway finances. The HSTs were a low-tech solution and the plan was to replace them eventually with the Advanced Passenger Train, which used tilt. Unfortunately, that idea foundered through the failure of the technology and a collective lack of nerve on the part of government and British Rail, as most of the glitches were on the point of being sorted out when the project was scrapped in 1986. Another scheme which did not see the light but on which much energy – and considerable cash – was expended was the Channel Tunnel Rail Link and the tunnel itself. A detailed plan was published in 1972 and work began but, after inevitable cost rises, it was put on hold in 1975 by Wilson.

Under constant pressure to reduce the deficit, which had briefly been wiped out in the early 1970s but soon reappeared, BR at last grasped the nettle of efficiency, boosting productivity enormously by cutting out swathes of bureaucracy and staff made redundant by new technologies. Both Marsh, and, to a lesser extent, his successor Peter Parker who took over in 1976, managed to drive through significant improvements in working practices which, in turn, ensured the survival of many marginal services. The tide had turned on closures, with BR now more ready to take into account the contribution made by passengers starting their journeys on the branch lines but continuing on the rest of the network. By the late 1970s station reopenings rather than closures were becoming the vogue but no new major lines were being considered.

Throughout the 1970s it was increasingly evident that the railway no longer needed a cumbersome and powerful regionally-based management system which bore no relationship to markets. This led to the creation of stand-alone businesses – InterCity, Network SouthEast, Provincial (later Regional) as well as freight and parcels – whose managers were expected to run them like commercial concerns by taking responsibility for marketing, investment and cost allocation. After a struggle, the powerful regions were largely phased out (though vestiges of the structure survived until the late 1980s) and the restructured railway began to assume the aspect of a modern, forward-looking business.

THATCHER'S DISCIPLINE

The election of Mrs Thatcher at the head of a Conservative government in 1979 brought an insistence that there should be greater financial discipline for the railways and that peripheral businesses, such as hotels, rolling stock manufacture and ferry services, should to be privatised. The railway soon came under attack from a government with little love for an industry still seen as archaic and a prime minister who famously once said that using public transport was a sign of failure. With modern high-speed trains and greater efficiency, BR had been booming, carrying almost a billion passengers in 1979, the highest since the start of the Beeching cuts. But recession was around the corner and the deficit was starting to rise again, going up from £692m in 1975 to £1,035m in 1982. The increasing losses, together with a prime minister hostile to the railways, led to the setting up of a commission on railway finances, a four-man committee headed by Sir David Serpell, a former Department of Environment senior civil servant, and a renewed debate about the size of the network.

On the assumption that the government still had a belief in the 'social railway', the British Railways Board had expected suggestions for a rational policy for sustaining and financing the network at its present size, even though it was obvious that major investment was needed on track, buildings and rolling stock after decades of under-investment. Instead, Serpell produced six options for a much-pruned British railway for the twenty-first century. His infamous 'Option A' chopped the 10,500 route miles of BR down to just 1,630, comprising only the main lines from Euston to Birmingham, Liverpool, Manchester, Glasgow and Edinburgh; King's Cross to Leeds and Newcastle; Liverpool Street to Norwich; Paddington to Cardiff; and a few key London commuter lines to the Essex, Kent, Sussex and Hampshire coastlines. There would, therefore, be no railway south west of Bristol, nothing in North or Mid-Wales, none north of the Scottish Lowlands, and not a single cross-country route.

By stressing this option, rather than some of the other more realistic ones, the BR Board managed to ensure that the Serpell Report created a storm of protest and was, therefore, quickly tossed into the bin. Instead, the Tory government surprised everyone by embarking upon a series of programmes that included modest investment in rural lines. This was prompted by a fruitful relationship between the new chairman, Sir Bob Reid, (the first chairman of that name who, confusingly, was succeeded by a namesake) and the secretary of state, Nicholas Ridley, which ensured that, for the first time, there was a dialogue about what the government wanted the railway to do. The fruits of this were seen in investment schemes such as electronic radio signalling, which scored notable successes in reducing costs in remote locations such as the West Highland and Far North lines in Scotland and in East Suffolk and, more important, the replacement of almost all the worn-out diesel multiple unit and locomotive-hauled trains on regional routes, all dating back to the late 1950s, with a modern fleet, many of which were air-conditioned.

BR was set the target of making InterCity profitable, which was achieved with a bit of fiddling over the inclusion of high-revenue routes such as London–Norwich and the omission of loss-makers, such as trains to Barrow in Furness and Cleethorpes, and some creative accounting that ensured costs were stacked into the heavily subsidised Provincial Railways sector. Freight, too, was supposed to be profitable, a much harder target. From an annual loss of £100m in 1984, InterCity broke even a couple of years later and then became highly profitable in the boom years of the late 1980s. This was achieved by more intensive use of rolling stock, good marketing and better yield management – raising fares in markets that could bear it. Indeed, for the first time, fare rises had been used deliberately by BR, under government instruction, to maximise revenue and bring down the deficit. Virtually every year from Mrs Thatcher's election to the mid-1990s, fares went up by more than the rate of inflation, which made sense in the narrow terms of cutting BR's losses but was nonsensical in environmental terms. Indeed, at times of boom, demand was deliberately choked off in order to damp down the need for investment in major schemes to increase capacity on the railway. Astonishingly, at the height of the late 1980s boom, Network SouthEast, the London commuter lines, broke even despite a massive investment programme. BR was again booming, with the number of train miles having increased by 18 per cent in the three years to 1988, while costs per passenger-mile had dropped by almost a third. BR was now arguably the most efficient railway in the world: subsidy was a mere 0.16 per cent of Gross National Product, compared with the European average of 0.52 per cent.[18] Subsidy had declined by a half in real terms between 1983 and 1989.[19] Indeed, according to the standard reference work, 'On statistical comparisons with almost all major European railways, showing the highest productivity and also the lowest level of funding by government. That did not affect public perception of shortcomings in service quality in some areas.'[20] In other words, the public might well have welcomed a bit more subsidy in return for a better service.

Railway economics are always highly dependent on the performance of the overall economy, and BR's new-found efficiency was no protection from recession. Just as BR had started to get things right, it suffered a sharp decline in patronage as a result of the post-Lawson recession – numbers travelling into London fell by 100,000 to 350,000 over a three-year period – and the situation was exacerbated when the railways faced yet another reorganisation. Although in hindsight this was in preparation for privatisation, the decision to sell off the railways had not yet been made, but the government wanted a more business-oriented structure. The scheme called 'Organising for Quality' resulted in virtually all aspects of the railway being devolved to the sectors. The British Railways Board would still set the objectives and standards (including safety), but the sectors would control everything else. InterCity was turned into six profit centres, Network SouthEast eight and Regional

Railways five and these would later form the future basis of the franchising system.

Through a combination of tight management under a good run of chairmen and some, though insufficient, investment, BR had largely got it right. The management had finally got rid of the regional baronies, they had developed a competitive – or market-orientated – fares policy, strikes were reducing, the passenger's charter had been developed as a means of measuring performance – which was improving – and they had even convinced the government to allow rolling stock to be leased. As mentioned above, efficiency was the best in Europe and productivity still rising. British Rail bore comparison with any major railway operation in the world. It was 'little short of miraculous in the circumstances',[21] as another former BR board member put it: 'By that time we certainly knew more about where the money went and what cost what than we do today, ironic given that transparency was one of the arguments for privatisation.'

Chris Green, one of the most forward-looking rail managers and now head of Virgin Rail, had developed the concept of Total Route Modernisation, concentrating scarce resources on one route to improve it radically. This involved the refurbishment of the track, signalling and stations, as well as new trains in order to create what was effectively a new railway. This was done on the Chiltern line which, not surprisingly, has managed to attract massive numbers of new passengers; but the demise of BR stopped the programme. The 1994 timetable, the last written by BR, was 'reckoned to be the best ever'.[22] Despite the row over the Settle–Carlisle railway, BR was now concentrating on reopening lines with over 200 new stations opened in its last decade.

Moreover, BR had developed two instantly recognisable brand names – InterCity and Network SouthEast – and the InterCity TV advertising campaign ranks among the all time greats. Although overall subsidy was on the rise, that was largely due to the economic downturn. As a former non-executive board member put it, 'I don't think the British railways were ever as well run as in the early 1990s.'[23]

As the first Sir Bob Reid said, 'Major organisational change is the remedy for a business which is in bad shape and ours is not.' Yet this was the point at which a government ignorant of railway realities chose to break up an efficient, publicly run, integrated railway. The recession which started in 1989 had weakened the railway and the numbers looked terrible because of the fall in passenger numbers and freight tonnage carried, the collapse of the property market and the costs of an investment programme predicated on a continued boom. The government failed to understand the simple economics and, pursuing its own ideological bent, embarked on its most controversial privatisation.

It would be wrong to paint BR immediately pre-privatisation as anything like perfect. There were still struggles to obtain investment and, inevitably, there were still inefficiencies and mistakes. However, it would also be wrong to dismiss the fifty-year record of BR as a failure because of errors such as the Modernisation Plan, the Beeching cuts and the perennial problems of under-investment. In fact, BR's record is much more mixed than its detractors would have us believe. Its biggest problem, which many see as an inevitable feature of a nationalised industry, was its vulnerability to the stop-go investment policies of the government. The railways need a constant level of investment in order to renew and enhance the network. Successive governments of both political hues blew hot and cold. During times of boom, the railway was positively swilling with money, but deficits built up quickly once there was an economic downturn.

The period of state control was characterised by a constant paradox that was never resolved: the railway was expected to be run economically but also to cater for rather vaguely defined social needs. As BR's official historian put it,

> The BTC had wanted to modernise the railways after years of neglect. The public wanted a modern railway network of roughly the same size of 1955. The government wanted the BTC to fulfil its obligation to break even. Much of the review activity was . . . about the attempt, made under government pressure, to reconcile these objectives. Not surprisingly, it proved impossible to do so.[24]

He was writing about the Modernisation Plan and Beeching but this analysis could apply equally to any part of the past fifty years of railway history.

These last two chapters demonstrate that, over the whole history of the railways in Britain, it has proved impossible for the state and the railways to reach a mutually fruitful relationship. There has been, at various times, too little or too much interference. Victorian *laissez faire* left us with an extensive network that did not necessarily serve social needs, but the attempt to rationalise the system after the First World War failed. Again, after the Second World War, the right structure seemed to elude the policy-makers and, sadly, it was only at the end that BR and the government had got many of the basics right. However, the biggest mistake of successive British governments has been the failure to think strategically and to develop the type of grand plan whose success makes the British so envious when they travel on the French TGV system.

CHAPTER 4

The poll tax on wheels

Mrs Thatcher may never have travelled on a train, but her political instincts were sufficiently well attuned to put her off privatising the railways. The idea of selling off the trains had been first mooted as early as the 1960s by the Conservative Research Department which rejected the idea as economically unviable.[1] The concept resurfaced when the Tories were in opposition in the late 1970s in a policy statement from the Young Conservatives and a pamphlet by Norman Fowler, the party's transport spokesman.[2] After the 1979 election which brought Thatcher to power, Fowler even managed to float, briefly, the idea of privatising Southern Region but there was overwhelming opposition from his colleagues. Clearly the time was not ripe for such a radical policy given that the whole concept of privatisation was still at the fledgling stage.

Contrary to conventional wisdom, Mrs Thatcher's government stumbled upon its massive privatisation programme largely by accident, and the sale of nationalised industries featured only obliquely in the 1979 election manifesto. There were plenty of easier targets than the railways. The first Conservative term was taken up with testing the water for privatisation through the sale of marginal state holdings like BP (5 per cent), Associated British Ports, Amersham International and British Rail Hotels, all as trade sales rather than open-market flotations. It was only in the second term, after the 1983 election, that the programme really got underway, and the next few years saw the sale of British Telecom, British Gas and the water companies, all as regulated monopolies with very little notion of competition, a fact which greatly disappointed the right wing of the Tory party who wanted privatisation to foster the opening up of markets.

Meanwhile, a more radical type of sale was taking place in the transport arena. The late Nicholas Ridley, a clever ideologue who had the ear of Mrs Thatcher, ended up by chance with the transport portfolio in the reshuffle caused by Cecil Parkinson's amorous indiscretions which had so embarrassingly come to light during the 1983 Conservative party conference. Following the passage of the 1985 Transport Act, Ridley set about breaking up the National Bus Company (NBC), a huge concern that ran most of the country's local bus services, into seventy separate companies, the majority of which were bought by management buy-out teams. He was driven by a singular vision of small-time capitalism. Ridley could see little difference between a local corner shop and a bus, and was in the habit of going round depots asking why the vehicles were not owned by the drivers.

The break-up of the bus industry is important for the subsequent sale of the railways because of the emphasis it placed on competition even though, by the time the structure of rail privatisation was being put in place, Ridley's much-touted belief in bus competition had been shown to be a chimera. At first, when the NBC companies were sold and the market deregulated by allowing virtually anyone to run services providing they fulfilled very basic minimum safety standards, there were fierce bus wars in many provincial towns (London escaped deregulation because the Tories rightly feared there would be vote-losing chaos). Dozens of operators thought there was a quick buck to be made by duplicating services on the profitable routes, but they were under no obligation to create the sort of network which is the lifeblood of an urban economy. They merely cherry-picked the best routes, creaming off profits that had formerly been used to cross-subsidise other services in a network.

These wars resulted in some towns like Sheffield and Manchester being swamped with battered old buses choking local people with exhaust fumes and in services that kept being chopped and changed almost daily to the confusion of the dwindling band of bus users. Within a couple of years, however, most of the smaller operators had been driven out of business by their larger rivals who used underhand tactics like putting on services a minute before or after their competitors, cutting fares below economical levels or even running free services. For example, Stagecoach, the most aggressive company, found itself facing investigation by the Office of Fair Trading thirty times in the decade after deregulation; but the authorities were powerless to stop such predatory activity.

Moreover, nationally, these big firms quickly consolidated and achieved monopoly status in large swathes of the country. (They were also to become the main bidders for the privatised rail franchises when these started being offered for sale in 1995.) Once they had carved out an area, they left their neighbours' territory well alone. With only rare exceptions, such as the fight between FirstGroup and Stagecoach in Glasgow, these large companies have avoided head-on battles with each other, knowing that such mega-bus wars would result in huge losses. The bus wars were, in effect, more a series of massacres of the weak than lengthy battles between well-matched competitors.

The bus fiasco sounded a further warning to Mrs Thatcher about privatising the railways, especially as she understood the special place that chuffa trains have in the hearts of the British people. Ridley arranged a meeting with Thatcher specifically to obtain her support for rail privatisation and received short shrift. A British Rail Board member told one writer:[3] 'She told him [Ridley] never to mention the words again and that was it. She said "Railway privatisation will be the Waterloo of this government. Please never mention the railways to me again."' Mrs Thatcher did not believe that privatising a loss-making industry was feasible as well as being concerned about middle England's affection for its railways. The Department of Transport, which had been testing the water with various ways of selling off the railways, realised that it was politically unpalatable and abandoned the idea.

Paul Channon, the secretary of state for transport appointed after the 1987 election victory, managed to put the idea briefly back on the agenda by announcing at the following year's Conservative party conference that rail privatisation was being considered by the government. He even started looking at some possible models for the structure, but by the time of the next party conference he had been replaced by Cecil Parkinson, who was told to play down the issue.

Thatcher finally changed her mind in the autumn of 1990, just before her demise, and Parkinson was able to tell Parliament that the government was 'determined to privatise British Rail'.[4] Her successor, John Major, shared none of her doubts and began to ask for more detail on how it could be done. He was, according to his colleagues, a more ardent privatiser than his predecessor. However, he apparently showed little direct interest in the issue, as there is no significant mention of rail privatisation in his autobiography but, in his typical bumbling way, he was open to the ideas being put forward by others without fully understanding what he was letting himself in for.

At this stage there was a key hurdle to overcome. Why privatise at all? It was bound to be a hassle since the public's attachment to the railways ensured the issue would be a political hot potato. It is surprisingly difficult to identify the political objectives behind such a key policy undertaking. There were the usual statements about the private sector being more efficient and market-focused. There was talk of extending share ownership, as with other privatisations. And there was the concept of freeing up the railways from the yoke of Treasury control. But none of these are convincing given that the railways were a well-run state industry that would always be in need of government subsidy.

In fact, the drive to privatise largely came from the Treasury, whose hyperactive privatisation unit had run out of things to do as all the obvious targets had been sold off by the time Major became prime minister in 1990. A working group of ministers and civil servants, mostly from the Department of Transport and the Treasury, was established late in 1990 to decide on a blueprint for the privatisation of British Rail and the liberalisation of the rail market.

It is here that the key decision that has done the most damage to the railway began to emerge. Although there were a number of different models, they can be categorised under two headings – integrated or fragmented. The ideologues in the group – largely Treasury mandarins – wanted to split off the track and infrastructure from the operations because this offered the potential for competition. They recognised that it was impossible to create competing tracks but felt that all other aspects of the railway should be subjected to competition. By separating out the track, different rail companies could compete against each other and, in the most extreme version of the model favoured by some Treasury thinkers, even bid in auctions for every individual train path to create real competition. Savour that thought for a moment: it was a serious suggestion that was only knocked on the head at a relatively late stage during one of the all too infrequent reality checks. The Treasury had been disappointed at the lack of competition introduced in most of the earlier privatisations and therefore wanted to ensure that the new structure of the railways involved as much competition as possible.

The Treasury, being the Treasury, also had another agenda in its sights – reducing subsidy. Averaging out the good years with the bad, the

railways cost the government about £1bn per year, though in the haphazard method of Treasury accounting, investment was lumped in with support for socially necessary routes. According to a BR board member of
the time, the Treasury officials leading the privatisation drive, notably
Steve (now Sir Steve) Robson who headed the privatisation unit, 'had no
feel for the industry and wanted a track authority like there was no
tomorrow. They thought the track authority would be free of subsidy
and therefore all they'd be doing is subsidising services.'[5] This drive to
save subsidy coloured all that was to follow because it resulted in a model
designed to deliver reduced subsidy towards a railway that was perceived
as being in long-term decline.[6]

If responsibility can be laid at the door of any one individual for the
model of privatisation eventually adopted, it must be at that of Robson.
It was he who pushed through the track authority model, which made
the rest of the debacle inevitable, and who managed to get mention of a
track authority – 'one part of BR will continue to be responsible for all
track and infrastructure' – into the Conservative party manifesto for
1992. Another former BR board member asked Robson how he managed
to win all the arguments with the politicians, and Robson replied that all
he had to do was point to the BR board, who were strongly in favour of
the BR plc model – privatising BR as one company, which the Treasury
saw as hopelessly monopolistic – and his view would prevail.[7] It may
seem unfair to suggest that a particular civil servant was responsible, and
there are certainly competing claims. A third former BR board member
suggests that Sir Richard Wilson, then Robson's boss and now cabinet
secretary, may have had responsibility for pushing the track authority
model.[8] And there is Sir Christopher Foster, a government adviser at the
time of privatisation (as well as having been Barbara Castle's adviser in
the late 1960s), who also wrote a seminal book on the privatisation of
nationalised industries in 1992 and was on the board of Railtrack for its
first six years.

However, the consensus of a large number of people involved in the
process is that Robson was the key player in driving through the model
that was accepted by the government and also, incidentally, later dreamt
up the hugely controversial plan for the Public Private Partnership, the
part-privatisation of the Tube, which has caused Labour and its transport ministers so much trouble. Robson hated British Rail and its executives. He felt they were plotting against privatisation and this belief was

reinforced by a story he tells about meeting Sir Bob Reid, the chairman of British Rail, by accident on a train. An 'old codger', a peer who had campaigned against privatisation, came up to them and, not knowing who Robson was, congratulated Sir Bob for having 'stuffed' the government in the debate and 'got over all the points you wanted to'.[9] Robson eventually left the Treasury in 2001 and admitted in an interview in the *Financial Times*[10] that rail privatisation had not been an unqualified success and that there were faults in the structure because Railtrack's revenues were not tied to passenger numbers and the operators were not given enough incentives to improve services: 'With hindsight, that was a mistake.'

The Treasury struck at the right time. After the good times of the Lawson boom, BR's finances collapsed in the early 1990s – the requirement for government support rose from £700m to £2bn because of safety expenditure resulting from the 1988 Clapham accident, the recession which saw usage fall by 10 per cent and the costs of improvements to lines leading to the Channel Tunnel.

The more cautious members of the committee examining privatisation wanted to retain a vertically integrated railway, and put forward two alternative ways of dividing up British Rail: regionalisation, which meant something like a return to the Big Four of 1923–48; or sectorisation, the sale of the three passenger businesses created in the 1980s – InterCity, Network SouthEast and Regional Railways. These suggestions, along with the idea of selling BR as one unit, were all dismissed. It was felt that a BR plc would preclude any competition and not have challenged the position of the strong nationally organised trade unions within the industry. Reducing the power of the trade unions was one of the hidden motives for rail privatisation, expressed privately by Tory ministers on many occasions but never boasted about in public.[11]

Given the divergent views on the committee, it was hardly surprising that the conclusions in its report presented to the Cabinet in mid-1991 were a compromise. The plan was to separate out the infrastructure and operations on most of the railway, but the London commuter area would be left vertically integrated because the lines were full and therefore there was no scope for new entrants.

Although Major's Cabinet agreed the principles of the report, the secretary of state for transport, Malcolm Rifkind (the transport portfolio is a revolving door for politicians on the way up or down), began to have doubts about the model that had been suggested. He started to think that InterCity should also be a vertical integrated railway, which effectively meant that the track authority would be a rather unattractive rump. According to one of the Treasury's privatisation team, 'Rifkind made heavy weather of whether InterCity should be vertically integrated. He was sulking in his tent and his officials hadn't been able to develop the idea [of how to privatise the railways].'[12] Downing Street then further muddied the waters by flying the kite of the regional model, which Major seemed to favour, once again. The Treasury felt this model was ridiculous as it was based on Major's strong nostalgia for the Britain of his youth, and had already rejected the idea because of the problems with trains which ran between different areas, thereby using other companies' tracks. This objection ignored the fact that well-established workable arrangements had existed to deal with running over other companies' tracks when the railways had been in the private sector before 1948. In reality the Treasury's obsession with pushing for competition meant that no proper consideration was given to any model other than that requiring the separation of Railtrack from the rest of BR. Major was bought off with the promise that the franchises would be regional.

The Treasury also argued that 'Brussels' required such a separation and this was widely picked up and used by ministers at the time. Indeed, in the run-up to the 2001 election, the Tories, now somewhat embarrassed by their own privatisation of the railways, cited the European directive issued in 1991 as an excuse for breaking up the railways in that way. Tim Collins, a vice-chairman of the Conservative party, said on BBC Radio 4's *Any Questions?*[13] that Major had wanted the Big Four model but had been prevented from introducing it by European rules:

> Separating track ownership from the responsibility for running the railway services . . . was imposed by Europe rather than by the national government. What John Major wanted to do was to recreate the pre-World War II situation where you had four national companies who would have been responsible for the tracks and the signalling and the train services in those areas. He was not allowed to do that because of European regulations.

The notion of the thoroughly Eurosceptic government of John Major bowing to European *diktat* was always unconvincing, and Collins was rewriting history. Europe did indeed pass directive 91/440 just before Britain embarked on rail privatisation, which, in order to stimulate open-access competition, required railway infrastructure to be separated from operations. However, the separation needed only to be an accounting mechanism and the sole open-access operators who had to be accommodated were international freight ventures, and not, as the Tories implied, any Tom, Dick and Harry who fancied running a railway. A report[14] analysing the European directive and its implementation gives the lie to the Tories' excuse that they were forced into their model by Europe. The report says that the directive's requirements were limited to accounting procedures but that it provided the British government with 'an important resource to legitimate its risky undertaking', preparing the way for what the politicians wanted to do anyway. The difficulty for the government was 'the radical and experimental character [of the railway reform] which created considerable uncertainty and risk for political leaders'. Where better to lay the blame than Brussels if anything went wrong.

According to the Treasury officials, Rifkind's dithering resulted in the loss of a year that should have been spent drawing up a detailed scheme to privatise the railways and this meant that the eventual scheme was implemented in much more haste than would otherwise have been the case. In order to find a coherent wording for the manifesto, Jonathan Hill, one of Major's advisers, 'walked round Whitehall saying, "We've got to have something in the manifesto on this,"' according to one official.[15] The eventual model of having Railtrack and a series of operators who held franchises to run groups of rail services seems to have been adopted at this point, although the Tory manifesto still kept options open by saying both that 'one part of BR will continue to be responsible for all track and infrastructure' but also that the new system would 'recapture the spirit of the old regional companies'.

Despite the radical but unspecific nature of the Tories' plans for Britain's beloved trains, there was precious little discussion of the railways during the April 1992 election campaign. Labour made very little play with the issue, and the media, expecting a Labour victory or at least a hung Parliament, did not examine the privatisation in any detail. This was fortunate for the Tories because, as we have seen, their scheme was not properly worked up and those senior ministers who had thought about the issue were hopelessly split over how to proceed.

After his surprise election victory, Major appointed yet another new transport secretary, John MacGregor, a pragmatic politician widely viewed in Westminster as a safe pair of hands. And so it proved, at least in the narrow sense of pushing through a controversial and unpopular policy. For the long-term future of the railways, however, he proved to be a hapless butterfingers. MacGregor realised that he had to act quickly. The imperative was to privatise the railways within the five-year Parliamentary term in order to ensure that the process was irreversible. The aim was even to try to ensure that the Tories could gain some electoral benefit from the privatisation, which meant that there was great pressure to get the sale process well underway within a couple of years of the election. Roger Freeman, the junior transport minister, talked of having privatised rail companies operating by 1994. In the event, the first privatised train ran two years later, but such wishful thinking demonstrated just how little ministers and their officials understood about the complexities of the railway industry. Moreover, the necessity to get things done quickly meant there was constant pressure to make decisions when there was insufficient knowledge on which to base them. This haste was to colour the whole process and allow a deeply flawed model to be implemented, even though, as the process unfolded, many Tories realised that it was by no means an ideal solution.

Chris Green, a former InterCity and Network SouthEast director, who is now in charge of Virgin Trains, argues that,

> The unique feature of rail privatisation is that the nature of the new structure was not decided by the experts working within the industry but by people from outside such as consultants, politicians and civil servants. They were acting out of a genuine desire to create economic freedom, competition and to break union power, though they could not say that publicly, and a belief that the industry was too big, unmanageable and inefficient.

There was no time for the niceties of a Green Paper, the consultative document which normally precedes a White Paper for such an important policy. Instead, realising he had been left with the task of implementing a policy for which there was no blueprint, MacGregor quickly cobbled together a White Paper called *New Opportunities for the Railways* which was published in July 1992. It was a thin, badly drafted and inadequate document which outlined, in very broad terms, the way the industry would be privatised. It set out, for the first time, the concept of franchising, but with just 100 short paragraphs it begged more questions than it answered. The paper explained that franchises were to be based on the provision of minimum service levels and quality standards, and that BR would continue running those services for which no bidder was found, a recognition that ministers were terrified that there would be insufficient private-sector interest. In launching the document, MacGregor said there was no 'universal template' for a franchise, as this would depend on the requirements of the private sector. More worryingly, he refused to rule out the possibility of closures and gave no assurances that the rail network would be preserved in its existing form.

While the White Paper promised that 'network benefits' – such as through-ticketing and a national timetable – would be retained, it then contradicted itself on the next page which said: 'It will be for train service operators to make arrangements to accept each others' tickets.' In other words, the operators could choose not to, which would have broken up the whole network. Moreover, there was no guarantee that the various railcards such as those for pensioners, young people and off-peak travellers in the South East would be retained, though the government said it believed 'operators will find it in their commercial interest to offer a range of discounted fares and travelcards.'

The spurious emphasis on competition remained. The franchises were to 'be designed, wherever possible, to provide scope for competition'. Even more radically, the White Paper specifically suggested allowing open access to the rail network for any private company that wanted to operate trains. This was, in effect, the dream of Malcolm Rifkind when, as transport secretary, he explained to the Commons his vision of seeing trains from different companies competing against each other on the same track. While in theory that sounded fine, once the logic of what was proposed began to be examined, it was patently unworkable and showed yet again just how little the architects of privatisation knew about how the rail network functions. The railway is not some kind of M1 for trains, because they have to run on tracks which have few passing loops and therefore services are greatly restricted by the availability of paths.

Yet, the structure of privatisation, and the legislation that created it, was very much built around this notion of open access. It was a blueprint for a madcap free-for-all on the railways based on a complete lack of understanding that the network was an integrated system with coordination and cooperation, rather than competition, as its bedrock. As a civil servant who went to Brussels frequently during this period to explain the ideas to his European counterparts said, 'I spent the whole time emphasising that the railways were a business and not a service. I was met with blank incomprehension.'[16]

The outline scheme set out in the White Paper was much more radical than the model eventually adopted and some of the former ministers who drew up the plan now claim that this was part of the political game. Fly a kite about killing all first born, and then, following an outcry, say you will only bump off one in ten. You then sound almost reasonable. Thus many of the more ridiculous aspects of the scheme were dropped as the legislation was dragged through Parliament and then implemented. For example, transport minister Roger Freeman suggested at first that there would be thirty-five or forty franchises, in order to maximise the potential for competition, but this was later reduced to twenty-five, largely based on BR's existing profit centres, because of the sheer complexity of dividing up the railway into so many parts. The notion of selling off stations separately by creating a Stations Authority was also quickly dumped.[17] The possibility of allowing the private sector to determine whether the various railcards were retained proved too unpopular, and guarantees that they would be kept had to be provided. Ticket inter-availability, a key plank of the network, was also retained in the face of widespread opposition to its withdrawal, but operators were given the right to issue cheaper tickets for use exclusively on their own trains.

These retreats were helped along by a guerrilla movement from within BR. Key papers outlining the battier aspects of the plans kept on being leaked to the media. One of this fifth column said:

> There were certainly some active attempts to sabotage privatisation by middle managers within BR. I came across a number of confidential privatisation papers circulating about fare levels and the impact on through and multi-modal tickets. These, when leaked (and they all implied fare rises and loss of multi-operator tickets), were, I think, instrumental in forcing the Tory government to regulate real fares downwards reversing the trend they had applied on BR. The movement to save the London Travelcard was greatly helped by a document, the revelation of which obliged Steve Norris [the junior transport minister] to guarantee its future by making it a franchise requirement.[18]

Indeed, fares regulation was one of the great victories for opponents of the privatisation. The original plan had been to regulate fares only where train operators had a virtual monopoly – such as on the London commuting routes and in rural areas – but ministers were keen to make privatisation more palatable and eventually, late in the process, a scheme to regulate season tickets, savers and some other fares was implemented as a sop to passengers. It was a marked reversal from BR's policy of using fares to restrict growth but, as with all aspects of privatisation, the implications for the economics of the railway were not thought through (see chapter 11).

After a series of very confused messages from the government, which resulted in ministers contradicting their own civil servants at a Commons committee hearing, John MacGregor was forced to concede what any 'A' Level economics student could have told him – open access was not compatible with the idea of selling franchises. Steve Norris, the sharpest of the transport ministers, had understood this straightaway:

> It was clear that no franchise for train operations could be let unless there were guarantees about where the potential revenue came from. If there were the prospect that any other operator could come along and cherry-pick the best bits, you've destroyed the basis on which you can make the bid.'[19]

Norris adds that total open access would, of course, consequently have required much higher levels of subsidy. The other objection to competition is that people do not want to be saddled with a ticket that is not useable on some trains. They do not care who the operator is – they just want to get on the first train heading for their destination

But Norris's colleagues were slower to cotton on to these contradictions. It was not until January 1993, when the Railways Bill was already in Parliament, that MacGregor realised somewhat belatedly that a free-for-all on the railways was both impractical and had the same potential to cause chaos as it had in the bus industry. He announced to a railfreight conference that 'If some franchises have to be exclusive in whole or in part, then they will be made so.'[20] There was, however, no explanation about how what came to be called 'moderation of competition' would be achieved. Instead, the buck was passed to the rail regulator, John Swift QC, who was appointed in January 1993. He recalls that in his initial meeting with officials, he asked, since Railtrack was a monopoly and it was being proposed to moderate competition, how he was supposed to fulfil that part of his remit which was to 'promote competition'. He relates, rather amusingly, that the permanent secretary asked the deputy secretary who in turn put the matter to the under secretary who mumbled something about it being 'a question of time'.[21]

After much consultation and backroom negotiation, Swift came up with a system which prevented Railtrack from selling train paths for journeys already provided by an existing operator. This was supposed to be relaxed in stages over the next six years but it was clear that this could only be done in a very limited way (and, in any case, Labour, which took over in 1997, showed no interest in promoting on-rail competition). Therefore, the whole basis for the creation of the complex model, which involved separating the track from the operations, was tacitly acknowledged to be a mistake. John Prescott, Labour's transport spokesman, spotted the contradiction straight away: 'If the [government's] proposals will not lead to competition in the provision of services . . . instead of the public monopoly about which the government are so concerned, we shall have what the secretary of state calls "exclusive service" – in other words a private monopoly.'[22]

The process of blunting the sharper edges of the policy continued throughout the Bill's passage through Parliament and the subsequent detailed implementation of the policy. The Bill, in fact, was widely criticised for providing few details as to how privatisation would, in practice, work. Oddly, it made no specific mention of Railtrack because the government was still hedging its bets over what sort of model would eventually emerge and the door was being left open to have vertical integration in some areas. Eventually, with the exception of the tiny Island Line on the Isle of Wight, this idea was dropped. The gaps in the Railways Bill demonstrated yet again the extent to which ministers were making it up as they were going along.

The government did not have a monopoly on daft ideas. In January 1995 John Swift, the rail regulator, came up with the notion that there would only be a requirement on operators to sell through tickets at 294 core stations rather than the 1,300 where tickets were currently available. The press quickly picked up the issue and Swift was ridiculed in Parliament by Labour's shadow transport secretary, Michael Meacher, who pointed out: 'Under the regulator's proposals, there will be an 88-mile stretch between Salisbury and Exeter, with Yeovil at its centre, with no core station. Thus a passenger wishing to travel from Yeovil to Birmingham will have to detour to Bristol or to Swindon to get a through ticket.'[23] Swift denied that this had been his intention and rapidly abandoned the notion of core stations. The episode demonstrated the ease with which opponents of privatisation could inflict political damage and showed Swift that he had entered a treacherous minefield.

Despite growing awareness that the Bill was deeply ill-considered, and the almost universal opposition, there was no question of the Tories abandoning what was now so obviously a flawed piece of legislation. They fought tooth and nail to push the Railways Bill through Parliament. It had a stormy passage; indeed, had it not been for the untimely death in the summer of 1993 of a key Tory opponent, Robert Adley, the Bill might not have got through without major changes. Adley, an old railway buff with a deep knowledge of the system, was a formidable opponent in a key position and his untimely demise was a major piece of good fortune for the government. Adley, who had coined the term 'poll tax on wheels' that was widely picked up in the media, was the chair of the Commons transport committee and his committee produced a couple of reports that were surprisingly damning given it was a Tory-dominated group commenting on a key Conservative government policy. The interim report produced in January got right to the heart of the contradiction over franchising and open access and may well have prompted MacGregor to drop the latter. The final report, in April, raised the fundamental point that the government had not set out what role it saw for the railways within the context of its wider transport policy.

The committee also expressed fears about fare rises and recommended that they should be regulated and tied to the rate of inflation. Surprisingly, this was later agreed by the chancellor, Kenneth Clarke, despite the fact that it resulted in having to pay more to persuade operators to take on the franchises. Key fares such as the saver return and season tickets were controlled, a move which, again, was part of the process of buying off the opposition to what became the least popular of all the privatisations.

The prospect of line closures, too, was dropped in order to soothe the opposition. The Bill introduced a closure procedure that was even more tortuous than the legislation it replaced. The difficulty of trying to make even small cuts to the timetable within the context of privatisation was demonstrated early on when Roger Salmon, the head of the Office of Passenger Rail Franchising (OPRAF, the body created to let out franchises to the private companies and to oversee them), made the mistake of trying to shut down a service, which served only to inflame the opposition to the whole privatisation process. He had identified the sleeper services to Fort William as deeply loss-making and barely used, calculating that the subsidy amounted to £450 per passenger – a figure that was widely challenged – and announced, in an unnecessarily provocative gesture, that he would not include these trains as part of the franchise process.

It was just the sort of move that the opposition had been waiting for. A variety of pressure groups, backed by much of the media, including *The Times* whose correspondent dubbed the train the Deerstalker Express because it was used by the gentry going to the Highlands on shooting trips, rallied around the cause and initiated a legal challenge.

Salmon, a political tyro, was trying to convince the Treasury of his credentials as a careful disbursor of government funds:

> One of the signals I wanted to give the Treasury and everyone else was that we were going to run this thing with some sort of coherent and sensible basis, and my thinking at the time was that if we conceded to the Scottish lobby over Fort William, how could we ever say no to anyone else wanting their local service?[24]

And so it proved. The attempt to scrap the service was lost in the courts on a technicality and Salmon quietly coughed up the extra subsidy in exchange for a revamped service. The row showed that, given the public's hostility and distrust regarding privatisation, it was impossible for the government to use the process to make cuts in services. The skirmish also highlighted the way that rational discussion of rail services had become impossible. The carriage of a few affluent but heavily subsidised visitors – the service is too expensive for locals – had no transport or social relevance. That is why wider questions, such as whether the affluent south-east commuters should benefit from subsidised rail services, are never discussed. Even the Treasury understood the lesson of the Deerstalker Express and, as we shall see below, greased the path to privatisation with large amounts of extra cash.

After that little fiasco, Salmon retrenched and did not try to cut any services. He did face a more important legal action, however, which nearly scuppered the whole process. The draft franchise contracts virtually replicated the existing timetable on all loss-making routes. Privatisation, therefore, far from threatening marginal services, enshrined them in stone at great cost to the taxpayer. On profitable services, however, the required frequencies were reduced, since Salmon argued that the service would be safeguarded by the self-interest of the operators who would wish to run as many trains as possible in order to maximise revenue. He was challenged by a union-backed group called Save our Railways, which won a partial victory in court in late 1995, just before the announcement of the letting of the first franchises. The court setback required a rapid redrafting of the regulations by the transport secretary, Sir George Young, but did not cause any further delay to the privatisation timetable. As it turned out, Salmon was right. The profit-making services, principally InterCity, did not need protection as operators have increased the number of trains since privatisation, quite dramatically on lines with some spare capacity such as Midland Mainline out of St Pancras and GNER out of Kings Cross.

Robert Adley's death in the summer of 1993 removed the linchpin of the Tory MPs' opposition to rail privatisation and, without a leader, their campaign subsequently waned. Given the tiny Parliamentary majority, MacGregor had been forced to spend a lot of time in the lobbies and bars of the Commons persuading sceptical Conservative MPs that the privatisation proposals were sound, but it proved to be more difficult to win over the Tory peers. Opposition on the Conservative benches was remarkably widespread, with even that old right-winger Nicholas Ridley, now elevated to the Lords, expressing doubts about the feasibility of the project, with a Delphic pronouncement in an article in the *Evening Standard*: 'I do not believe it is possible to privatise the railways. Nor does the government.'[25]

Oddly, opposition in the Lords centred around the right of British Rail to bid for franchises. A former transport minister, Lord Peyton, moved an amendment to this effect but ministers were opposed because they felt it would reduce interest from the private sector. In a cunning political coup pulled out of the bag just as defeat in the Lords seemed inevitable, the government granted this concession subject to the discretion of the franchising director. Since the franchising director was a creature of government who acted under the instruction of ministers, this was a rather dishonest ruse, but Peyton and his allies were fooled. They must have felt stupid when, inevitably, Salmon began to let the franchises and simply barred any bids from BR.

The Labour opposition did not distinguish itself during the privatisation battle. It was easy for the party to capitalise on the public opposition and its string of spokespeople during that Parliament – Prescott, Michael Meacher, Brian Wilson, Clare Short and Andrew Smith – made all the appropriate noises and pressed the right buttons. Remarkably, Tony Blair was even moved to make one of his most radical sounding speeches when he promised to restore a 'publicly accountable, publicly-owned railway', and yet, when asked precisely what this meant and whether a major renationalisation was on the agenda, he prevaricated.

BR's position throughout this process was hopelessly muddled. As we have seen, there were some insiders trying to sabotage the process but, according to one, they were in a minority: 'Most people protect their own backsides. Only a very small proportion of us made any real contribution, but some were in quite influential positions.'[26] This individual feels that most of BR's senior staff agreed with him privately:

> 'I had made my position as a dissident known to John Welsby [the chief executive] and Bob Reid [the chairman]. In effect they agreed with me, saying the proposed structure was not one they supported, but as it was government policy, it was their duty to work with it and try to get pragmatic changes made. The only alternative was resignation, and that they felt would play into the government's hands as they would be replaced by people less experienced and more compliant, to the further detriment of the industry. I am not sure I agree with their analysis, as I think their resignations would have severely shaken the process.'

In fact, the government had long lost faith in Sir Bob Reid (the second incumbent of that name) but the departure of Welsby, who was eventually very helpful in smoothing the path to privatisation, might have held up its progress.

Most BR staff were implacably opposed to privatisation, not just out of fear of redundancy, but also because of a genuine belief that the plans would be bad for the railways. Others, however, saw the potential for making money out of privatisation through management buy-outs which were actively encouraged by the government. Indeed, it is remarkable that the railways kept running during the run-up to the sell-off given how many managers were drawing up management buy-out plans while simultaneously running services as well as restructuring the railway for privatisation. The unions, too, made little real fuss. They fought pitched battles over pensions and staff travel, but did not make any real attempt to stop the process, not least because ASLEF, the drivers' union, quickly realised that it was onto a winner.

As we have seen, British Rail was in an optimistic phase. It had sorted out its structure and there were a lot of very good senior managers running the railway. The chairman, Sir Bob Reid, was himself strongly opposed to the way that privatisation was evolving, even though he had been appointed by Cecil Parkinson from the private sector (Shell) to oversee the sale. Sir Bob favoured a much more gradual approach, involving the contracting out of all peripheral activity, such as renewal and maintenance, while leaving the core service in the hands of the public sector. He even went on radio to express his doubts, causing a furore, but although the tone of his remarks implied extreme disenchantment with the process, he remained in his post for the reasons cited above.

The civil servants at the Department of Transport and their ministers felt that BR was being obstructive and quickly decided to ignore any arguments put forward at meetings by BR's managers, thus ensuring that the eventual structure failed to take into account the needs of the railway. There was, indeed, a bias against using anyone with railway expertise in the process. Both regulators, Swift and Salmon, were outsiders with no railway experience – a competition lawyer and a merchant banker respectively – and railway staff appeared to have been systematically excluded from the appointments process for these posts. Whenever expertise or advice was needed, consultants were called in. According to a Parliamentary answer,[27] a staggering £450m was spent just by the government on consultants (not including the amounts paid out by BR and Railtrack) during the run-up to privatisation and many of these consultants had no prior knowledge of the industry. It was a case of the blind advising the deaf.

Moreover, there were some real opportunities to stop the process had Labour really wanted to do so. If the party's spokespeople had, unequivocally, said that the railways would be returned to public hands, then the process would have been stopped in its tracks. Labour was consistently ahead in the opinion polls throughout the 1992–7 Parliament and therefore private sector investment would have looked too risky. In fact, the taxpayer got the worst of both worlds. Clare Short, the shadow transport secretary, warned that 'Anyone contemplating bidding for any part of the rail network should know that there will be no gravy train for fat cats out of this one and that Labour intends that the rail system should remain in public ownership.'[28] This deterred bidders for the lucrative rolling stock companies (Roscos), the first major part of British Rail to be put up for sale, and significantly reduced the amount of money which was obtained from their disposal. Indeed, Short's sidekick, Brian Wilson, even gloated when NatWest, a bidder for the rolling stock companies, pulled out: 'I warmly welcome this decision by NatWest which I am sure other key investors will follow. Labour's message is that they should stay clear of this high risk and totally unwanted privatisation.'[29]

This guerrilla war on the privatisation process would have been perfectly valid if Labour had really intended to stop the sale. But it did not. New Labour, as it was now calling itself, wanted to distance itself from its old image of being hostile to the private sector. The crunch moment came during the sale of Railtrack (described in the next chapter) scheduled for the spring of 1996, when there was a genuine opportunity to undermine the process fatally. In the run-up to the sale, Labour's transport team, led by Short together with Prescott, Geoff Norris from Tony Blair's office, Lord Williams of Elvel and Andrew Smith from Gordon Brown's team, cooked up a scheme to stop the flotation of Railtrack. The plan was simple. Labour would announce that, once in office, it would swap Railtrack's shares for preference shares, which, like bonds, only pay a fixed rate of interest, rather than dividends that depend on the company's performance. Williams had checked out the scheme with City experts who pronounced it watertight. But it had to be inserted into the Railtrack sales prospectus that was to be issued in May and Gordon Brown vetoed the idea because it represented a public expenditure commitment. Interestingly, following the collapse in value of Railtrack's shares after Hatfield, the chairman of the company, John Robinson, privately suggested a similar idea to the government.

Labour's cries of 'wolf' had, however, cost the taxpayer dear. The sale of the three Roscos which had taken over all of BR's 11,260 locomotives and coaches and which represented about half of BR's assets, turned out to be deeply disappointing, with very few bidders coming forward despite a massive and expensive round-the-world sales pitch by Hambros, the merchant bankers in charge of the marketing operation. Partly this was a result of Labour's opposition which the politically naïve City and, in particular, the large American leasing companies, unable to spot a bit of grandstanding, wrongly perceived as a genuine threat.

Sandy Anderson, who led the management buy-out team for the £526m purchase of Porterbrook which, only six months later, was sold to Stagecoach for £300m more, allowing him to pocket around £40m for a personal investment of just £120,000, is in no doubt as to who to thank for his good fortune: 'If anybody says to me, why was I able to get Porterbrook so cheap, I say I'd like to thank the Labour Party.'

Anderson is being a bit glib because, despite Labour's dishonesty, the main culprits were, of course, the Tories who cut a lot of corners to ensure that the Roscos were sold quickly. They had been desperate to boost their rail privatisation programme with a big sale in order to show that it could be done. Moreover, the rolling stock companies were, along with Railtrack, the principal source of potential receipts. But selling quickly, as the subsequent National Audit Office (NAO) report into the sale demonstrated, would result in a lower sale price. One reason was that the bidders would not know who their customers were to be since the franchises would not have been let, although if the City whizz-kids had been cannier, they would have realised that most of the rentals were guaranteed by the government in any case. The Roscos had only just been carved out of BR and divided up arbitrarily into three companies in order to provide competition, and therefore they had no proven financial track record to provide a basis on which bidders could determine a price. To compound this uncertainty the government never even bothered to obtain up-to-date valuations for the three Roscos because, according to the Department of Transport, this was impossible, a view challenged strongly by the NAO.

By the completion of the bidding process there were only four companies in the race – three management buy-out teams and one outsider, GRS Holding Company, a consortium including Babcock and Brown. Although the NAO says Hambros managed to keep the lack of bidders secret, there were rumours flying around the industry and this absence of competition must have affected the eventual price. In the event, the three Roscos went for £1.8bn in early 1996, and within two years all had been resold for a total of over £2.65bn. The NAO estimated that even on moderate assumptions about the state of the market, the Department should have been able to get £2.5bn – £700m more than was obtained. The requirement that any company should only be allowed to buy one Rosco meant that GRS's higher bid for Porterbrook had to be rejected, at a cost to the taxpayer of £55m.

The sale of the Roscos was all the more disappointing because they had been deliberately fattened up to make them more attractive to the potential purchasers. The government had created a complex pricing regime which made the older rolling stock almost as expensive to franchisees as the newer, with the idea of encouraging the purchase of newer trains. This Treasury-inspired attempt to manipulate what were supposed to be market mechanisms meant that the new Roscos were leasing old rolling stock at prices which bore little relationship to their balance-sheet value. This generated enormous surpluses which were supposed to be reinvested in the railways. But, instead, since the Roscos were entirely unregulated, there was nothing to stop the owners from taking these large surpluses out of the industry or simply rewarding their shareholders with dizzyingly large dividends. Thus, for example, Porterbrook became an amazing cash cow for Stagecoach, generating in its first six months £63m in profit on a turnover of just £136m. It was virtually a licence to print money especially as, to make the Roscos saleable, the government had guaranteed 80 per cent of the income from the initial leases, which had between four and eight years to run at the time of the sale.

Fattening companies up in this way with public money to ensure they were saleable at a good price was another consistent feature of the rail privatisation process, used, for example, in the sale of Railtrack and the thirteen companies which maintained and renewed the track (see next chapter). The fact that in the longer term this meant extra subsidy and cost to rail travellers was irrelevant. The Tory government was only interested in the short-term – obtaining capital receipts and selling off the railway – rather than in the long-term financial viability of the industry, let alone any wider considerations such as the need to boost rail travel for environmental reasons and to reduce congestion on the roads.

The flawed sale of the Roscos was the greatest scandal of privatisation in terms of cost to the taxpayer but cannot be blamed entirely on the politicians. It also exposed the weakness of the market for rail companies, none of which, by definition, had any independent financial record. The sale demonstrated the City's wariness of new markets and its failure to understand that the Roscos were an excellent deal with a guaranteed income flow and virtually no risk. The aspect which had most concerned the City was the fact that the leases were relatively short while trains have a thirty to forty year life-span. Potential backers were worried about what would happen when the leases ran out. They did not understand that since the trains had to keep on running, the train operators would most likely sign new leases. Instead, in estimating the worth of the Roscos, many City firms simply assumed that the trains had only a token value at the end of their leases. This 'residual risk' problem dogged the whole sale and reduced the number of bidders. In fact, at the prices achieved for the

Roscos, they were terrific bargains even if the residual values were assumed to be zero.

Despite the failings of the Rosco sale and the paucity of bidders, with £1.8bn in the bag, the government felt sufficiently confident to go full out on the sale of the twenty-five rail franchises. Three sets of lines – Great Western, South West Trains and London, Tilbury and Southend (LTS) – had been selected as the first to be sold. Although the government claimed that thirty-eight potential purchasers had prequalified, many of these were no-hopers going along for the ride and, in fact, there were very few solid bidders for these initial franchises. While the transport secretary, Brian Mawhinney, who had taken over from MacGregor, was gungho in public, saying the high number 'was a vote of confidence in rail privatisation', behind the scenes, according to Roger Salmon, the franchising director, there was a state of panic: 'We were short of bidders. There was a terror that there were not going to be enough bidders, like with the Roscos.'[30]

The sale of the Roscos had little public impact and the government was in a desperate hurry to get the franchising process going to demonstrate to the electorate that privatisation would become a reality. MacGregor had said, rashly, that half the railway would be franchised by April 1996. This was an empty politician's promise based on unfounded optimism and the forlorn hope that there could still be benefits of privatisation to present to the voters at the next election. The impossible target led to a major rift between Salmon and ministers, who felt he was not moving quickly enough. Indeed, only ministers' concern that sacking Salmon would delay the process prevented them from showing him the door. In the event, Salmon, sick of the pressure from ministers, announced his departure as soon as the franchising process was underway.

Opposition to the whole process continued unabated, putting ministers under continued pressure. The official watchdog, the clumsily named Central Rail Users Consultative Committee, was very wary of the whole privatisation process and, in his swansong, the outgoing chairman, the steadfastly non-political Major-General Lennox Napier, said that while he did not oppose privatisation, the model chosen by the government was wrong and he warned, with great prescience, that financial problems were likely to arise: 'So I end rather looking at a pantomime. Pantomimes should have a happy ending. At the moment there isn't a

Prince Charming called Finance or Investment yet in the script.'[31] Sir
George Young, the transport minister and responsible for appointing
Napier's successor was incensed and hit back arguing that 'Privatisation
offers the opportunity for stronger investment and better services.'

Given this political climate, ministers were so terrified by the prospect
of not having any interest from business that they gave special incentives
to encourage the management buy-out teams to bid. Despite much
behind the scenes arm-twisting among supporters of the Tories, the
major players in the City and industry could not be induced to bid. Even
companies in other transport industries which the government had
hoped to attract, such as the airlines and shipping companies, largely
stayed out of the process because they saw it as too complex and unremu-
nerative.

The government was, however, saved by the bus companies created,
as we have seen, by their mid-1980s privatisation and, in particular,
Stagecoach, which was prepared to go where others feared to tread and
was richly rewarded with a highly profitable franchise, South West
Trains. Stagecoach, created by a buccaneering and aggressive brother-
and-sister team from Perth, Brian Souter and Ann Gloag, had earlier had
its fingers burnt over rail privatisation. It had tried to launch Stagecoach
Rail, the first private main-line trains in fifty years, which offered cheap
seats for overnight travellers between London and Scotland, but the initiative had failed miserably, partly because of lack of cooperation from
BR, but principally because of a severe misreading of the market. Unde-
terred, Stagecoach, which along with the French conglomerate CGEA
was the only substantial outside bidder for the first franchises, ultimately
bid for them all, though very conservatively, which meant they did not
win any others apart from the tiny Island Line.

The first three franchises were eventually put out to tender in May
1995, and in November that year news leaked out that they would go to
Resurgence Railways (Great Western), Stagecoach (South West Trains)
and the management buy-out team (LTS). In the event, of these three
only one, Stagecoach, finally took over its franchise, compounding the
sense that the privatisation process was spinning out of control. Resurgence quickly fell away when the company, a start-up venture created by
a Thatcherite former BR freight manager, Mike Jones, failed to obtain the
required bank guarantees. It had not been helped by a report in the
Financial Times revealing that its finance director had headed up a

double-glazing firm that had gone bust. The franchise had to be hastily awarded to the under-bidder, the management buy-out team which had backing from FirstBus (later renamed FirstGroup).

The media coverage remained implacably hostile, with much fun being made of the fact that the first privatised train due to run early on Sunday 4 February 1996 was, in fact, a bus running on a substitute service for Great Western. And it got worse for the government when, just as the management team for LTS was about to take over, an auditor uncovered a petty little scam that involved creaming off revenue from London Transport to the nascent rail company. This was leaked to the BBC by one of BR's fifth columnists in time to maximise embarrassment for the government. Sir George Young, the patrician aristocrat who had replaced the universally disliked Mawhinney as transport secretary, had no choice but to pull the plug on the management buy-out team's deal and relaunch the whole bidding process for the line.

The collapse of Resurgence and the LTS fiasco meant there was a miasma of sleaze which so infected the privatisation process that the government never managed to clear the air. Nor did Stagecoach's reputation, referred to above, help matters. The company's already dreadful image was made worse by the publication of a 1995 MMC report on its activities in Darlington, which the MMC called 'deplorable, predatory and against the public interest' because Stagecoach had run free buses that had proved the final straw in bankrupting the ailing but long-established local municipal firm.

Despite the constant mantra from Sir George, who described every franchise announcement as 'great news for the taxpayer and for passengers', there was only one criterion for determining the winning bid – the lowest level of subsidy being demanded by the bidder. Stagecoach's success on SWT set the tone. The OPRAF press release struggled to say anything exciting about it and merely mentioned a couple of bus links, a tighter passenger's charter and 'improved customer information on stations'. A few franchisees, like Midland Mainline, made some obvious improvements, such as doubling the number of trains between London and Leicester, but there was no overall strategy or any attempt to try to boost numbers using the railways.

The process speeded up in 1996 and the machine which Salmon created became adept at letting out the franchises. Encouraged by Stagecoach's involvement, other established companies like Sea Containers and National Express successfully entered the fray, while Prism, another start-up created specially to bid for franchises, picked up four.

Most of the franchises were for seven years, a compromise between the Treasury, which had wanted very short ones, and the bidders, who had lobbied government for much longer terms in order to provide stability (and profits). A few of the deals, requiring the leasing of new rolling stock, were for periods of up to fifteen years but the franchisees were not otherwise committed to provide any investment. Indeed, the train operating companies bear little resemblance to other transport businesses: they do not own the rolling stock, the stations or the track, merely having a license to run services for the duration of their contract. They had no incentive to invest, nor to provide any extra services beyond those which could be squeezed out of their existing rolling stock. The one truly exciting scheme was for the West Coast Main Line but this had needed a total refurbishment in any case. However, Virgin had bravely signed up for a deal which meant that by the year 2012, rather than receiving £76m in subsidy (as it did in 1997/8), it would be paying the Exchequer £227m (in 1997/8 prices) for the right to run main-line services along the route. Whether the company would ever be in a position to fulfil the awesome terms of that contract was highly doubtful even before the Hatfield chaos; moreover, the arrangement represents a ludicrous tax on rail travel and a marked contrast to the near-identical service on the East Coast Main Line whose franchisee would not be paying a large premium.

The contracts all required subsidy levels to decline over time in this way, putting enormous pressure on the operators to cut costs even though BR, as we have seen, was relatively efficient. Cutting staff was, therefore, essential and many middle managers found themselves redundant, a loss to the railway that would later affect performance. Frontline staff were cut, too, which meant that far from enjoying the promised improvements, some passengers found that even more stations became unstaffed.

Labour had a final opportunity to stop the franchise process at this stage and retain at least part of the railway in public ownership. Most of these late franchises involved Passenger Transport Executives in the large conurbations like West Yorkshire, Greater Manchester and Tyne and Wear, which funded commuter and suburban services (through government grants). OPRAF could not have let these franchises without the agreement of the PTEs, which were all Labour-controlled. Given that negotiations stretched into early 1997 with the increasingly desperate OPRAF officials making more and more generous offers, it would not have taken much for the local Labour politicians to sabotage the deals or delay the process until the election, which had to be held that spring. But they were under instruction from Andrew Smith, who had inherited the shadow transport role from Clare Short, to reach accommodations on the best possible terms because Labour did not want to be saddled with a hybrid railway after the election.

After the initial reluctance by many companies to bid, the later franchises, much to the delight of ministers, were the subject of fierce competition as more players entered the fray, seeing the opportunity to make what they felt would be easy money. They made a classic mistake, however. The later franchises were mainly those that required the most subsidy, covering regional and rural lines. Most of the income, therefore, came from the taxpayer; but OPRAF, under orders from the Treasury, nevertheless built in sharply declining levels of subsidy to these franchises. This was to cause problems for several operators (see chapter 6).

Most of the twenty-five franchises went to bus companies who were in the mind-set of managing declining businesses through cutting costs and staff and who overestimated the similarity between the two industries. Only three management buy-out teams managed to get a stake in a franchise, the rest being defeated by their lack of access to cheap capital. However, most of the managers who led unsuccessful bids were retained by the new franchises because of their experience of running trains. Therefore it is hardly surprising that there was very little of the much promised innovation which the Tories said privatisation would bring to the railways and few benefits to passengers, apart from the ubiquitous – and often horribly garish – new liveries for the trains.

There had also been a damaging hiatus in any new train orders, a gap of nearly three years, which not only caused massive financial hardship to the rolling stock manufacturers but also meant that many older new trains in desperate need of replacement were still running on the tracks.

The biggest irony was that, in order to coax through the privatisation of the railways, the Treasury was prepared to throw money at them and double the initial subsidy paid to the train operators in order to ensure that private companies would take them on. The figures are somewhat difficult to decipher because the proceeds from privatisation are not separately listed in the government accounts but were merely used to offset grants from the Treasury; but in broad terms the grant to British Rail in 1993/4, the last year before the break up of the railway in preparation for privatisation, was £1.1bn which almost doubled to £2.16bn the following year.

Under the franchise plans the level of subsidy was scheduled to drop to just under £1bn by 2002/3 but the Labour government's ten-year transport plan, announced in the summer of 2000, reversed that decline and, indeed, promised unprecedented levels of financial support for the industry. Given that several rail operators had already got into trouble meeting their financial targets even before the Hatfield accident and its aftermath, it is doubtful that those 'savings' were ever realistic, but they looked good enough on paper to allow the Tories to argue that privatisation saved money in the long term (see chapter 10 for a fuller assessment of the financial impact of privatisation). BR managers were incensed by the level of largesse disbursed to smooth the path for privatisation, arguing that had they been given this amount of money, they would have been able to create a modernised railway without the disruption engendered by privatisation.

Ministers were too concerned with ensuring that the whole edifice was broken up and sold in time for the 1997 election to bother much about the short-term financial effects or the long-term robustness of the structure they were creating. The fact that they succeeded in disposing of the railway so quickly was, in many respects, a remarkable achievement since it was the most complex of all the privatisations. However, any chances of making political capital out of the sale – which had always been pretty thin anyway – were lost when Stagecoach, which had taken over the South West Trains franchise, found they had allowed too many drivers to claim redundancy and started cancelling hundreds of trains. The debacle started in February 1997, just as the prospect of a general election was heating up the political climate. Over the next two months, the company was forced to cancel 2,000 trains and, instead of apologising, the Stagecoach chairman, Brian Souter, poured petrol on the fire by suggesting that some of his customers had nothing better to do than write letters of complaint in office time and wondered whether their bosses knew they were doing this.[32] The new franchising director, John O'Brien, threatened to fine the company £1m, and passengers even staged a takeover of a train being taken out of service. Eventually Stagecoach managed to wriggle out of paying the fine because the enforcement regime was so weak, but the political damage had been done.

One inexplicable aspect of the sale of the railways is that the Tories did not seem to have learnt from the failure of competition in the bus market when they drew up the model for rail privatisation. The whole new structure of the rail industry was predicated on the notion that there should be on-rail competition, even though the bus example had shown the difficulties of allowing unfettered market forces to hold sway in a loss-making industry providing a basic public service which cannot be allowed to go out of business. Furthermore, public transport – with the possible exception of parts of the London commuter market – always faces competition from the ubiquitous motor car or, in the case of long-distance travel, airlines. The ideological obsession with competition resulted in a scheme that was flawed from the outset. And the error was about to be compounded. For the Tories were now set on selling off Railtrack, even though they had initially said it would stay in the public sector until the next Parliament.

CHAPTER 5

Compounding the catastrophe: the sale of Railtrack

Railtrack was, initially, not part of the privatisation plans for the railway. When the White Paper had been launched in 1992, John MacGregor, the transport secretary, intimated that Railtrack would remain in public hands until after the following election. There were good reasons for this. Railtrack was not an easy candidate for privatisation. Hived off from BR in 1994, it was the owner of a national asset, built up over 170 years, which was difficult to value and much of which had long been written off anyway. Moreover, Railtrack was a monopoly dependent on subsidy and responsible for a massive programme of investment largely funded out of public money. Even the most enthusiastic privatiser within the Tory party realised that selling Railtrack would be difficult.

Therefore, as we have seen, public attention during the passage of the Railways Bill in 1993 was largely focused on the passenger services and there was little mention of the fate of the infrastructure, not least because Railtrack, as explained in the previous chapter, was not even mentioned in the Bill. The feeling within the Department of Transport was that Railtrack would remain in the public sector while all the other parts of the railway were sold off. The model envisaged was not unlike that of London Transport Buses where a central public-sector organisation determines the routes and frequencies and owns the infrastructure but the buses are actually owned and run by private firms. Railtrack was therefore little discussed or considered during the long debate over privatisation.

However, this step-by-step transition to private ownership was to be quickly undermined once Railtrack had been carved out of British Rail, and an aggressive oilman previously sacked by BP, Bob Horton, was appointed as its first chairman in February 1993. Horton had a reputation as an abrasive but strong-minded manager, and he immediately started lobbying for the privatisation of Railtrack. He was convinced that it was essential to sell Railtrack:

> I always felt that the long-term funding requirements were for the infrastructure and we would not get these amounts of money unless we were privatised. I started lobbying ministers, strongly pointing out that it was likely that there would be a change of government and that this would leave Railtrack in the public sector. This would mean that the whole point of privatisation – the renewal of the system – would not be achieved because Railtrack would still be constrained by government rules.[1]

The creation of Railtrack was not easy. Horton, who had little railway experience, having been on the BR board only since December 1992, had the task of separating out the organisation very quickly, as the government wanted the company to become free-standing, although still state-owned, by April 1994. It was a massive logistical task, with the lawyers playing a prominent role as they had to draw up the contracts to govern relationships between Railtrack and the 100 other businesses created out of BR. These relationships had previously been informal and the key task was to change the industry from being a command structure, where orders were passed down clear hierarchical lines, to one where everything was set down in contracts. It was a Herculean task that absorbed hundreds of millions of pounds in fees. John Edmonds, Railtrack's first chief executive, recalls that, for example, setting up the freight access agreements required 224 separate legal documents.[2] The creators of this paper mountain argued that its construction was no more than a necessary formality, as, once signed, the contracts would remain in the bottom drawer; but clearly they failed to grasp the nature of such arrangements or to appreciate that the relationship between the various players in the industry would, as a result, be necessarily antagonistic. The instinctive mode within the industry changed from cooperation to conflict.

When Railtrack became a legal entity in April 1994 it assumed ownership of 11,000 route miles of track, with associated signalling, 40,000 bridges, viaducts and tunnels, and 2,500 stations. It was done in extreme haste and, necessarily, corners were cut. As Richard Middleton, the technical director of Railtrack, put it, 'When they did the same thing of separating out the infrastructure on the Austrian railways, they took five years over it.'[3]

Again, outside advisers played a central role in the development of the structure with little input from old BR managers, not least because most experienced railway staff were opposed to separating the track from the services. Middleton, while supporting the creation of Railtrack because he felt it would be better able to manage the expansion of the railways, nevertheless accepts that the changes were made too hastily: 'Our industry was not ready for it. They tried to change too much too quickly.'[4]

No sooner had Railtrack been carved out of BR and started operating independently, then the process of preparing it for privatisation began. Horton's lobbying had been successful, although a formal announcement about the proposed flotation was not made until November 1994. But it had not been only his efforts that had brought about the change in policy. A former senior civil servant in the Department of Transport recalls that there was a strong push from civil servants, eager to please ministers, to get Railtrack privatised:

> Key officials like Steve Robson at the Treasury and Nick Montagu at Transport pushed very hard for the sale of Railtrack because they were very exasperated by the lack of progress, which, they felt, was down to a lot of ex-BR managers who were sabotaging the process. They argued that, without privatising Railtrack, the whole thing would get bogged down because the managers would ensure that progress was halted. It was a 'sod it, let's get the bastards' kind of attitude. They lobbied hard and were successful. Indeed, during the whole process Robson nearly always got what he wanted.[5]

Horton and his allies in the Department were, in any case, pushing on an open door as far as ministers were concerned. While the long-term implications of a privatised Railtrack for the railways did not figure in the debate, there was the prospect of a short-term cash bonanza. Indeed, Kenneth Clarke, the chancellor of the exchequer, soon realised that there was the potential of a sizeable capital receipt and this was quickly incorporated into his budget plans, setting in stone the plan to sell Railtrack in the financial year 1995/6.

Imperceptibly, therefore, the model for the privatisation of the railways changed, but not for reasons that had anything to do with the better operation of the railway. Moreover, there was no debate about the implications of a private sector infrastructure provider. As the former civil servant quoted above remarked, 'There was not much discussion about what was a very significant change. Just, suddenly, it was going to happen.'6

Separating Railtrack from the rest of the industry was crazy enough. But trying to turn it into a conventional profit-making company was even madder. Railtrack is an infrastructure provider, highly dependent on subsidy and only able to make money from selling train paths, whose price was arbitrarily determined. The best comment on the idea was made by a rail executive from Japan, where the railways have been successfully privatised as integrated entities. He wrote – before the Ladbroke Grove accident and so with remarkable prescience – about the British privatisation:

> The first point I have difficulty with is that Railtrack, which had been expected to run up deficits, is making profits, paying dividends and has listed its shares on the stock market. Operation of infrastructure resulting in profits is unthinkable in Japanese railway operations. If profits by Railtrack have resulted from high levels of usage rates, the UK government should reduce its subsidies to operating companies and insist on cuts in track usage fees, as would certainly be the case if this happened in Japan. If the profits of Railtrack have come about by cutting costs required for upkeep and maintenance of infrastructure, *there would be problems regarding operational safety*.'7 (my italics)

Even before Railtrack was put up for sale, another crucial mistake was made in the way that the railways were being carved up, which was to have a deeply damaging effect on their performance. When Railtrack was created, the thirteen track maintenance and renewal companies – British Rail Infrastructure Companies, or Briscos – were not included as part of its structure. Instead, they were also in the process of being separated out from BR and put up for sale.

As with the rolling stock companies, the Briscos had to be fattened up in order to make them saleable. This was done by granting them seemingly generous contracts with Railtrack. Not only were these regionally based companies guaranteed to be the sole contractors within their areas for between five and seven years, but Railtrack had very little control over how the work was carried out. Indeed, one former Railtrack manager explains how it was impossible for the company, still state-owned, to get information out of BR about the nature of the contracts: 'BR were saying that the contracts were commercially confidential. They didn't want us to know what was in them. Eventually, we won a bit of a concession as we were given auditing rights over them.'[8] In other words, BR, under instructions from the government, was setting out the terms of contracts between two third parties, Railtrack and the Briscos.

Again, the combination of haste and political opportunism meant that the needs of the railway industry and, ultimately, those of passengers did not come into the equation. The government forced on BR the separation of the maintenance and renewal companies, an artificial division that was widely seen as 'inappropriate'.[9] Several Railtrack managers had resisted this separation, trying to keep as much of the industry together as possible. A compromise, which Middleton says was a better option, would have been for Railtrack to have inspection and monitoring resources to identify what work was needed and then call in contractors to do it. However, that would have required an engineering department and it was felt that there were not enough good, qualified engineers within the old BR to staff a Railtrack department and leave sufficient people to run the Briscos. Until the reorganisation prompted by the Hatfield crash, Railtrack therefore did not have an engineering department. Instead, it had to take on a lot of contract managers, mostly from outside the industry, to oversee the engineering work.

In order to make the Briscos saleable, the terms of the contracts were progressively weakened as the sales process got under way. Incredibly, by the end of the process, according to Middleton, 'The contracts were so weak that Railtrack was not even allowed to withhold payment if work were not done. The infrastructure companies decide what is done, how it's done and where. We have no power to tell them, for example, to replace a specific set of points.' Railtrack was therefore saddled with contracts over which it had very little control and which it did not have the resources or ability to monitor. At first Railtrack did not even check the work after it was finished, raising serious concerns about safety (see below). While a checking process was gradually introduced during the first couple of years after privatisation, it was still greatly inadequate. Some of those involved in the process argue that the contracts might have been sufficient had Railtrack monitored them as intended. As one put it, 'We were under constant pressure from Norman Broadhurst [Railtrack's finance director] and the regulator to cut costs and that meant not having enough people to do the checking. Only one of the ten zones audited the contracts properly.' Other former insiders argue that the contracts were fundamentally flawed in that the auditing and monitoring provisions were not sufficiently robust. As early as 1998, Railtrack had begun to recognise that the contracts were unworkable but could not impose changes without incurring massive losses. Instead, the company began drawing up a new form of contract involving a partnership between contractors and the company, with both benefiting from cost savings. However, these new contracts, which started taking effect in 2000, still placed an emphasis on costcutting rather than ensuring that the railway was in the best possible condition.

While the terms of the contracts were loose, not even specifying set outputs, and were virtually unpoliceable, they were also insufficiently profitable for the contractors because the level of payments for the contracts had started from a relatively low base. Under pressure from the Treasury, BR had cut back on maintenance and renewals in its last few years, knowing that it was to be privatised. The maintenance contracts were let in 1995 and the price was set at the old BR cost, which was historically a low figure. Therefore, the contracts were underpriced and, moreover, they were fixed by the regulator to be increased by 3 per cent below the rate of inflation per year, a substantial cut in real terms, particularly as wages were rising. The contracts were 'closed book' which meant that Railtrack had no idea what the real costs were, nor how much profit the contractors were making. The maintenance contractors had no incentive to ensure the track was in the best possible condition. They made their profit by spending as little as possible provided they met the vague standards set out in the contracts, which, for example, specified the intervals at which work had to be carried out. The contractors were under constant pressure to make a profit which meant that Railtrack's contracts managers, according to a former Railtrack executive, 'spent all their time dealing with claims and variations, rather than making sure that delays were being kept to a minimum, or, indeed, that the system was safe.'[10]

The Briscos were mostly bought by established engineering companies such as Tarmac, Jarvis and Balfour Beatty who were experienced at making the most out of such deals and arguing over every variation and claim. This combination of unpoliceable contracts and the pressure to reduce costs proved to be lethal, as the story of the Hatfield crash, outlined in chapter 9, shows. The sale of the Briscos brought in £169m but money had not been the only motivation of ministers in separating them from Railtrack. The Tories wanted to break up the unions. They feared that if Railtrack had included the Briscos, that would have created an organisation of around 40,000 employees, which would mean the unions retained their strong central bargaining position. By devolving maintenance and renewal to thirteen regional companies, the position of the unions was greatly weakened. As a manager involved in the creation of Railtrack commented, 'This was the unspoken agenda. Ministers told us in private that they wanted to break up the unions, but of course they did not say that in public.'[11]

The arbitrary division of the Briscos into maintenance and renewal companies was another mistake which contributed to the lack of control that Railtrack had over the management and maintenance of its own assets. This little-noticed decision was, again, an ideologically driven move which had no historic basis in the way that the railways traditionally functioned. This distinction had not existed under BR and further complicated the process of getting work down. As Steven Marshall, the chief executive of Railtrack from November 2000, explained,

> If a rail needs replacing, the maintenance company has to go to us and ask us to agree that the work needs doing. With only limited information, we have to decide whether it was the result of poor maintenance or because it was simply worn out by age. Then we have to pass the work onto the renewal company which has to fit in the work with its existing programme of possessions [track closures].[12]

There is even a set length of replacement track which determines whether the work is carried out by the maintenance or the renewal company – 60 feet for jointed rail and 600 feet for continuous welded rail. For other work, maintenance contractors carry out work worth up to £25,000 per job and bigger contracts are put out to the renewal contractors. It is all extremely time-wasting and costly. This system also meant that it was impossible for Railtrack to make proper judgements about when rails should be replaced or maintained. As one insider put it, 'While the amount of investment going into the industry rose after the first two years of privatisation, there was no way of knowing whether that money was being spent wisely because so much was wasted by putting work out in this way.'

Without the Briscos, Railtrack was a very lean company with just

10,000 employees, around two-thirds of whom were signallers. This leanness made the company much more attractive for privatisation. Indeed, had it included the 30,000 people who worked for the Briscos and all the associated problems, some City analysts reckon Railtrack would have been unsaleable, since there had already been concerns over the disruptive strike by signallers in 1994.

Nevertheless, there were still problems in making Railtrack appeal to private investors. A roadshow toured the City institutions and was relatively successful because the Railtrack team and their advisers stressed the potential for cost reduction in the new company. However, the City was less convinced about the company's growth potential, and the government decided that at least one major project, Thameslink 2000, had to be included in the prospectus to demonstrate that the shares would be a growth stock.

Again, haste and political expediency overrode the aim of maximising revenue for the Exchequer or, indeed, any consideration of what would be best for the railway. Ministers clearly wanted a scorched earth policy that left no part of Railtrack in public hands. S.B.C. Warburg, its advisers, recommended that there should be a 100 per cent sale, as retaining a minority stake would lead to worries among investors about whether this might be a Trojan Horse for subsequent renationalisation by a future government. Moreover, such a residual stake was perceived as a way that the government could influence the company, in particular pushing it towards expensive investment schemes.

The subsequent National Audit Office report[13] pointed out that these fears could easily have been allayed. A new government, it said, would require primary legislation to renationalise the railways and legislation would have protected Railtrack's private shareholders against adverse effects of government pressure to overspend on investment. Moreover, the NAO suggested that proceeds of the sale – which grossed £2.5bn if debt transferred to the company is included – would have been increased by a quarter (£600m) had the government retained a 20 per cent holding in the company at the time of the flotation in May 1996. A 40 per cent stake could have enhanced proceeds by an impressive £1.5bn, almost doubling the amount received by taxpayers, because the share price soared in the months following the flotation.

Taxpayers also lost out through the timing of the sale. Under pressure from the chancellor, and concerned about their wafer-thin parliamentary majority that was being eroded at every by-election, ministers pushed for the earliest possible sale. The problem was that Railtrack did not have a financial track record, though Norman Broadhurst, the finance director, cobbled one together by going through the BR accounts, with some difficulty because they had been drawn up on a completely different basis. But the City, which is slow to adapt to new markets and is very risk-averse, still did not really understand the rail industry. As the NAO report put it, 'The timing of the sale may have had an adverse impact on the value achieved, since it was carried out at a time when the market was only beginning to understand the new commercial and regulatory structures within the rail industry.'

The NAO was told by institutional investors that a higher price 'would have probably [been] obtained for the company'[14] had the sale been postponed just for a few months. Such a delay would have allowed investors to learn more about Railtrack's business and the complicated regulatory regime. The Department of Transport told the NAO that it believed that market confidence would have been damaged by a delay until the autumn, putting at risk both the flotation and the privatisation scheme generally but, in the measured language that is used for these reports, it is clear that the NAO completely disagreed with the department's analysis: 'In our view, a delay to the sale of Railtrack, even only to the autumn of 1996, would have been helpful to institutional investors and analysts as it would have enabled them to gain a better appreciation of Railtrack's business within the privatised rail industry.'[15]

Another obstacle on the course to a successful sale was the large burden of debt carried over from British Rail days. Right from the outset, it was clear that the company could not be saddled with large amounts of BR's historic debt, as this would make share the offer too unappealing. According to the NAO, Railtrack owed £1.5bn to the public sector, which was cancelled on privatisation and replaced with new debt of £586, a write-off of around £900m, equivalent to half the eventual receipts for the company. The reduction in debt was partly a result of Railtrack's hard bargaining over the Thameslink 2000 project. The government had wanted to show that privatisation would boost investment but Railtrack was anxious not to take on the burden without compensation. After protracted negotiations, the level of Railtrack's debt was reduced further by £225m to cover much of the cost of the project, with the Department arguing, disingenuously, that Railtrack's value would be boosted by £240m because of lower debt payments and a boosted share price due to investors' enhanced perceptions of the company's growth prospects. However, when the NAO spoke to investors, most said that the Thameslink 2000 project 'did not have a significant influence on their valuations'.[16] The NAO reckoned, therefore, that of the £225m additional write-off, £125m was wasted.

The most blatant fiddle was the way Railtrack was compensated for another potential risk which might have made it more difficult to sell. In an effort to improve punctuality and reliability, a performance regime was introduced in April 1995 based on the passenger's charter, which recorded the percentage of trains that were cancelled or which were more than five minutes (for short distances) or ten minutes (for longer journeys) late. Under the new system every delay was to be allocated either to Railtrack, if the problem was with signalling or track work, for example, or to the operator, if it was a result of, say, a train failure or an absent driver. The system measures the delays not just at the end of the journey, but also at various points *en route*. Railtrack became responsible for the fault attribution, although train operators also took on staff whose sole function was to quibble over who should be penalised for particular delays.

In an extraordinary decision the rail regulator, John Swift, under pressure from ministers sweetened the pill for Railtrack by allocating the company an extra, inflation-protected £75m in track access charges to compensate for any possible losses on the performance regime.

The level of track access charges was originally determined by a group of civil servants and Swift had realised that the level set was too high which, potentially, would have allowed Railtrack to be too profitable. So Swift announced a reduction of 8 per cent for 1995/6 and in subsequent years Railtrack was to be allowed increases of inflation minus 2 per cent. The cut in charges angered ministers and officials in the Department of Transport who were worried that the reduction would jeopardise the flotation of Railtrack. So the addition of the supplementary access charges, supposedly to cover for the performance regime, was a compromise between Swift and the government with, yet again, the taxpayer footing the bill.

In the event, Railtrack performed well in 1996/7, and therefore it received £111m out of the performance regime, money which again largely came from taxpayers and most of which (£77m) was the result of these supplementary access charges. It was, in effect, a 'heads Railtrack wins, tails Railtrack wins' kind of regime which removed some of the pressure on the company to improve performance. As with all Swift's decisions, he was hamstrung by the fact that he had to ensure that he did nothing which actually jeopardised the flotation of Railtrack – as opposed to eliciting whinges from Railtrack's managers – because part of his remit was to ensure that the company could be sold.

Track access charges are Railtrack's principal source of income, worth, at the beginning of privatisation, around £2.3bn annually and are paid by the train operators who, in turn, receive subsidy from the government (worth £1.8bn in 1997/8 but declining to £1.15bn in 2001/2). The access charge regime, which is necessarily complex and arcane, demonstrates the arbitrary way that privatisation was designed. Swift did not particularly like the system that he had inherited but he could not change it as there was not sufficient time. Although too complex to describe in detail, the system essentially determines how much Railtrack should invest in maintaining and renewing the railway and then sets the access charges to ensure that the company has sufficient funds to do the work and to reward its shareholders. It is very unwieldy and the amounts are largely fixed, with only 9 per cent of the charges being variable. In other words, Railtrack gets very little extra money (and in many cases none at all) when additional trains are run on its tracks, a situation which was to cause the company much grief when operators started putting on many new services in the late 1990s (see chapter 10). The privatisation was supposed to have made the whole of the rail industry transparent and to expose the costs of running the railway in order that rational economic decisions could be made on the viability of many marginal services and lines. However, the way that Railtrack was valued meant that this transparency never emerged from the fog of railway economics.

The regulator proved to be equally generous towards Railtrack in making a decision about what should happen to the company's income from property sales. Here, the government had learnt from previous privatisations, notably the sale of the bus companies where purchasers had made large, quick profits by flogging off town centre bus stations, and ensured that the company only took on operational railway land while property that could no longer be used for railway purposes was left to be sold by the British Rail Property Board that remained state-owned.

However, this still left Railtrack with many sites that had great development potential, which, along with rental income, was expected to bring in £250m in profits over a five-year period. Rather than imposing a blanket clawback clause, Swift allowed Railtrack to retain 75 per cent of any extra profits beyond the £250m, with the remaining 25 per cent going towards reducing access charges. This was another climbdown by Swift, as ever under ministerial pressure, as earlier he had intimated that Railtrack would only be able to keep a small proportion of these windfall profits. Horton, however, had lobbied hard to be allowed to retain the bulk of the proceeds, arguing that it would boost the image of Railtrack as a high-yielding utility with the added spice of potential development windfalls. Critics saw the move as encouraging Railtrack to focus on its property portfolio rather than on its main task as the infrastructure provider for the rail industry.

In fact, the way the industry was regulated gave little encouragement for Railtrack to invest. Indeed, the most amazing omission in the new structure of the industry was that there was no obligation on Railtrack to spend money to improve the railway. Although the track access agreements included specific items of investment that Railtrack was obliged to carry out, it was under no obligation to follow an investment plan set out by the rail regulator. In other words, he had no powers to direct Railtrack to carry out particular bits of work or, most important, any enhancements. This omission was later remedied by the addition of licence Condition 7, agreed between Railtrack and Swift in 1997, which specified Railtrack's duties in maintaining and improving the network, but this was still a vague requirement. The regulator has no power to force Railtrack to invest in particular projects.

All these decisions were taken in order to make Railtrack more saleable and to allay the fears of Horton and his colleagues. As we saw in the previous chapter, the Labour party had threatened to stymie the sale but its statements of intent became progressively weaker as the time for the privatisation approached. Even as late as February 1996, just three months before the eventual flotation, Brian Wilson, Labour's pugnacious transport spokesman, said: 'Without public ownership of the infrastructure, a Labour government would be hamstrung in its determination to expand and develop the railways. . . . These practical considerations must dictate our view on Railtrack.'[17] Yet despite the clear message that renationalisation was on the agenda, by the time the statement had to be drawn up for the Railtrack prospectus a couple of months later, Wilson's boss, Clare Short, had dropped any commitment to renationalise the railways in a speech setting out the party's position in relation to the flotation, arguing it would be 'irresponsible'[18] for Labour to threaten potential investors that, once in government, the party would take back Railtrack.

When the prospectus was issued in the run up to the sale, Labour's U-turn was all too evident. The attempt to put flesh on Blair's commitment to a 'publicly owned, publicly accountable railway' still left the bones exposed. While criticising the privatisation, arguing that 'We do not believe that increased investment and a more intensive use of rail can be achieved with the current structures proposed for the privatised Rail-track,' Short only promised tighter regulation and, bizarrely, 'reconstituting British Rail' to encourage and foster partnership between public and private finance in the rail network. On the big question of renation-alisation, the formula was hardly threatening and contained more weasel words than the average lawyer's briefcase: 'Dependent on the availability of resources, and as priorities allow, seek, by appropriate means, to extend public ownership and control.' In other words, given big Gordon is not going to prioritise buying back the railways, we'll let you get on with it.

This removed any remaining doubt about the flotation. The price of the shares was set relatively conservatively at 390p, after a bookbuilding exercise – involving investors being approached individually – had proved successful. The company was sold in May 1996 for £1.9bn, although, since it assumed the debt of £586m, the total receipts were almost £2.5bn. The offer was seven times oversubscribed, which led the NAO to criticise the fact that the share price had not been raised during the bookbuilding process. Since, as we have seen, around £900m had been written off by the government, the net receipts were £1.6bn and the company was receiving around £1bn per year in subsidy, Railtrack was not so much sold as given away.

Railtrack quickly began to attract much of the opprobrium that had been levied at British Rail, made all the worse by the fact that its share price was soaring and its directors were paying themselves inflated salaries. The public sensed that Railtrack was not acting in its best

interests and the company quickly became the target of widespread criticism. As I put it in the *Independent on Sunday*, 'Railtrack has succeeded
where generations of British Rail managers failed: it has made BR popular.'[19] In the autumn of 1995, for example, it had produced its first 2,100-
page *Great Britain Passenger Railway Timetable*, having taken over the job
from British Rail, and it had so many mistakes that two supplements
totalling over 300 pages had to be produced simultaneously, a fiasco
which led Barry Doe, a timetable expert, to say, 'I have timetables going
back to the 1950s and this is by far the worst I have ever seen.'[20] To make
matters worse, Railtrack had charged each train operating company
£100,000 to produce the timetable. Eventually it pulped the whole
80,000 print run and offered previous purchasers a free copy on production of the old cover.

Everything that was wrong with the railways was being blamed on privatisation and, quite often, on Railtrack. Remarkably, even Her Majesty's
Inspector of the Constabulary joined in. In his 1996 report he wrote that
there was 'a direct link between the increase in crime [on the railways]
together with the reduced number of detections and some of the changes
that had occurred within the railway industry'.[21] It seemed far-fetched
but he cited reduced staffing, open access to premises and reluctance of
staff to 'patrol some late night services'. In fact, in fairness, all of these
trends had developed under BR, and the inspector seemed to be jumping
on the anti-privatisation bandwagon.

Even the relatively compliant John Swift found Railtrack's behaviour
intolerable. As he commented, 'Railtrack "got greedy" sometime in
1997.'[22] He detected an unwillingness to invest which he found troubling
(see chapter 11) and this is what led him eventually to introduce the new
licence Condition 7.

While the sale was a success within its own narrow terms, having been
achieved on time and having attracted 665,000 applications, Railtrack's
early behaviour in the private sector was disastrous for the railway. As a
company with a conventional structure, its legal duty was to its shareholders and, freed from government, Railtrack's directors decided that
they only had one purpose in life – to satisfy those shareholders and maximise their dividends.

But the directors didn't know what to do with their new-found freedom. There was no strategy, no vision, not even an idea of precisely what
Railtrack was for. Edmonds, the chief executive until the autumn of 1997,

was an experienced railwayman but was not a good delegator and ran the organisation as his own fiefdom. Moreover, he had a long-term dislike of engineers that was to prove very damaging to the company. He did not share his vision, if he had one, with his colleagues. As Richard Middleton, who was a zone director at the time, put it, 'We pottered along. After privatisation, we did not know what to do next. People were dabbling in this or that, but there was no clear sense of corporate purpose. We hadn't decided it was a growing business and therefore there was no objective to deliver growth.'[23] Railtrack never set out a corporate strategy, or even figured out what its role was. The early Network Management Statements, the agenda for investment which the company was obliged to produce, reflected that. They were thin documents full of banalities: 'Over the next ten years, we will spend more than £1bn annually to make our vision of the world's best railway a reality', and 'Our privatisation freed us from public-sector constraints on spending.'[24] (As we shall see in chapter 12, in reality Railtrack became even more heavily dependent on subsidy than BR, as evidenced by Railtrack's 1999/2000 annual report which said: 'It is clear that the level of government subsidy for the railway will need to rise.'[25])

Initially, investment of £10bn was promised over the first ten years. While that sounded a big number, it was only sufficient to ensure the track and infrastructure remained in the same condition without any improvements. Indeed, in the 1996/7 statement, maintenance was forecast to go down from the current level of £740m to just £500m a decade later; and renewals were scheduled to be at the same level of £600m in 2006/7 as in 1995/6, with a bit of extra expenditure during the intervening years (see chapter 11 for a discussion of the problems with investment on the railways since privatisation).

In the absence of any other guiding purpose, profit maximisation became the holy grail. Gerald Corbett, who replaced Edmonds as chief executive in the autumn of 1997, was swept up by that agenda. Corbett was a conventional big company executive, having previously been financial director of GrandMet (now Diageo), and therefore did not question Railtrack's ethos. As he stated to the House of Commons Transport sub-Committee in late 1998, 'We believe very strongly that profits and investment are two sides of the same coin. The more profitable Railtrack is and the stronger Railtrack is, the more money we can raise and the more we can get done.' The purpose of the company was to manage the infrastructure to reduce delays which were attributable to Railtrack so that it could make a profit out of performance. The view of Railtrack executives was that it was a separate company from the rest of the industry with a limited remit to do its bit. Corbett believed that Railtrack's job was to manage the assets in such a way that the company maximised profits and initially went about that task aggressively before he realised that Railtrack's remit included a wider public agenda.

Railtrack's management systems were rudimentary for a company that, overnight, became a member of the FTSE-100. Corbett said that when he took the job he was told there was a target to improve performance by 15 per cent:

> I asked what the performance plan was. The managers said it was 15 per cent. So I said, 'What's the plan?' And they said, 15 per cent. But, I said, 'How are we going to get there?' – blank look. There was no plan. There was no suggestion of how you might want to do it, or how you could go about it. There was no thinking about what they were capable of achieving. Some of the better ones put a few things down on paper, but the others just exhorted the troops to do better.[26]

Corbett set about trying to change this with a massive operation devised by McKinsey's, the management consultants, called Project Destiny which was an attempt to formulate a plan about what Railtrack should do and how it should set priorities for investment. There were some improvements – investment increased and performance got better but, as we shall see in chapter 9, the strategy was flawed.

Not surprisingly, the City loved all this. Railtrack became one of the great privatisation successes, with its share price soaring to reach a record level of £17.68 by the end of 1998, over four times the original offer price. Railtrack's managers clearly got over-excited, ordering that a daily notice with the previous evening's share price be posted on every signal box noticeboard.

To be fair to Corbett, he eventually understood that Railtrack could not simply aim to maximise its profit without regard to wider social issues. He changed his tune completely. In April 2000, in an interview in the *Observer*,[27] he said: 'We have moved completely off the profit agenda and the shareholder agenda. After we were privatised, we stayed on a profit and shareholder agenda for too long. We have now gone over to the public service obligations agenda as agreed with Tom Winsor [the rail regulator].' Corbett had learnt what, as we shall see, the Labour politicians have not, unfortunately, yet understood – that the railways cannot be run as a conventional business. Partly, too, this was a clever ploy. He set up a regulation department with twenty-five people whose main task was to ensure that Winsor gave the company a favourable settlement in the access charge review. This was hugely successful – Railtrack eventually got £15bn, double the previous level.

THE RESPONSIBILITY FOR SAFETY

Safety was the dog that did not bark – at least initially. Throughout the privatisation process there had been fears expressed by trade unionists and other anti-privatisation groups that safety would be compromised by the fragmentation and privatisation of the railway. John Edmonds later wrote: 'While the financial elements could be manipulated to meet the demands and expectations of the market, a single serious accident involving loss of life would have scuppered the entire process and all those closely involved were well aware of this.'[28] By chance – or perhaps mischance – the fatal accidents caused by privatisation were to happen after the sales process had been completed.

The break-up of the industry necessitated a completely new approach to the management of safety on the railways. Traditionally, under BR, the industry had been largely self-regulating. Her Majesty's Railway Inspectorate (HMRI) investigated accidents, but it was a tiny organisation staffed by former senior army officers with barely half a dozen inspectors and it had no day-to-day role in relation to safety, as this was seen as the responsibility of everyone in the industry. BR employed inspectors to cover all aspects of its work.

Safety improved gradually in the railways through the rather crude but effective process of learning from accidents. All the major improvements in safety came as a result of applying the lessons from disasters and through investment in new safety measures. The prevailing philosophy was that there was no such thing as absolute safety, but that it should be the aim. However, it was also recognised – which is a point that the public is less prepared to accept today – that there would be accidents and even fatalities.

The management of safety began to change after the Inspectorate was criticised by the Fennell report into the 1987 Kings Cross disaster for not taking on a pro-active role in preventing accidents. The Clapham disaster the following year resulted in the Hidden report that was also critical of HMRI. Stan Hall, author of several books on railway disasters, feels Fennell and Hidden misunderstood the role of HMRI, setting in train changes which led to the bureaucratisation of the safety process in the industry: 'HMRI was not responsible for overall safety. Its remit was to investigate accidents and trends, to oversee, gently, any works and to keep ministers informed. The industry was self-regulating.' But, insists Hall, it worked because there was mutual trust, a culture of pride in the railway and great respect for the inspectors.

This came to an end when BR accepted the Hidden recommendations and, as a result, HMRI was incorporated into the Health and Safety Executive (HSE). Safety then became the responsibility of an outside body with a large bureaucracy, and that process was extended further with privatisation, which necessarily led to a massive expansion of this bureaucracy.

There was no longer any question of the industry being self-regulating, given the fragmentation of what had been BR into so many parts. The government commissioned a report from the Health and Safety Commission (which oversees the HSE) to work out how safety could be regulated in a fragmented industry. Called *Ensuring Safety on Britain's Railways*, the document recommended that every company involved in the railways set out a safety case, which involved assessing all the potential risks and putting forward strategies on how they would be kept to a minimum. This was a concept developed successfully in the nuclear and offshore oil industries and would now be applied to rail.

On the recommendation of the HSE, another controversial decision was made without proper consideration of the implications. Following the Clapham accident, British Rail had set up a Group Standards Organisation which set standards for all aspects of British Rail's operations, ranging from driver training to the maintenance of locomotive wheels. There was a fierce debate over whether this should remain intact as an independent unit or as part of the HSE. Oddly, the HSE did not want it, suggesting instead that Railtrack should take over the organisation, creating what became the Safety and Standards Directorate (SSD).

This idea was opposed by many people in the railway industry because of fears that the company would be influenced by commercial considerations when making decisions on safety requirements. Moreover, it gave one commercial company, Railtrack, a role over others in the industry, something that neither party would be happy about. Railtrack felt it was being burdened with a role for which it was not suited; the other companies feared that Railtrack could exercise control over them by masking commercial considerations under the guise of safety considerations. Nevertheless, the government adopted the HSE's suggestion, partly allaying fears over the profit motive by ensuring that part of Railtrack's licence condition was to fund SSD adequately and that it was to be independent of Railtrack's commercial business. It was an arrangement that failed to recognise that the perception of the management of safety was almost as important as the reality itself. Inevitably, therefore, the status of SSD as part of Railtrack was highlighted in the aftermath of the Ladbroke Grove disaster and it was quickly hived off into a separate subsidiary, Railway Safety.[29] Railtrack was thus given the role of monitoring the safety cases of all the other companies working in the industry, while its own safety case was vetted by the HSE. While the safety case system is considered to be robust, there is a tendency for it to lead to 'ticking boxes' and an attitude which sees the objective as fulfilling bureaucratic requirements rather than improving the safety of the industry.

Even before privatisation, Railtrack's safety management had become the subject of criticism from the Health and Safety Executive. In a report published in March 1996,[30] following the HSE's most extensive inquiry ever carried out on the railways, the deputy chief inspector of the railways, Vic Coleman, warned that there were severe weaknesses and poor management in Railtrack's safety systems.

Railtrack's position at the heart of the railways' safety system is constantly undermined because it is not seen as an impartial player and because it has a lot of responsibility without any real power. One former senior Railtrack manager, for example, cites the example of a drivers' training programme:

> If you are a zonal director and find that the programme is inadequate, you tell SSD and then the whole thing takes ages because they have to do an audit and getting an audit from SSD is like being stroked with a feather duster. And then SSD, if they are unhappy, go to the HSE. It should be that if there is an

issue with a train operator, Railtrack should be able to tell them to deal with it, but in practice it doesn't work like that. Railtrack does not have the power to issue enforcement orders, so if the operator told them to bugger off, the whole thing would just have to go through SSD.

The only other option for Railtrack is the nuclear one of denying the train operator access to the tracks, but, in practice, that is so draconian it would never happen unless the railways were in imminent danger.

Safety was considered to be a given to such an extent that it was not included as a measure of the performance of the railway in the same way as 'minutes delay'. Therefore, the performance regime outlined above did not measure or reward the safe running of the railway but focused only on punctuality and the number of cancellations. This created a potential conflict between safety and performance that was to contribute to the Hatfield disaster (see chapter 9).

It was not only safety that had been compromised by the rushed privatisation of Railtrack. The railway was suddenly transformed from an integrated service into a fragmented business. Moreover, the complete overhaul of a long-established system which had, despite all the difficulties and the criticism, been functioning relatively well was carried out in an incredibly short time. Railtrack, carved out of BR so hastily, never had a chance to bed down before it was prepared for privatisation. Railtrack was a bastardised construct at the heart of a dysfunctional railway, neither truly in the private nor in the public domain; but due to luck and happenstance it took a couple of years to be found out.

In the meantime there was always the hope of something better on the horizon. By the time of the 1997 election the new rail system was showing few signs of its problems, at least so far as the general public was concerned, and those that had come to prominence, such as the Stagecoach drivers fiasco (see chapter 4), were dismissed as teething problems. At the time of the interminable campaign leading up to the 1997 election there had been no major accident since the privatisation of Railtrack, and the railways figured little in the campaign. Any chance the Tories had of capitalising on the sale had long gone because of the delays, which meant most private companies had only just taken over running services, and, of course, because of the huge media coverage generated by Stagecoach's appalling management of the South West Trains franchise.

In any case, everyone knew that Labour would win the election and had promised a 'publicly accountable, publicly owned' railway, whatever that meant. Which was not much, as it turned out, even though Labour won the election on 1 May 1997 so convincingly that it seemed, for a while, that anything was possible.

CHAPTER 6

Labour fails to grasp the nettle

After winning the 1997 election so handsomely, Labour was expected to introduce rapid changes to the rail industry. The election manifesto, however, had been guarded, a sign that Labour was preparing to hoist the white flag on the railways. The manifesto recognised that 'the process of rail privatisation is now largely complete' (omitting to say, as we saw in chapter 4, that the process had been helped along by Labour) and suggested there would be no major changes to the structure or ownership of the industry: 'Our task will be to improve the situation as we find it, not as we wish it to be.'

John Prescott, the deputy prime minister, was given a brief that suited his girth and his ego as head of a specially created department which combined environment, transport and the regions. Gavin Strang was made minister of transport, also with a place in the Cabinet, which suggested that transport would be high on the new government's agenda.

But it was not. Transport was not perceived as being a key political issue. Tony Blair had shown little interest in transport in opposition and he largely ignored the subject after the election, which, as ministers later admitted privately, was a big mistake. Transport policy is a long-term business and not doing anything much in the first couple of years of what turned out to be a four-year Parliament was short-sighted. Mistakenly, Prescott did not press the issue. He wanted time to draw up a White Paper, get the transport legislation through Parliament and then obtain the money. He managed to do this, but it took all four years of Labour's first term and therefore there were to be precious few achievements in those four years.

Unpopular road schemes would be scrapped or 'reviewed', as

promised by Labour in opposition in order to garner the environmental vote, but nothing much else was on the agenda. In any case, the railways could not be reformed without primary legislation and it quickly became clear that none would be forthcoming in the first two years of Labour rule.

Instead, a White Paper on transport was commissioned, with the promise that it would set out a vision for 'integrated transport', an oft-repeated but ill-defined slogan. The Tories had already produced a quite commendable Green Paper, which, surprisingly, had little emphasis on building roads and stressed the need for public transport, but this was consigned to the dustbin.

The development of a coherent transport policy was not helped by a series of spats between Prescott and Downing Street over the nature of the policy. Blair was terrified of frightening the ever powerful motoring lobby and his policy team at No. 10 actively briefed against Prescott's carrot-and-stick approach aimed at encouraging people out of their cars and onto public transport through a mix of extra charges on road use and improvements to rail and bus services. The differences between Prescott and his boss came to a head in a TV interview by the deputy prime minister when he referred to Geoffrey Norris, the forty-something who held the transport brief in No. 10's policy unit, as a 'teenybopper'.[1] The put-down was a response to Norris's temerity in writing to Prescott to warn him that the prime minister was concerned that the proposed White Paper on transport was too green and too anti-car.

Prescott, in need of allies, instead wooed Gordon Brown, the chancellor, and won some key concessions from him, but they came at a heavy price. Prescott managed to persuade Brown to allow councils the right to spend any money they raised through congestion charging on local investment schemes for transport, including rail and bus as well as roads. He even obtained a promise from Brown that any future revenue from the fuel tax escalator would be earmarked (hypothecated) for national transport spending, but this was to prove a Pyrrhic victory since the automatic escalator was abolished in the 2000 budget and then buried by the fuel tax protests that autumn. Moreover, congestion charging was a long-term prospect and needed legislation before it could be introduced.

The price Brown extracted was Prescott's agreement to two controversial part-privatisations, the London Underground and National Air

Traffic Services. While the latter is beyond the scope of this book, the Tube has relevance because the Public Private Partnership proposed is similar to the railways, in that the infrastructure is to be separated from the operation of services, although in the case of the Tube, the infrastructure is split and privatised while the operations remain unified and publicly controlled. The plan is to have three private sector infrastructure consortia each responsible for three or four tube lines, while the operation of services is to remain in the hands of the publicly run London Underground. However, concerted opposition to the scheme led by the mayor, Ken Livingstone, elected in May 2000, particularly in the wake of the Hatfield crash, resulted in a lengthy political battle. Just as the campaign for the June 2001 election got underway, the government made a big concession when it allowed Livingstone's appointee, Bob Kiley, to take over the tube and the negotiations with contractors over the terms of the PPP. However, Kiley was soon sacked after the election as ministers continued to push through the scheme despite widespread opposition. Transport industry experts were remarkably united against the scheme and few could understand why the government was so intent on pushing through the plan despite the fact that the Hatfield crash had demonstrated the disadvantages of separating the management of maintenance from the running of services.

Prescott tried to disguise his inability to do anything much on transport by making a lot of noise, the usual politician's trick of masking lack of action with words. He rashly announced in a press conference that he would persuade people out of their cars and made a commitment that few thought he would ever be able to keep: 'I will have failed if in five years' time there are not many more people using public transport and far fewer journeys by car. It's a tall order but I urge you to hold me to it.'[2] So far as the railways were concerned, given the retreat from renationalisation, Prescott was forced to tinker at the margins. Soon after the election new instructions had been issued to the franchising director which removed the requirement to push privatisation, and, importantly, this was replaced by a new emphasis on growth. But a more radical move, regulation of the rolling stock companies in order to control prices, was blocked by the rail regulator, John Swift, who argued that it was unnecessary.

Instead, Prescott took his aggression out on the train companies, barracking them rather impotently from the sidelines and taking every opportunity to criticise them. When FirstGroup, the large bus company, took over Great Western Holdings' three franchises from the management buy-out team in March 1998, the original directors, former BR managers, became instant millionaires. The managing director, Richard George, saw his £40,000 investment turn into almost £3m, while Brian Scott, the chairman, got £4m for his stake of £37,000 just two years after the franchise had started operating in the private sector. It was all the more galling for Prescott because Great Western had been the company whose driver was at fault in the previous year's Southall train crash in which seven people died (see chapter 7). Prescott tried to stop the takeover but ultimately he was advised that he did not have the power to do so. Instead, he extracted a few new coaches and a stricter performance regime out of FirstGroup, which, along with other measures, were optimistically valued at £75m.

Much to Prescott's consternation, there was a steady trickle of news about the creation of yet more rail industry fat cats and massive profits for rail companies. It was the rolling stock company executives who did the best out of privatisation, which is why Prescott had tried unsuccessfully to regulate them. John Prideaux, a former head of InterCity, made a staggering £15m from the sale of Angel Trains to the Royal Bank of Scotland, and Andrew Jukes, the managing director of Eversholt, did even better with £15.9m when the company was sold to Forward Trust – though neither of them became as fat a cat as Sandy Anderson, who, as we have seen, made around £40m when the third rolling stock company, Porterbrook, was bought by Stagecoach in the summer of 1996, barely half a year after it had been privatised.

Railtrack, too, was booming, with annual profits of £339m announced in June 1997 for its first year in private ownership, and Prescott let it be known that he had told Sir Robert Horton (who had been rewarded with the knighthood he apparently craved in John Major's final honours list) that 'Railtrack must no longer put the needs of its investors above those of the taxpayer.'[3]

Even in abandoning the renationalisation commitment at the 1997 conference, Prescott had attacked the new railway barons: 'To purchase Railtrack would cost over £4bn,' Prescott said, and 'not a penny piece of this money would go into investment or indeed rail safety. It would go into the pockets of Railtrack shareholders. I don't believe you really want me to use public money next year to make fat cats even fatter.' In order to defeat a rail unions' motion calling for renationalisation, Prescott suggested that there might be a role in future for the public sector in running the railways, but this was clearly an empty gesture since all franchises ran at least until 2003. Indeed, when the refranchising process eventually started in 2000 there was no suggestion that any would return to the public sector.

Prescott went even further in his criticism of the rail companies at the following year's Labour party conference. After many delegates had been delayed by a series of mishaps on Virgin trains, he departed from his planned speech to call the train companies 'a national disgrace' and later summoned them to a rail summit.

Prescott's attacks on the rail companies were widely seen within the industry as the railings of a powerless man who everyone knew was hamstrung by his leader's fear of alienating business. Given a free hand, Prescott would have renationalised the railways, cost or no cost, but he knew that that was impossible because of Blair's conservative approach. As Steve Norris, the former Tory transport minister put it, 'Prescott doesn't like the private sector. He tolerates it. He is one of those dangerous people who actually think the public sector runs things better than the private sector.'4 Instead, sullenly, Prescott used every opportunity to criticise the railways, a futile gesture which damaged morale in an industry that was already the target of a disproportionate number of media attacks.

But the system was against him. The Tories had deliberately engineered much of the government's role out of the railways. Prescott therefore saw the White Paper, the first on transport for twenty years, as the instrument through which he would regain control of the industry. By the time it was published, in July 1998, the lacklustre and taciturn Strang was already on the way out, to be replaced by John Reid, a sparky *bon viveur* Scot who was on the fast track to the Cabinet. (Reid was followed a year later by Helen Liddell, who lasted barely a couple of months before being replaced by Lord Macdonald, a technocrat who was good on TV, making it clear that the revolving-door policy for transport ministers, long operated by the Tories, had been retained by Labour. Prescott remained throughout Labour's first term, but he had little time for detail given that he had to deal with everything from global warming and aviation to rural policy and local councils.)

The White Paper, *A new deal for transport: better for everyone* lacked clarity and, as its wordy title implies, a hard edge. It was a typical piece of Blairite inclusive politics that eschewed the hard choices that must be made in a complex policy area such as transport. Prescott wanted to present it as a radical shift away from the old emphasis on roads, but he could not be seen to be too radical because of Blair's fear that Labour would be labelled anti-motorist. The use of public transport, walking and cycling were to be encouraged, whilst, overall, the need for travel would be reduced through better land-use planning and technological innovation. The White Paper announced plans to allow congestion charging and taxes on company car parking, and there were plenty of other good ideas and suggestions but it was short on firm commitments. While the White Paper represented a marked shift away from the 'predict and provide' model of road building – whose ultimate logic was the paving over of much of southern England – a few radical edges had been knocked off on Downing Street's orders, such as a suggestion to tax supermarket car park users. More importantly, there was no date for implementation since there was no commitment to a Transport Bill for the 1998/9 Parliamentary session. As the *Daily Mail* observed accurately: 'A quick reading could lead to the impression that the Paper contains hard and decisive policies. Unfortunately, closer examination suggests there is less to his proposals than meets the eye.'[5]

Rail was to be at the heart of the programme, with investment and improvements inducing people out of their cars and on to public transport. As Reid put it, 'If we don't have a decent train system, we can't handle the other problems in creating an integrated transport policy. Train is the central element in solving all our transport problems.'[6]

There was to be a Commission for Integrated Transport to act as a government advisory board and, for the railways, the White Paper confirmed the creation of the much-trailed Strategic Rail Authority (SRA). The idea was that this would inject some long-term thinking into the industry, a blatant gap left in the Tories' model, and would also take over the role of disbursing subsidies. The SRA was presented as a way of bringing together a fragmented industry, but this was not strictly true. It was, rather, an addition to the panoply of organisations with their fingers in the railway pie and its power to crack heads was limited, as events after the Hatfield disaster were to show.

Yet Prescott was desperate to be seen as doing something for the railways and much play was made of the creation of the SRA. A draft bill was published in the summer of 1999 but this was only a fig leaf to cover up the fact that legislation would not pass through Parliament until the following session. In fact, because the creation of the SRA became part of a complex Transport Bill, it did not actually reach the statute books until the autumn of 2000, over three years after the Labour government had been elected. The SRA only achieved its statutory status just a couple of months before the 2001 election but it started operating in July 1999 in shadow form. Sir Alastair Morton, the former chairman of Eurotunnel, who was widely credited with having saved the channel tunnel project from bankruptcy, was appointed as its part-time chairman (see chapter 10 for an assessment of the SRA's performance).

Not only did the hapless Prescott not have any legislation until three-quarters of the way through Labour's parliamentary term, he also didn't have any money to improve train services. The Tories had set subsidies for the train operators at sharply declining rates, with the level of payments reducing by £2–300m per year from the initial level of £1.8bn in 1996/7. That meant the train companies faced a constant squeeze on their finances. Nor was there was any prospect of extra money since Gordon Brown had pledged Labour to respecting the Tories' spending plans until April 1999.

The well-targeted Tory taunts that Prescott had done nothing for transport apart from the publication of the White Paper prompted him to announce the preparation of a ten-year transport plan which was eventually published in July 2000. The headline commitments in the document, *Transport 2010: The 10 year plan*, when it was published in July 2000 looked, at first glance, impressive. The staggering sum of £180bn, equally split three ways between roads, rail and other modes of travel, would be spent on transport in the first decade of the new century. However, as with all such documents, closer examination revealed a less generous picture, not least because the figures included increases for inflation (see chapter 11 for an analysis of the ten-year plan).

While both the White Paper and the ten-year plan contained measures aimed at making significant improvements on the railways, the delay in producing them, together with the fundamental policy differences between Prescott and No. 10, resulted in Labour losing the political initiative on transport. With such a large majority, Labour had a brief opportunity to launch radical policies whose benefits would have begun to percolate through in time for a general election. Instead, Labour got the worst of both worlds because its relatively radical rhetoric, even though it had not been backed up by corresponding action, helped provoke a backlash. At the time they left office the Tories had realised that a transport policy based solely on making life easier for the motorist was counterproductive, but under a more right-wing leadership the party now reinvented itself as the motorists' friend. Their supportive rottweilers in the tabloid press could be unleashed at the slightest whiff of anti-motorist policies.

The roads lobby, that powerful coalition of interests representing bodies as varied as the Automobile Association, car dealers and truckers' organisations, had been relatively silent in the final years of Tory rule. Margaret Thatcher had feathered their nest with the country's biggest road-building programme but the plans had ground to a halt during the late Major years as result of concerted opposition from local residents and roads campaigners, combined with the Treasury's realisation that most schemes were not good value for money. When the Tory party changed its tune after the 1997 election, the roads lobby returned from the wilderness and quickly pointed its guns at Prescott, which it perceived to be an easy target. He bore the brunt of many attacks, provoked by, for example, his idea of creating a bus lane on the M4 near London and his spectacularly stupid 200-yard drive along the Bournemouth sea front at the 1999 party conference, allegedly because his wife, Pauline, had been worried about her hair blowing about, although Prescott claimed it was for security reasons. The M4 bus lane proved, later, to be a great success, reducing journey times for both bus passengers and cars, but that never made any headlines. (Pauline's hair, though, stayed immaculate.) The ease with which the roads lobby could whip up support was illustrated when both the *Daily Mail* and the *Daily Express* declared that there would be a 'war on the motorist' on their front pages[7] when reporting the 1999 Queen's speech, merely because Tony Blair said the forthcoming Transport Bill would include measures that would 'reduce road congestion'.

The backlash culminated in the great petrol price revolt in the autumn of 2000. A group of pasty-faced farmers and beer-bellied truckers brought the country to its knees on the ludicrous premise that petrol prices were excessive. In fact, the overall real cost of motoring had remained virtually unchanged for two decades but the fuel tax escalator, which ironically had been abandoned in the previous budget, together with a hike in the world price of oil, had led to record prices at the petrol pumps[8]. The government dithered and for inexplicable reasons the tanker drivers felt unable to cross the picket lines at the depots while the police behaved with kid gloves, in marked contrast to their confrontations with the miners during the 1984 strike. The country almost came to a standstill as the pumps ran dry and, despite a few local hiccups where operators found themselves short of fuel, the railways enjoyed a momentary boom (only to lose their new-found customers a month later following the Hatfield disaster), while many people enjoyed the freedom of the relatively traffic-free streets for a few days.

The petrol price revolt exposed the lack of coherence in Labour's transport policy. Its ministers, Tony Blair included, refused to go on the offensive and argue for the need for high prices to protect the environment. Instead, Labour politicians justified the high price of fuel on the basis that it paid for schools and hospitals, a simplistic argument which the public saw through.

By the time Labour went into its successful 2001 election campaign, its transport policy was utterly incoherent. While the railways were scheduled to benefit from the ten-year plan, roads would do even better and, unlike the rail passenger, the motorist could see that the investment was already beginning to come through. In December 2000 the government announced a £1bn programme of by-passes and dual carriageways, including many schemes which had previously been postponed in the roads review carried out in the wake of the election. Blair's pandering to the motoring lobby ensured that Prescott's grand schemes for getting motorists out of their cars and for massive investment in 'integrated transport' were stillborn. Prior to the 2001 election Tony Blair made no significant mention of public transport during the entire campaign.[9] The bankruptcy of Labour's ideas on the subject was shown by the manifesto which had barely half a dozen paragraphs on transport and these were based on the promise to 'improve and expand railway and road travel' – does that suggest Labour wants to see more cars on the road? Despite the collapse of Railtrack's share price during the election campaign, the issue did not feature at all at the hustings.

Even more than Blair's lack of interest, Prescott's muddle-headedness blighted the first Labour government's policy towards the railways.

Prescott was a fan of the railways but could never contain his hatred of the companies that ran them. So he never talked up the industry and its successes, such as the sharp rate of growth, or provided what Gerald Corbett referred to as 'air cover' when there were disasters such as Ladbroke Grove and Southall. Instead, by allowing a damaging briefing by Alastair Campbell, the prime minister's official spokesman, in the aftermath of the Ladbroke Grove accident (see chapter 8), he not only undermined Railtrack but encouraged the overly conservative response of the industry in the aftermath of Hatfield. Prescott seemed to act like an opposition politician in relation to the railways. Twice, for example, in 2001 he criticised fares rises – by Silverlink and then Virgin – and yet did not attempt to impose more regulation of fares, which was in his power, through the Strategic Rail Authority and the refranchising process. As one rail insider put it, 'Prescott undermined the industry rather than supported it.'[10] He appointed a regulator, Tom Winsor, who was more interested in being at war with Railtrack than in regulating it. Prescott also made the mistake of thinking the SRA could pull together the fragmented industry, when, in fact, the events after Hatfield showed that the structure was wrong. In short, the industry felt that the government had always asked for the impossible and then criticised the rail companies when it was not delivered.

While the railways toiled, the roads blossomed. Labour's road-building programme was potentially even more ambitious than that of the Tories during their whole eighteen-year rule. As two academics put it at the Royal Geographical Society in early 2001, Labour's support for road-building was 'completely inconsistent' with the party's earlier support for integrated transport.[11] The railways, then, were no longer at the centre of transport policy as John Reid, the long-departed transport minister, had once promised. In an interview with *Modern Railways*[12] Reid had said that 'The train is the central element in solving all our transport problems'; now this priority for railways had been lost. Instead, Prescott had taken the easy way out, promising lots of money for all modes of transport. The ten-year plan was a step forward, but the numbers in it are not sacrosanct beyond the Treasury's usual three-year spending horizon. Given the lack of a real political commitment to the railways, the industry finds itself just as much at risk from the vagaries of the nation's economic performance as before. In a crisis the old battle between spending on roads and rail will be re-enacted and, in the past, roads have always won. Four years of shambolic transport policy under Labour have revealed nothing that suggests that this would not be the case again. Stephen Byers, Prescott's replacement, who took over at the renamed Department of Local Government, Transport and the Regions (DLTR) after the June 2001 election, inherited a tough legacy.

CHAPTER 7

A moment's inattention

The disaster which Railtrack's first chief executive, John Edmonds, had feared would halt the sell-off process never happened. The major accidents which are examined in this book all occurred after the completion of the privatisation process. There was one serious accident near Watford in August 1996 when a passenger train went through a red light and hit an empty one crossing its path, killing a woman passenger, but the train operating company, North London Railways, was still operated by BR at the time and the issue of privatisation never came into play.

Despite the superb record of the railway in the early and mid-1990s, safety became a key issue in the privatisation debate as critics of the process expressed concerns that the fragmentation and sale of the railways would increase the risks to rail passengers. It was not only the many opponents of privatisation who raised this issue; far more importantly, they were also given resonance by the highly critical report from Her Majesty's Railway Inspectorate[1] (HMRI, part of the Health and Safety Executive) published in March 1996, which said weaknesses in Railtrack's systems 'cause concern' that rail travel could become less safe as a result of the changes. In particular, the Inspectorate highlighted the system of contracts and legal agreements that was at the heart of the new way of running the railways. The report, the biggest single project in HMRI's history, listed a series of incidents in which management failures had led to safety defects. In one, remarkably, a signal was not reinstated after work on the track. More systematically, the report said that, while Railtrack was dependent on technical audits to monitor the performance of the railways, the HMRI 'found little evidence of technical auditing taking place'. Vic Coleman, the then deputy chief inspector of the railways, said: 'We have found a management system which does have a number of weaknesses and we believe that those weaknesses need attending to.' As the Hatfield crash was to show, Railtrack did not sort out a lot of these weaknesses and, indeed, possibly exacerbated them over the subsequent years (see chapter 9 for more details of this report).

There was also evidence that Railtrack was taking a more commercial attitude towards safety issues. In the 1996/7 annual safety report from the Health and Safety Executive, the chief inspector of railways, Stan Robertson, criticised Railtrack for its nit-picking approach to safety. He cited the example of Railtrack's appeal against an improvement notice seeking better fencing on the Foord viaduct in Kent. Railtrack, he said, 'spent almost as much money on assessment etc to avoid compliance as would have been necessary to provide the additional safety feature required by HMRI in the first place.'[2]

The derailment of a train at Bexley in February 1997 raised further concerns about standards of maintenance and of communication between Railtrack and its contractors (see chapter 9 for details of this incident, which highlighted similar issues to the Hatfield disaster). This was the inevitable result of creating a railway where relationships between various parties were based on contracts rather than on an established hierarchical structure.

The bigger question that naturally arose from all these incidents was whether privatisation was affecting the trend towards better safety on the railways. This long-term improvement had been a facet of rail travel almost since its invention because of the way that lessons were learnt from disasters. There were fewer deaths in railway accidents in each post-war decade than in the previous one: the 344 deaths in the 1940s and 337 in the 1950s compare with just 75 in the 1980s and 46 in the 1990s. In fact, until the two accidents on the main line out of Paddington, Southall in 1997 and Ladbroke Grove in 1999, the 1990s had been an excellent decade for rail safety with three years in which there were no deaths and a total of just eight in seven years.

Privatisation occurred in 1996/7 and the two disasters after that killed a total of thirty-eight. It would be a misuse of statistics to place too much emphasis on the fact that the two major incidents of the decade occurred in the three years after privatisation, but nevertheless it is a disturbing point, especially as the third major post-privatisation disaster, Hatfield, in 2000, was unequivocally caused by the new structure of the railway (see chapter 9). The rail network and the management of safety within it

was the product of 175 years of steady evolution. The privatisation and
fragmentation brought about an unprecedented upheaval. Of course,
there had been changes and reorganisations before but nothing on the
scale of those of 1996/7. It was revolution rather than evolution. As a
lawyer would put it, privatisation has a *prima facie* case to answer that
will be examined over the next three chapters.

On the face of it, the accident at Southall on 19 September 1997
appears to be a run of the mill railway disaster that could have happened
at any time under British Rail. But on closer examination it is clear that
the recent fragmentation and privatisation of the railways contributed in
several ways to the collision.

The accident involved a Great Western Trains high speed train from
Swansea to Paddington which smashed into a goods train crossing its
path at Southall in West London. Seven people died and over 100 were
injured. The immediate cause was the inattention of the driver of the
high speed train, Larry Harrison. With the train travelling at its maximum permitted speed of 125mph, he had failed to notice first the double
yellow and then the single yellow signals which, on British railways,
always precede a red. By the time he saw the red, which was protecting
the junction that the goods train was using to cross the high speed train's
path, it was too late. Although Harrison applied the brakes, a collision
was inevitable and the passenger train smashed into the middle of the
goods train, consisting of empty aggregate hoppers, at a combined speed
of between 80 and 90mph.

Driver Harrison clearly should not have passed the red signal – in the
industry this is called a SPAD, a signal passed at danger, which, interestingly, is one of the few technical railway terms to have gained currency
among the general public. But, as with nearly all major transport disasters, the underlying causes are much more complex. The Uff report into
the accident, published in 2000, highlighted, in particular, the absence
of the Automatic Warning System as a key factor, but there are several
other issues worth examining.

The Automatic Warning System (AWS) is a device which alerts drivers that they are approaching yellow or red signals. A couple of hundred
metres before each signal, between the rails there is a box containing
magnets and this triggers off the warning device in the cab. If the signal is
green, a bell rings and a black aspect is shown on a little display in the
driver's cab. If the signal is double yellow, single yellow or red, a horn

sounds and there is a yellow and black 'sunflower' shown to the driver. The sunflower is displayed until it is reset to black by the next green signal, thus giving the driver a visual reminder that he or she should proceed with caution. If the driver does not acknowledge the horn, by pressing a reset button, the brakes are applied automatically. Crucially, on the day of the Southall disaster the high speed train's AWS had been 'isolated' – turned off.

The background to why the AWS was not functioning is both very complicated and highly revealing of the way that the massive changes in the industry had unexpected consequences relating to safety. A fault in the AWS in locomotive 43173, the one which was at the front of the high speed train when it hit the goods train, had occurred the evening before the accident when the train was pulling into Oxford to pick up passengers. The driver, Allan Taylor, found he could not reset the system after it was triggered by the red light at the end of the platform and consequently the train came to a halt halfway along it. Taylor then isolated the AWS in order to be able to proceed and was allowed to take the train, with passengers, to Paddington, even though the safety device was not working.

At this point there occurred one of those little oversights, insignificant in themselves, that might have made all the difference as to whether or not the name of Southall joined the roll call of rail disasters. At Oxford, driver Taylor had told the station supervisor (who worked for a different company, Thames Trains) that the train had stopped because of the AWS. The supervisor then passed this information to Richard Parker, the signalman (who worked for Railtrack), but Parker remembered only that the brakes had come on and did not recall anything being said about AWS. Consequently, he did not pass any information to Operations Control in Swindon (run by Great Western Trains) which would then have logged the failure onto the fault reporting system, known as RAVERS, and this would have been picked up by the depot at Old Oak Common in West London where maintenance is carried out. Taylor did make an entry in the defects repair book on the train which said, 'AWS isolated, unable to cancel', but when he took the train to Old Oak Common after the journey to Paddington, he failed to fill in a defect report form or an incident report form as required by the rules, both of which would have ensured the fault was logged onto RAVERS.

The train was due for an 'A' examination at Old Oak Common, a series of checks carried out every three to four days. However, as a result of the failures by driver Taylor and signalman Parker to report the fault, the only record of the problem with the AWS in locomotive 43173 was contained in the defects book on the train and the fitters only came to it late in their shift since they had other faults to fix.

Old Oak Common had been the subject of a reorganisation after Great Western Trains took over operations from British Rail in February 1996. The number of staff had been reduced and, as Uff put it, 'The men were working under more pressure, and cannot have been motivated to spend more time than the minimum necessary to carry out the required tasks.'3 In fact, there were only four fitters on duty as opposed to the six who had been employed prior to the 1996 reorganisation.

GWT's post-privatisation reorganisation had already given rise to concerns about its impact on safety. While the history of problems over the standards of Great Western's maintenance work stretched back to BR days, its roots were in the separation of Railtrack from the operations in April 1994. Sloppy maintenance at GWT had caused a train fire at Maidenhead in September 1995 which resulted in the death of a passenger who fled from the fire into the path of an oncoming train. The fire had started when the rear fuel tank on the front locomotive fell off after its retaining nuts worked loose due to insufficient maintenance. The following year there was renewed concern from Railtrack about a series of nine incidents between June and November 1996 attributed to defects in GWT's rolling stock. The subsequent investigation, carried out by an independent safety auditor, David Parkes, found, according to Uff, that 'key activities had lapsed and key safety posts had been withdrawn without adequate resources being provided.'4 A new internal audit system covering fleet maintenance was introduced early in 1997 as a result of these concerns, but it was allowed to lapse in August 1997, just before the Southall accident.

Moreover, the depot still showed signs of bad management. Training was inadequate and haphazard, with poor record keeping. There was a lack of clarity about precisely what work should be included in standard maintenance procedures such as the 'A' exam. Uff was scathing about the failings at Old Oak Common: 'It must be concluded that maintenance procedures at Old Oak Common were far from robust. Whatever the effect of the reorganisation of 1996 . . . there was, in September 1997, a lack of attention to details, some of which were safety-critical.'5 Uff is careful not to blame any particular individual but, instead, focuses on the failings of management which had allowed the depot to become so badly run.

As a result of only finding out about the faulty AWS in 43173 during the latter part of their shift, the maintenance engineers gave it a cursory examination which found that it was functioning normally. In fact, it would have taken a much more detailed test to reveal that the problem was caused by a rogue bit of polish on a contact whose presence the inquiry and investigators never managed to explain.

So the train left Old Oak Common with what appeared to be a fully functioning AWS. On the morning of the accident, driver James Tunnock took the train to Paddington using the locomotive 43173 which was at the London end of the train. The AWS was functioning normally and at Paddington he shut the engine down and walked to the other end, locomotive 43163, where he found the guard/driver buzzer was not working. He went back to 43173 and it was at this stage that he found, like driver Taylor the previous night, that he could not cancel the AWS. Again, there was further minor sloppiness which contributed to the accident. Tunnock claimed – and Uff believed him – that he phoned Operations Control at Swindon to alert them to the problem. But no proper record of that call was taken.

The confusion over the messages and precisely who was responsible for 'control' became an issue in the enquiry. The rule book made frequent references to 'Operations Control' but, as it had not been updated since privatisation, the precise meaning was unclear. In the days of BR, of course, the driver, signaller and control staff were within the same organisation and part of the same hierarchy. As Uff put it, 'One of the potential difficulties created by privatisation was the split, first between the driver and signaller, who would work respectively for the train operating company and Railtrack; and secondly, between the signaller and Control, which might refer to either Railtrack or the train operating company.'[6] There was, in fact, a Railtrack control and a Great Western control. While the two were in contact, as Uff pointed out, this was not recognised in the rules and added to the confusion over who was responsible for reporting and dealing with faults.

Back to the train. Tunnock drove the train to Swansea as the 0700 service from Paddington, with the AWS working as there was no problem with 43163. However, when he arrived a few minutes before 10 a.m.

the fitters he expected to find waiting for him on the platform were not there. His message to Swindon that he needed fitters to fix both the guard/driver buzzer and the AWS had never been passed on. Tunnock contacted the station services manager who in turn telephoned the GWT Landore depot ten minutes away and the fitters arrived around 10.15, just seventeen minutes before his scheduled departure. They were not able to fix the guard/driver communication system but, more importantly, they did no work on the AWS because they were not advised that it was out of order, although Tunnock believed they had previously been advised of the problem.

So a series of mishaps and minor mistakes contributed to the fact that the train started off from Swansea with no AWS. The fault in the AWS could not, in fact, have been repaired at Swansea, as it needed to be worked on from a pit, for which the train would have had to go to a depot. But the train could have been taken out of service or turned around.

Here we have to consider the ambiguity in the rules surrounding AWS, which requires a quick look at the rule book. AWS is a relatively simple and crude system that was introduced over the space of thirty years following disasters at Harrow and Wealdstone in 1952 and Lewisham in 1957 which, respectively, killed 112 and 90 people and both of which were caused by drivers going through signals at danger. Although not foolproof, because drivers get into the habit of unconsciously resetting the device, and also less effective than it could be because both yellow and red signals trigger the same sound, it has played an important role in reducing the number of SPADs. However, AWS has never been made mandatory, having been installed gradually and almost imperceptibly on the great majority, but not all, of the signals on the rail network.

Back to 43173's last journey. One other way of dealing with the faulty AWS would have been to adopt the simple expedient of turning the train around. Here we get into theoreticals but they are, nevertheless, worth considering. If the controllers had been alerted about the faulty AWS, would they have ordered the train to be turned around so that the functioning AWS could be used? This was an easy manoeuvre at Swansea as there is a triangle of tracks allowing trains to turn around, but the answer is 'probably not' because of the industry's ambiguous view of the importance of AWS. Moreover, while in BR days turning a train would have been easy, now Great Western would have incurred charges from Railtrack for using up an unscheduled train path, and, had this caused a delay, possible penalty payments as well. In other words, there were built-in obstacles to carrying out this simple manoeuvre that would have prevented the disaster.

The rules governing what happens when the AWS stops working are unclear. While operators are keen to ensure that the safety system is working, they are also desperate to avoid taking trains out of service unnecessarily, especially as, since privatisation, that puts them at risk of financial penalties as well as loss of revenue. The rule book for drivers, devised by British Rail but passed on to Railtrack, said at the time of the accident that 'a traction unit must not enter service if the AWS is isolated' and a bit later that 'if it is necessary to isolate the AWS the driver must inform the signalman at the first convenient opportunity. The train *must be taken out of service at the first suitable location without causing delay or cancellation*' (my italics). As Professor Uff puts it in his report, 'These provisions are, and were perceived to be, ambiguous.'[7] It is unclear whether they mean the train should have been taken out of service once its AWS was found not to be working. Indeed, at the inquiry hearings, various experts even differed about precisely when the train 'entered service'. Did it 'enter service' that morning at Paddington when the first passengers got on or, at Swansea when it began the fateful return journey that was never to be completed?

The root of the problem is whether AWS is regarded as simply an aid to drivers' vigilance or whether it is a vital piece of safety equipment without which trains should not run. The former view was the historic conventional wisdom but gradually managers in the industry had started to realise that AWS was essential for the safe running of trains. As Uff commented, wryly, 'No one was to be heard justifying the decision to allow [the train] to run normally between Swansea and Paddington with its AWS isolated. Yet, with very few exceptions, such concerns were not expressed before the accident.'[8]

In his conclusions, Uff said that the responsibility for the non-functioning of the AWS on the train 'rests firmly with GWT, first in having inadequate maintenance procedures to eliminate known faults, and secondly through inadequate procedures for communicating and taking action following AWS isolation'.[9] However, he also blamed Railtrack for the 'existence of ambiguous and confusing Rules as regards action to be taken in the event of AWS isolation', and says that the company should have initiated a review on this issue.

Another post-privatisation change which had a bearing on the accident was that the requirement to have a second driver at speeds over 110mph had been negotiated away with the unions. The tradition came from steam days when there was a driver and a fireman, and the latter sometimes helped with spotting signals, but the evidence about the safety benefit of having a second person in the cab is ambivalent, as the two people can distract each other. At the Cowden accident, for example, where five people were killed in October 1994, the guard, who had ambitions to drive trains, was, contrary to the rules, in the cab with the driver, both of whom were killed. (Unlike the case of airline pilots where clearly two will always be required because of the possibility of sudden illness, there is a 'deadman's handle' which ensures the train stops should the sole driver be incapacitated.) Uff is equivocal on the issue and, indeed, seems to contradict himself: 'The crash would probably not have occurred had there been two men in the cab, but it would not be right to conclude that the adoption of single manning above 110mph was itself a contributory cause of the accident.'[10] Nevertheless, in the specific circumstances of a train with a malfunctioning AWS, having a second person in the cab would reduce risk and, indeed, such a change was recommended by the internal railway inquiry into the Southall accident.

Driver Tunnock's duty ended at Cardiff and he was replaced by Larry Harrison, a driver with a good but not unblemished past record. There were a couple of incidents in the 1970s when Harrison went through signals at danger at slow speeds and one in 1996 when he started a train without the proper signal from the guard. Nevertheless, he was categorised at the highest level of competence. Driver Harrison drove routinely from Cardiff towards London, although the inquiry heard that passengers at both Bristol Parkway and Swindon reported that he was driving with his feet (or a foot) up on the console.

There was one more safety device which could potentially have prevented the disaster – Automatic Train Protection (ATP) – but it was not functioning. It is replete with irony that, although only two lines in Britain were fitted with ATP, both the Southall and Ladbroke Grove accidents happened on one of them. The reason why Harrison did not have a functioning ATP was not a technical one, as with the AWS, since the ATP on both the train and the trackside was working, but an administrative and political one.

Again, a bit of history is required here. ATP is a system which physically prevents a train from going through a red light. The device constantly monitors the speed at which a train is approaching a red signal and ensures that it can stop in time. In the case of Southall, Harrison's train would have been slowed down before ever reaching the red signal that was protecting the goods train.

The report of the Hidden inquiry into the 1988 Clapham train disaster recommended the network-wide installation of ATP, a rather strange decision given that Clapham was not caused by a SPAD but by the faulty wiring work of a signals engineer. However, the Hidden inquiry also looked at two other accidents, Belgrove and Purley, both in March 1989 and both caused by a signal passed at danger. Indeed, even before Clapham the British Railways Board had already approved plans for the development of an ATP system, and it seemed only a matter of time before the device would be introduced throughout the network.

Two routes, parts of the Great Western between Paddington and Bristol and of the Chiltern line out of Marylebone, were selected for pilot schemes. At first, development progressed well. Driver training started in August 1991 and the equipment began to be fitted to locomotives and to the trackside. There were, of course, teething problems, notably those caused by slipping on the wheels of the high speed trains which could result in unnecessary emergency brake applications. The antennae were frequently damaged by flying ballast because there was nowhere suitable to put them. And retrofitting – putting the equipment on old rolling stock – proved much more difficult than installing ATP on new trains such as the cross-channel Eurostars, Heathrow Express and Chiltern's new stock. However, by April 1994 when Railtrack was separated out of BR, the trackside infrastructure was largely complete: all GWT's locomotives had been fitted and it only remained for the full pilot scheme to be put into operation.

Then privatisation intervened. The costs of ATP were proving much greater than expected – £750m, possibly £1bn[11] – and the newly separated Railtrack began to express concerns over this. However, the British Railways and Railtrack boards knew that dropping ATP would lead to widespread public criticism in the event of an ATP-preventable accident. A memo to the Railtrack board written in December 1993 by Simon

Osborne, the company secretary, and Andrew Sim, its legal advisor, warned of the potential risk of manslaughter charges in the event of an accident, and suggested that 'At the end of the day, the most difficult question which may have to be answered is why many foreign administrations have introduced APT [sic] but the British network has not.' The memo clearly reveals that Railtrack's intention was simply to get out of commitments to network-wide implementation of ATP that had been made by the BR chairman Sir Bob Reid at the Hidden inquiry into the Clapham disaster and by his successor, also called Sir Bob Reid, in the board's safety plan for 1991. The memo concludes that the risk of manslaughter charges could, 'with care', be reduced and therefore 'These risks, *per se*, do not warrant the board taking the line that it is already committed to ATP.'

How the Railtrack executives, so eager to privatise the company, must have cheered. As Peter Rayner, a former BR manager who has been highly critical of the post-privatisation safety regime put it, the meeting held to discuss the memo was 'taking up public funds to protect the backs of people who are already trying to find ways and means of not implementing ATP'. The Railtrack memo recommended a series of actions to reduce the risk of a future manslaughter charge, including a 'meticulous study of the benefits of ATP based not only on trials in the UK but also the experience of ATP in foreign administrations', a consideration of cheaper alternatives to ATP and a full cost-benefit analysis. In the event, only the last was carried out because there was not time to do a more detailed study as ATP was threatening to disrupt the privatisation timetable. The memo, however, makes clear that this was not an open study to assess the value of ATP but one which was being used to endorse a decision which had already been made – the dropping of the network-wide commitment to ATP. The cost of implementing ATP was clearly an unwelcome encumbrance to privatisation.

On the day before BR formally handed the infrastructure to Railtrack, Sir Bob Reid sent the cost-benefit analysis of ATP to the Department of Transport and also set out what BR would have done if responsibility had stayed with it. He said the Great Western and Chiltern pilots would have been put into full operation and that ATP would have been installed on any new high-speed line.

The BR report which accompanied his letter raised doubts over the cost of ATP, suggesting that it would cost £10.9m per life saved to install, well above the norm of £1m usually applied for such safety schemes. For selective implementation on the busiest lines, the most likely estimate was £5.5m per life saved, still well above the industry norm.[12] (See chapter 11 for a fuller explanation of the cost-benefit analysis process.)

British Rail's report on the economic viability of ATP was referred by the government to the Health and Safety Commission which, after some backroom dealing, backed the decision not to proceed with Hidden's recommendation for network-wide implementation of ATP. The HSC, however, warned that it was not entirely satisfied with the remit of the BR report. In his letter to Brian Mawhinney, the transport secretary, Frank Davies, the chairman of the HSC, said that the calculations only applied to the forms of ATP that were being trialled on Great Western and Chiltern and 'do not necessarily apply to the generic concept of automatic train protection'. Moreover, he warned that the report did not take sufficient account of the wider damage caused by major disasters: 'What does seem clear is that in any catastrophic accident, the damage in terms of public confidence, additional costs, and harms and risks to people quite aside from the number of deaths is substantially greater than damage connected with the generality of risks to individuals.'[13] In other words, a much higher price per life saved might be worth paying because of the long-term damage caused to the industry by catastrophes. Davies was being prescient because, of course, there were to be three such ATP-preventable disasters, Watford, Southall and Ladbroke Grove, within three years of each other.

Mawhinney, an impatient man not noted for careful consideration of issues, brushed aside any such doubts and used the HSC report to dispose of the ATP problem. He received the report in December 1994 but took three months to issue a press release which killed off ATP as an aspiration for the whole network. The press release made the statistical point that 'Accidents involving SPADs, overspeeding and buffer stop collisions which ATP could prevent are infrequent and account for about 3 per cent of fatalities and injuries (excluding trespassers and suicides).'[14] That figure was totally meaningless. In his response, Mawhinney had lumped together all train incidents, including passengers being run over by trains or falling over drunk at stations, and all injuries, even very minor ones, to reach the figure of 3 per cent. In fact, of deaths in major train crashes in the previous five years, according to Stanley Hall, the author of several books on rail safety, about a third would have been prevented by ATP.[15]

Despite abandoning ATP on such flimsy grounds, there was no commitment to introduce a cheaper system, but merely a statement that 'Railtrack is giving high priority to the development of appropriate
techniques for analysing the costs and benefits of all safety projects
addressing [the] risks associated with signals passed at danger, overspeeding and buffer stop collisions.' It was not so much kicking ATP into
touch as completely out of the ground.

Having abandoned ATP, Railtrack showed no sense of urgency about
looking for a cheaper alternative. British Rail had been developing a
Train Protection and Warning System that would greatly reduce the
number of SPADs (and the impact speed of those it did not prevent) but
Railtrack merely asked for assessments about costs rather than trying to
ensure progress in the development and installation of TPWS (which is
discussed fully in the next chapter).

Although ATP had been dropped as a national objective, all the parties involved said they were committed to ensuring that the two trials,
Great Western and Chiltern, would be fully implemented. Uff, however,
is pretty sceptical about this commitment. He wrote: 'Privatisation
remained contentious and inevitably the abandonment of ATP altogether in 1995 would have had political implications. ATP pilots represented enhanced safety on Great Western and Chiltern, there was no
realistic alternative to their going ahead.'[16]

In other words, it was politically unacceptable to drop the trials, but
no one was particularly interested in pursuing them since they were a BR
initiative and BR was dead. For the manufacturers there was no longer
the prospect of a national scheme which would have been highly lucrative. The train operator, Great Western Trains, the management buy-out
team that took over the running of services in February 1996, was, from
the outset, lukewarm about the whole project, which its managers saw as
a hassle and a cost with little discernible benefit. And that lack of interest
from train operators was to contribute to both the Southall and Ladbroke
Grove disasters. Furthermore, implementation of ATP became much
more difficult with fragmentation. Whereas previously only BR had been
involved, now there were three parties – the rolling stock companies,
Railtrack and the train operators. Therefore it would have taken extra
effort to ensure that the system was fully implemented.

And GWT was not prepared to make that effort. Quite the opposite.
This was made clear at the Southall enquiry by the testimony of Richard

George, the GWT executive who made £3m out of the sale of Great Western to First Group (see chapter 6) and who was responsible for safety. George, who happened to be a passenger on the ill-fated train, denied that GWT had shown no commitment but admitted the company had not been very interested in pursuing the ATP pilot. He told the hearing: 'I will say again that we could and should have shown greater commitment to the project than we did.'17

George highlighted the way that the fragmentation of the railway made such investment much more difficult to justify, given that there were now shareholders and a whole host of complex contractual agreements. He told the hearing that the privatised railway had created an environment where everything had to be set out clearly on a contractual basis or else 'there is no legal basis for expenditure'. Therefore, in 1996, when it was found that £350,000 was needed to pay for modifications to the ATP antennae, Great Western baulked at having to foot the bill. So did Angel Trains which owned the locomotives. A memo of a meeting on the subject, read out at the hearing, said that 'GWT expressed clearly that they would not, at this stage, fund any part of the modification programme as the system belonged to Railtrack.'18 George claimed that this was a negotiating ploy in order to ensure there was a 'strategic understanding' of progress on the scheme and, in the event, it was agreed that the cost should be shared between Angel and GWT but no order was actually placed for the antennae. At a meeting just a week before the crash, GWT reiterated its complaint that the unreliability of the equipment was the major obstacle to its wider implementation but, as Uff found, 'Lack of driver training was the sole reason why ATP was not able to prevent the crash.'19

This lack of commitment to ATP at management level percolated down to the maintenance staff. A report into the ATP project by Electrowatt highlighted the situation, saying that while staff at one depot, Landore, were enthusiastic about ATP, 'They are [a] minority in the company [as the] general view is that ATP is at best an inconvenience to the running of trains services and, at worst, an unfair imposition on the company. It is tolerated while its use remains at the present low level, about 13 per cent of train services overall.' That low level of use showed just how little regard was being paid to ATP by GWT. Uff commented that the ATP project 'came close to being abandoned before the Southall crash'20 and, indeed, Railtrack was preparing to ditch the project before the publication of the Electrowatt report which recommended its full implementation.

The neglect of the ATP trial was also demonstrated by the absence of a coherent training programme for drivers. Various witnesses, whose statements were read to the inquiry,[21] related how ATP training was not listed as a particular competence for drivers and therefore no attempt was made to match suitably trained drivers with trains that were due to run using ATP. Amazingly, the resource centre that allocated drivers' duties had no record of which drivers were capable of using the system. Moreover, the driver training manager for the period prior to the accident was not even ATP-trained himself and therefore could not train people in the use of the equipment. ATP refresher courses had stopped entirely in January 1996, and were not resumed until after the Southall accident.

In a way it is unfair to be too harsh on George, who had the good grace to admit that there was no 'sense of urgency' about the ATP trial. He had a good reputation as a railwayman within the industry and was deeply affected by the accident and its aftermath, bursting into tears at the inquiry hearing. He just happened to be in the right (or rather wrong) place at the right time to be seduced by the bright lights of privatisation and the opportunities which it afforded a few lucky managers like him.

The new structure meant that decisions were no longer taken in the general interest of the railway. Viewed narrowly, of course, the ATP trial was a hassle and as it was no longer to be implemented nationally, why should GWT and its managers have taken much interest? They were little people for whom the big picture was an irrelevance. That is why the failure to have a fully functioning ATP on Harrison's train was not really George's fault, but that of the system of which he was part. There was no ownership of the project and therefore no one was thinking that ATP could actually be a vital back-up should AWS not be working.

So back to the hapless Larry Harrison getting into his train at Cardiff. Despite the host of technical difficulties which had dogged the ATP trial, the train which Larry Harrison took over at Cardiff had a functioning ATP system. But Harrison did not turn it on for several reasons. First, he felt he was not properly ATP-trained. He had been on a course some years previously and claimed to have asked for refresher training, though Uff did not believe him. He had, in any case, never driven a train unsupervised with the ATP switched on. Secondly, GWT's rules actually prevented ATP being switched on *en route*. When the ATP system was switched on, according to the rule book, there had to be a four-minute start-up test to ensure it was working properly. This led GWT to tell drivers that the system should never be started up at an intermediate station because of the delay the start-up process would cause. However, by 1997 there was no reason to maintain the rule since the start-up test had been reduced to two minutes and therefore would not create any appreciable delay; but, again, the implications of a set of changes had not been thought through because of the lack of management of the project, which, as Uff puts it, 'lost its urgency and impetus'. He concludes that 'The willpower and commitment to take the steps which can now be seen to have been required to bring the ATP pilot into full operation simply did not exist before the Southall crash.'[22] He found that there was not even a proper legal framework for the continuation of the ATP trial.

However, Uff's conclusion is, perhaps, too general when viewed in the context of what happened in neighbouring Chiltern, the other line used for an ATP trial, albeit with different technology. There, much better progress was made with the system, not least because the management showed commitment to it right from the beginning. Although Chiltern had newer rolling stock and the initial fitment was 'significantly less troublesome than the Great Western trials',[23] the attitude of the new private management contrasted very strongly with that of Great Western. The company that took over the franchise, M40 Trains, had an immediate commitment, not only to retaining ATP but to extending it, despite the cost. Adrian Shooter, the gangly and genial managing director who was a career railwayman, stresses that 'my first job has always been to run a safe railway and to make sure that we do everything we can to make it safer'.[24] Although the trial had been 'drifting' when M40 took over in July 1996, Shooter says, 'We got hold of it by the scruff of the neck. We knew we had a system that was a valuable safety feature and that we had to make it work.' Moreover, when, soon after taking over the franchise, Chiltern became the first of the privatised franchises to order new trains, the company insisted that they must be fitted with ATP. According to Shooter, 'That raised a few eyebrows as people had expected us not to because of the cost.' And the cost ran into hundreds of thousands of pounds because there was only one possible supplier of the equipment 'who had us over a barrel'. Chiltern's already strong commitment to ATP was reinforced after the Southall accident, and the company now has a policy of taking trains out of service if the ATP is not working.

Uff appears rather naïve when assessing the role of privatisation in the lack of commitment to ATP. He says, 'It has been suggested that Railtrack's cost-benefit analysis of 1994 was inspired by anticipation of privatisation.'[25] In fact, the memo to Railtrack's board shows this is undoubtedly true. Uff, however, goes on to argue that such an analysis of the costs of ATP would have taken place anyway. That may be the case, but it would have been politically impossible for a government to abandon the scheme in the face of opposition from BR whose chairman, Sir Bob Reid, and director of operational standards and safety, David Rayner, had given specific undertakings for its fitment. In any case, the letter from the second Sir Bob Reid, written on the eve of Railtrack's separation, makes clear that the commitment to the ATP trials was solid.

Would the various circumstances which led to the Southall accident have arisen under BR or, more pertinently, had the changes in the industry been less dramatic and slower? The answer is almost certainly no. There are minor caveats. Some of the failings arose from practices that had their roots in BR days and, moreover, the commercial pressures which played a key role in the disaster were not solely a result of privatisation since BR, too, was becoming more business-focused. That said, it is impossible to get away from the fact that the Southall crash has its roots in the fragmented railway created by privatisation. The reorganisation of the depot would not have happened in that way under BR; the train may well have been turned around or taken out of service under BR; there would probably have been a second driver had BR still been operating services; the development of ATP would undoubtedly have proceeded more coherently had not privatisation intervened; the confusion over 'control' and the split between the driver, the signaller and operations would not have existed; and so on. There were other factors too, such as the way privatisation put pressure on greater use of rolling stock – sweating the assets as the bean counters call it – and therefore taking a train out of service was likely to be more disruptive since there were fewer spare sets.

Another decision resulting from the break-up of the railways, whose wider implications were not properly considered, was the change, instituted by the regulator, in the priority given to different types of trains. Under BR, high speed passenger trains always had priority over goods trains, which sometimes sat in sidings for a long time before being allowed to proceed. John Swift, the first regulator, changed that after consultation with the industry, creating a system of minimum overall delay. This was, as Uff points out, 'driven, to an extent, by privatisation and the perceived need for commercial equality in the face of the penalty payment system'.[26] The change was introduced without any risk assessment having been undertaken, a failing which was highlighted by several parties at the inquiry hearings, but, surprisingly, there was little controversy over the introduction of the change. Railtrack, keen to minimise the cost of delays, ran 'track access awareness' sessions for signallers, which outlined the penalty system. The new rule Swift introduced said that various factors had to be balanced in train regulation, including 'protecting the commercial interests of Railtrack and each affected train operator'. While there is little evidence that signallers considered commercial matters when making decisions and Uff judged that the 1996 regulation policy did not have safety implications, Tom Winsor, who became regulator in 1999, clearly did have such concerns. He told the inquiry that this requirement had been put in against his advice in 1995 (when he was legal adviser to the regulator) and, as regulator, he promptly removed it in November 2000.

While Uff was reluctant to rule definitively on the role of privatisation in causing the accident, presumably because he felt that the issue was somewhat beyond his remit, the evidence is unequivocal. It is the structural way that privatisation contributed to the disaster which is the most compelling evidence. The significance of the break-up of the clear decision-making process that had been a key safety feature of the way that BR operated, and the difficulties over interfaces between the various players, emerges several times in the story of the Southall accident. Even with all the safety case paraphernalia, decisions were taken in isolation from one another, as there was no one to consider the whole picture. So, for example, the decision about having a single driver for high speed trains should have been considered in relation to what happened if the AWS were not working, but there was no one to suggest that there would always be a second driver should the train not have a functioning AWS. As Uff notes, when the requirement to have a second person at high speeds was removed, 'no consideration was given to running High Speed Trains without operative safety systems and the EQE [the technical consultants] report appeared to place some reliance (which was quite misplaced in the circumstances) on the avail-ability of ATP'.[27]

Moreover, privatisation put Great Western Trains in charge. While it was the same management team as had been with BR, their remit changed because they were working to shareholders rather than a gov-ernment-owned board. That they misused the freedom which their new positions as railway bosses gave them is not in doubt.

It was little solace to the relatives that in July 1999, before the inquiry was held, Great Western had been fined £1.5m – a record for any health and safety matter – after pleading guilty to breaches of the Health and Safety at Work Act, 1974. Driver Harrison had originally been charged with manslaughter but the Crown decided not to proceed with the prose-cution. Charges of corporate manslaughter against GWT were rejected on legal grounds by the judge, Mr Justice Scott-Baker, much to the fury of victims and the bereaved. As presently constituted, British law makes it difficult to proceed with corporate manslaughter charges, because there needs to be a 'controlling mind' who is clearly identifiable. To have pro-ceeded against Harrison without pursuing GWT's rich executives would have seemed patently unfair to the victims and bereaved, as well as to the general public. The Home Office is currently reviewing the law on corpo-rate manslaughter, which could have a significant impact on the opera-tion of the railways.

Unfortunately, the Southall inquiry, which did not start until the autumn of 1999 because of the criminal proceedings, was overshadowed by the Ladbroke Grove crash, which occurred just as the inquiry had got underway. It was, as the next chapter shows, another accident in which privatisation played a key role.

CHAPTER 8

Disaster at signal SN 109

The disaster at Ladbroke Grove on 5 October 1999, the worst railway accident since the Clapham disaster eleven years previously, also has its roots in the changes made as a result of privatisation and fragmentation. Thirty-one people died and 425 were injured when an inexperienced Thames driver, Michael Hodder, unaccountably ignored a red light and went down a prohibited piece of track. Hodder's 8.06 a.m. Thames Turbo train bound for Bedwyn smashed head-on into the Great Western High Speed Train Cheltenham Flyer just a couple of miles out of Paddington station.

The aftermath of the collision was one of the most horrific ever witnessed on a British railway track. The combined impact speed was reckoned to have been 130mph, at that time[1] the highest ever on British railways, and the front coach of the Turbo quite literally disintegrated. Visiting the floodlit site that evening, I was particularly struck by part of the side of the Thames train which hung gruesomely over the largely intact middle coaches of the HST. The aluminium-built Turbo, weighing a total of 90 tons, never stood a chance because the leading vehicle of the HST was a heavy, wedge-shaped locomotive pulling a 400-ton train that brushed it aside like a bird bouncing off a car windscreen. All but seven of the dead were in the Turbo, mostly in the front coach. All the dead in the HST, apart from the driver, were in the leading coach, first class carriage H, which quickly became engulfed by fire. The report[2] by Lord Cullen contains much detail about the crashworthiness of the vehicles involved and consideration of the means of escape but such matters are largely an irrelevance. No trains can be built to withstand impacts of this speed and, indeed, it is a great tribute to the solidity of the HST carriages that everyone outside coach H survived, though, of course, there were many very severe injuries. The high death toll which, at one point, the police suggested might be over 100, and the proximity to London's media HQs – the BBC's Television Centre is a mile down the road – turned Ladbroke Grove into one of the biggest news stories of the year which, in turn, ensured a powerful political involvement. This, as we see below, has proved highly damaging to the railways. Of course, even if the accident had happened somewhere more remote, there would have been extensive coverage, but there is no doubt that its location, along with the fact that it took nine days to recover the bodies and remove the last coach, heightened and prolonged media interest.

Although the primary cause of the accident was the fact that Hodder went through a red light, as with most accidents, many other factors contributed to the disaster, including the way that the industry was fragmented. The key issue was the high incidence of Signals Passed at Danger (SPADs) in the Paddington 'throat' in the six years since it had been remodelled and electrified with overhead line equipment in order to accommodate the Heathrow Express trains. According to Lord Cullen,[3] there had been sixty-seven SPADs in the area in that period, many more than would be expected, even for such a complex section of track.

Most significantly, the signal which driver Hodder unaccountably – the Cullen report sheds little light on the reasons – went through at red had been passed no less than eight times during that period. SN 109 was an unusual signal in that it was shaped as a reverse L, with the red not, as is usual on Britain's railways, at the bottom of the set of lights but to the left at the same level as the lower yellow lamp. This unique set-up had come about because of concerns about the signal's visibility, as it is partially obscured by a bridge, a problem that had not been realised until the equipment was actually fitted.

While four of the SPADs at SN 109 involved only tiny overruns, such a spate of incidents clearly pointed to the fact that this was a more than averagely troublesome signal. The four other SPADs all gave cause for concern. In February 1995 a Thames driver admitted he misread an adjacent signal as relating to him and he told the inquiry how the signals were difficult to see because of the bridges and that he would normally count across from the leftmost signal to check which one related to him. He passed the signal by 105 yards. Another incident, in March 1996, also involving a Thames train which overran by 146 yards, was put down to 'driver inattention', a conclusion at which the train companies were all too ready to arrive, in the same way that airlines like ascribing accidents to pilot error since it implies that no significant changes to systems need to be made. The report of the last incident, in August 1998, an overrun of just three yards, is also highly relevant because, as driver Offen later told the Cullen inquiry,[4] the signal was obscured by the bridge: 'It didn't register as well as it should have done. . . . The moment I seen [sic] SN 109 I reacted to it . . . I realised it [SN 109] was there and red as it come [sic] into view under the bridgework.' In other words, from these accounts, it is clear that this was a very difficult signal because of the bend and the bridge, a fact that was confirmed by the post-accident research into the visibility of the signal.

However, the most significant incident, which was almost a dress rehearsal for the disaster, took place on 4 February 1998, twenty months before it occurred. This involved a Great Western HST whose driver mistakenly thought he was on the main line, where he would have expected a clear set of greens, rather than on the track controlled by SN 109. Fortunately, the driver, having confidently accelerated to 70mph after the previous yellow, spotted 'six signals in a line'[5] and realised his error but only managed to stop 432 yards after the signal. The oncoming train, a Heathrow Express shuttle, had, by then, also come to a halt as the signaller managed to turn its signal, SN 120 – just a few metres away from the collision point of the Ladbroke Grove disaster – to red. While the cause of the driver going through the red light was investigated, crucially no one noticed that the near miss highlighted the potential danger of a SPAD at SN 109 – the fact that the way the track was laid out and the points were set meant that a train going through that signal would end up directly in the path of an oncoming train.[6] (See diagram p. 146.)

The high rate of SPADs in the Paddington area led, almost inevitably by the law of averages, to one collision. This occurred at Royal Oak, less than a mile outside the station, in November 1995. It was not SN 109 but a similar gantry signal, SN 74, which was passed at danger. A Thames driver, approaching the station, thought that a neighbouring signal referred to him and, although he realised his error and managed to stop, it was too late to avoid a low-speed collision with a Great Western High Speed Train heading for Swansea. There were no injuries but an inquiry was held which made fourteen recommendations in March 1996.

Here, the first clear evidence of Railtrack's failings emerges: the company had no procedure to ensure that the recommendations of such inquiries were implemented. Of the nine Royal Oak recommendations accepted by a safety review group, Railtrack failed to implement seven. While a couple were not proceeded with because they were superseded by other events, the others seem to have disappeared into an administrative black hole, not actioned or followed up by the person given the task, who, in any case, did not know that he was responsible. Several of these recommendations were ways of improving the visibility of signals in what was recognised to be a difficult area for the drivers. Similarly, four of the five recommendations arising from the inquiry into the very serious February 1998 SPAD were not followed up, including the suggestion that there should be a risk assessment of bi-directional working – the practice of using the same lines for trains travelling in both directions – in the Paddington throat.[7]

At that time Railtrack was divided into seven zones, and the Great Western zone, broadly covering the routes out of Paddington, had a troubled history with frequent senior management changes and a poor reputation among train operators. Cullen found that the zone simply had 'no procedure for the tracking of recommendations'. The report's account of the recommendations on the SPAD seems to have been taken out of a manual on how not to run a successful organisation:

> Recommendations 3,5 and 6 were allocated for Mr Wiseman [Railtrack Great Western zone's business development manager]. He was unaware of this fact until over 18 months later [i.e. after the disaster, suggesting that he would never have found out otherwise], apparently as a result of Mr Sutton [the zone's performance services manager] failing to notify him. Recommendations 4 and 7 were allocated to Mr Wilkinson [the zone's production manager]. It appears nothing was done.'[8]

Wilkinson told the inquiry that the recommendations were simply sent to headquarters and he did not attempt to progress them. Sutton, the zone's performance service manager, claimed that it was impossible to follow all recommendations since the zone was swamped with 4–500 of them. Cullen, however, says this was an exaggeration and that there was nothing like this number of recommendations to be dealt with. Nor did the zonal manager responsible for following up such recommendations do so. He was, in any case, described by Chris Leah, Railtrack's director of safety, as 'more of a register and not a chaser and closer down of recommendations'.[9] Revealingly, Leah confessed to the inquiry that the system was flawed and that the problems with it would not have been uncovered had it not been for the evidence given to the inquiry.

As an aside, the very title of Peter Wiseman's job – business development manager – betrays much about that was wrong in the way that Railtrack was structured. Implementing safety recommendations, which necessarily implies adding costs to the production process, is hardly compatible with the notion of 'business development'. There is a strong parallel with the Hatfield accident (see next chapter) where engineering decisions ended up being made by contract managers who knew nothing of the discipline. While it is wrong to suggest, as the tabloid media often do, that commercial decisions have no place in the railway because safety has to be paramount, Railtrack's structure was far too weighted towards placing responsibility in the hands of managers whose primary function was commercial. Of course commercial issues have to be taken into account – it is just that they must not be allowed to dominate in the way that clearly they did within Railtrack.

While it is impossible to assess whether the implementation of any of these two sets of recommendations would actually have prevented the accident, it is clear that there was a fundamental failing in the way that Railtrack dealt with safety measures arising from incidents. While no particular measure can be identified as the one that would have saved the thirty-one lives, their collectivity most probably would have done.

Given that Railtrack did not even manage to implement recommendations of a formal inquiry into an accident, it was hardly surprising that the series of SPADs at SN 109, none of which had resulted in a collision, failed to trigger an adequate response. This part of the background to the accident is just as damaging to the reputation of Railtrack's management and has even more direct relevance to the accident. The fact that SN 109 had been passed at danger eight times in six years clearly should have rung alarm bells throughout the zone. Indeed, there are set procedures for calling signal sighting committees – a team of experts – to assess the visibility of signals if they have been repeatedly passed at danger. According to the rules, a signal sighting committee should be called where a signal has been passed at danger more than once within a year, or three or more times in any three-year period. If this rule had been followed, six of the eight SPADs at signal SN 109 would have resulted in the convening of a signal sighting committee. None was called, even though a meeting of the SPAD action group on the day after the February 1998 incident said that committees should be convened for both SN 109 and another signal, SN 63, within a month.

The reason for the failure to call a meeting is, again, taken from the manual of how not to manage: there was no one charged with that responsibility. A number of Railtrack witnesses to the inquiry thought that it was the job of Symon Murrant, the zone's train operations liaison manager. Murrant admitted to the inquiry that he had tried to call these committee meetings, but he was not aware it was actually his responsibility and was just attempting to show the train operators that he was trying to do something. His bosses were unaware that signal sighting committees were not being held and Murrant gave the inquiry three explanations as to why he had not convened them: difficulty in obtaining safety permits for possession of track; the lack of qualified people; and the lack of a clear direction from senior management. However, on being pressed, he admitted that he had never tried to get any possessions, nor had he made much effort to find suitable people. Cullen totally dismisses the third explanation, saying that convening the meeting was not an option but 'mandatory' and therefore nothing to do with the view of senior management. Cullen concludes that the whole episode 'betrays a culture of apathy and lack of will to follow up promised actions'.[10]

It would be wrong to single out hapless junior managers like Murrant, as on further investigation the story gets far worse. When internal auditors from Railtrack Assurance and Safety came to visit the zone, six months before the disaster, a random sample for the report revealed that sighting committees had not been convened following SPADs at SN 63 and SN 109. Moreover, the zone was found to be the worst performing of Railtrack's seven zones in terms of safety matters. But the auditors were reassured by the fact that a larger exercise, checking all the signals in the two miles out of Paddington, was being undertaken. 'This,' they reported cheerfully, 'and other initiatives by Great Western zone demonstrates a pro-active stance on this issue.'[11] If only. In fact, this referred to the intention of Bernard Melanophy, the operations manager, to commission W.S. Atkins to review the signalling between Paddington and Ladbroke Grove. Unfortunately, as Cullen says, the auditors were under a mistaken impression 'since Mr Melanophy did not in fact commission W.S. Atkins or anyone else to review the signalling'.[12] In other words, someone pulled the wool over the auditors' eyes. The auditors said there should be a signal sighting committee but this was still ignored by the local managers and a follow-up audit in September 1999 again found that no action had been taken. However, Chris Leah, Railtrack's director of safety, must have also been misled because in December 1999 he told an industrial tribunal hearing, which was appealing against the Health and Safety Executive's post-accident decision to shut down signal SN 109, that such a meeting had been held after the February 1998 SPAD.

Cullen concludes, 'The failure to have signal sighting committees convened was persistent and serious . . . [and] was due to a combination of incompetent management and inadequate process.'[13] Cullen is being too kind. The behaviour of various managers in the zone seems to reflect an appalling lack of concern about safety in what is, above all, a safety-critical industry. Treating recommendations of inquiries as if they were irrelevant, persistently failing to take a course of action which was clearly set out in the rules and misleading the company's own auditors is symptomatic of a culture of almost venal ineptitude and perhaps even deliberate dishonesty.

The real tragedy is that convening a sighting committee was not a mere technicality but would very likely have prevented the accident. As Cullen says, it would have led to changes, possibly including the replacement of Gantry 8, the one holding SN 109, and of other signals on the routes out of the station. This is because, as the subsequent investigation revealed, the signal broke all the rules. Right from the beginning there should have been a signal sighting committee for SN 109, which was first commissioned as part of the new Paddington lay-out in 1993 before the overhead wires were installed. Twice, subsequent changes should have led to a signal sighting committee: first, in the following year, when the signals on the gantry were lowered because the view was being obscured by Golborne Road bridge which is 100 metres in front of the gantry;[14] and secondly when, in 1995, overhead line equipment for the Heathrow Express was installed which further obscured the view of the signals on Gantry 8. As a result of the overhead line equipment, the signals as seen by train drivers would disappear temporarily and reappear. The experts who, after the accident, carried out the signal sighting exercise found that SN 109 was not compliant with the rules which specified that it should be seen for at least a full seven seconds from the cab of a train approaching it at the line speed of 60mph. Moreover, they concluded that, because there are five other signals on the gantry, the situation presented to drivers was very confusing. Of course, as driver Hodder was killed in the crash, one can only surmise about why he missed the red aspect, and Cullen draws no conclusions, except to point to the difficulties of seeing the signal.

There are few heroes in this story, but one of them is Alison Forster, First Great Western's director of operations and safety. She persistently expressed concerns over the series of SPADs in the Paddington area in a series of letters and tried to get Railtrack to do something about them. Her efforts demonstrate the extent to which Railtrack was impervious to outsiders' concerns. Her evidence to the inquiry was chilling and must have been the most harrowing for the survivors and the relatives of the dead. She spoke of meetings where lots of ideas were generated but no follow-up was instigated. There was a lack of clarity about who at Railtrack was supposed to deal with reducing SPADs and, worse, many of her letters were simply ignored. In August 1998, for example, she wrote to Les Wilkinson, Railtrack's production manager, about signal SN 109, asking if 'you would advise me as a matter of urgency what action you intend to mitigate against this high risk signal',[15] and she told the inquiry, 'I have never received a full response to that.'[16]

Overall, Forster said that Railtrack took a narrow view of safety concerns:

> The organisation does not look very often at some of the big-picture issues. They tend to be reactive to incidents and single-issue problem-solving processes . . . and sometimes not taking a broad risk based approach to the management of safety, which I do not think is helpful for long-term improvements that we need to see . . . they do not seem to be a learning organisation.[17]

Forster was not listened to because, in the structure of the railways, she was a mere customer working for a train operator. Her warnings to Railtrack were received in much the same way that retailers' 'customer liaison departments' deal with pushy complainants. One can almost hear Railtrack's reaction – 'Oh, it's that bloody Great Western woman again, send her standard letter B this time.' Tom Winsor, the rail regulator, would argue that there is a contract between the two companies which is legally enforceable. But the real world does not work like that. Railtrack is supposed to provide a properly functioning and safe railway to its clients, but working out the precise meaning of that vague requirement is impossible for middle-ranking executives such as Ms Forster. How could

she press her case? Had she, however, been working for the same organisation under a unified structure, then it would have been much easier.
There would have been clear lines of communication and responsibility.
Her warnings would have carried extra force and her superiors would
have known precisely what weight to give to her expressions of concern.
There would have been the in-house expertise to assess them and to carry
out the work. Instead, Railtrack with its 'business development managers' and its commercial concerns had its attention focused elsewhere.

One of the key mistakes in separating the operation of track from services was the fact that it meant that there were no 'Fat Controllers' – general managers, as they were in the earlier days of BR and later directors of
sectors such as InterCity – who were responsible for all aspects of the railway. Such a figure would have picked up fundamental flaws in the lay-out
at Paddington (see diagram p.146) which received insufficient attention
in the Cullen report. After SN 109, there was a distance of 700 metres
before the track merged into the up main line on which the Cheltenham
Flyer was travelling. About half way between the gantry and the junction
there is a set of points – 8059 – which, had they been switched the other
way, would have taken the Turbo back on to the down relief line from
which it had come. That may, conceivably, have led to a collision, though
this would have been unlikely and, in any case, would have involved a
side-on hit at a much slower speed.

The lengthy overrun of the Great Western HST in February 1998
would have alerted the Fat Controller to the major flaw in the lay-out,
which is that a down (away from London) train passing SN 109 at red is
routed into the path of an oncoming up train with nothing in between
to stop it. The logic behind that lay-out was that this gave a longer safety
overlap than if 8059 were set in such a way that the train was routed
back towards the down relief line. The assumption was that no driver
would ever go through SN 109 by 700 metres because they would realise
they were going down a prohibited piece of track. But this failed to take
into account what would happen if a driver did make this mistake and,
vitally, the respective consequences of the way the points were set – a
head-on collision if the points were set towards the up (towards
London) main, or alternatively either a side-on crash or a rear-end shunt
if they were set the other way. It is quite possible that Hodder, at this
stage, was lost, which would explain why he actually accelerated after
passing the signal and, unaccountably, cancelled his AWS.

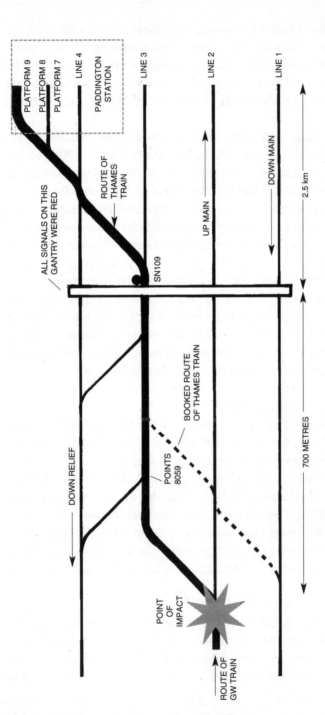

A simplified detail of the track layout at Ladbroke Grove. The Thames train should have stopped at signal SN 109, where it would have remained stationary until the Great Western HST had passed the two sets of points on the up main line (line 2) on its way into Paddington. SN 109 would have then turned green allowing the Thames train to proceed on its booked route, taking it across line 2 and onto line 1, the down main. Had points 8059 been set towards line 4, the down relief line, there would have been a risk of a train passing SN 109 at red hitting a train going the same way on line 4, but no danger of a head-on collision. In fact, the points were set the other way because, first, that route provided a slightly longer, 700-metre, safety overrun and, second, as line 3 ceased to be bi-directional after points 8059, it was assumed that any driver passing them would realise he or she was going the wrong way on a one-way track.

Two principal reasons for the failure to provide what is called 'flank protection' in the industry were given to the inquiry: that the alternative offered a longer overlap and, secondly, that the line was expected to be provided imminently with Automatic Train Protection. As we shall see below, Thames trains were not fitted with ATP and, once this was realised, there should have been a reassessment of the decision, but by then, with the fragmentation of the industry, there was no chance of such a reconsideration ever getting on to the agenda, despite the frequent SPADs at SN 109. Even more astonishingly, points 8059 were left in whatever sense they had been used by the last train. Had a train gone that way previously, then the accident would never have happened.

Cullen's conclusion on this issue is particularly lame. He merely says, 'It is, of course, necessary to make a comprehensive assessment of not only the need for flank protection but also the risks to which its use may give rise. For that reason, it is not possible for me to determine that it should have been provided or should not be provided.'[18] In other words, the issue was too complicated for him to consider properly; but at least one of my contacts suggests that there will be another accident like Ladbroke Grove in the near future, as there are many similar track lay-outs.

The other criticism of Railtrack by Lord Cullen was directed towards the signallers in the Slough Control Centre and the failure to ensure they were prepared for such an emergency. In the past, the only way of contacting a train was through the signalling system and when there was a SPAD the standard reaction was to put all signals to red. However, following other accidents, a system called cab secure radio has been installed in most trains in order to improve communication, but the signalling procedures have not really changed to take account of this technological improvement. Therefore, theoretically, it would have been possible for the signallers to send a stop message to driver Hodder after his train had passed SN 109.[19] However, no such action was taken until a second or two before the crash. It took the ill-fated train twenty seconds to travel the 700 metres between signal SN 109 and the point at which it smashed into the HST. Could the signallers have done anything in time? Cullen certainly thought so, but only if they had been properly trained. He calculated that by the time they could reasonably have realised that the train was heading for disaster, they had between 7.35 and 9.25 seconds in which to send the vital message to Hodder to stop the train, which might have reduced the speed of the accident or even prevented it altogether. Instead, the signaller in charge, David Allen, decided to 'monitor' what happened, only taking action at the very last moment.

The issue is confused by the fact that the various signallers in the control centre at the time gave misleading accounts of their actions, which Cullen does not entirely trust. Cullen, however, does not blame the individual signallers for their actions but the way in which they were managed and trained and, indeed, suggests, 'It is surprising that [these] deficiencies were not picked up by senior management.'[20] It emerged clearly that the signallers were not properly trained. Even though there had been an average of a SPAD per month in the area covered by the Slough control centre, there was no proper training of the signallers on how to deal with them or any attempt to learn the lessons of previous incidents. The use of the radio was not really properly considered because of this lack of training and no signaller had received any training in the use of the radio in emergencies. Cullen concludes, 'The general picture which emerged was of a slack and complacent regime, which was not alive to the potentially dire consequences of a SPAD or of the way in which signallers could take action to deal with such situations.'[21] The attitude of the signallers was very much that SPADs were a matter of driver error and nothing to do with them. While this is an inheritance from BR culture, clearly the fact that drivers and signallers now work for different organisations did not help create a sense in the signallers that they were the last line of defence against errors by their fellow railway workers. Moreover, Cullen's judgement on the signallers is harsh. They faced a very difficult situation and really had very little time to do anything.

Railtrack was the subject of most of the criticism in relation to the Ladbroke Grove accident, both in the Cullen report and the subsequent media coverage. But this too was unfair. The primary cause was the fact that driver Hodder went through a red light, and certainly the role played by Thames Trains, who allocated him to the most complex and difficult layout in Britain without proper training or knowledge of the route, is as significant as Railtrack's failings. Hodder was only two weeks into his job and on only his twenty-first trip out of Paddington when he made his disastrous mistake. He was by all accounts a model pupil, having previously been in the Navy, although one of his references was from a relative and the other was not taken up. He was never asked to fill in an application form and therefore did not disclose a recent minor

conviction arising out of a fight. This readiness to ignore the proper procedures was a result of the fact that Thames was desperate for drivers and
had only recently started recruiting from outside the industry when
Hodder applied in February 1999.

Under British Rail, there had been a minimum training period of
forty-three weeks and most drivers were already experienced rail workers, familiar with the rules and the railway, but there was no set period
for driver training after privatisation. Instead, there was a Group Standard to ensure basic competence but each train operator individually
certifies its drivers when they are judged to be competent. Incredibly, in
the privatised industry there is no independent assessment of driver
competence.

Thames had already been criticised in the Royal Oak inquiry which
found in March 1996 that 'The methods of route learning into and out of
Paddington appear very informal.'[22] The inquiry also recommended that
SPAD briefings should be held for drivers, including the use of videos.
However, at the time, Thames was not recruiting and, as Cullen puts it,
the company's 'corporate memory was weak' in that it failed to heed
these recommendations when it started taking on drivers again over two
years later.

Indeed, very little attention seems to have been paid to SPADs in the
training programme, even though, for example, six of the eight SPADs at
SN 109 were by Thames drivers. Again, the auditors, this time the Railway Inspectorate, had the wool pulled over their eyes when Thames
claimed in September 1996 that all drivers were receiving briefings on
SPADs as part of the strategy to reduce them.

Thames's programme was lax in the extreme. No particular consideration was given to the fact that recruits from outside the industry would
need different training from those who already knew about the railways.
There was no clear syllabus and, most amazingly, there seemed to be no
coherent assessment of the performance of the trainee. As an expert, Professor John Groeger of the University of Surrey, told the inquiry, 'There
were no specific criteria . . . to determine whether the driver had compe-
tently handled a situation; [and] there was a lack of definition as to how
frequently the driver should have to perform in similar situations before
being assessed as competent.'[23] As Cullen put it, the praise for Hodder
was all very well, but it was in the context of the fact that 'His teachers
were working with a less than perfect programme.'

The training programme was particularly deficient in relation to warnings about the risks of SPADs. Terry Worrall, Thames's director and general manager, admitted to the inquiry that the course had failed to instruct '[Hodder] directly about the risks of SPADs at particular signals like SN 109', or to ensure 'that his route learning assessment specifically covered the area between Paddington and Ladbroke Grove'. Nor had Hodder attended a SPAD awareness day.

Most astonishingly, Ray Adams, Hodder's instructor, said that route learning was not a matter for him: 'I was not there to teach Michael the routes. I was totally [sic] to teach Michael how to drive a Turbo.'24 Hodder started training on 1 February 1999 and took his first solo shift on 22 September, thirty-three weeks later, some ten weeks fewer than the BR minimum. This whole pattern suggests the operation of Thames's course was tailored not so much to ensure competence, as to meeting their need for new drivers. Thames had abandoned driver training and then, suddenly aware that there was likely to be a shortage, recreated a programme that was clearly inadequate. It was no comfort to the victims and their families that, even before the accident, Thames had realised that its procedures were inadequate and that subsequent trainees were on a much improved course.

The other aspect of Thames's culpability which arises from the privatisation is the fact that its trains were not fitted with Automatic Train Protection. As we noted in the last chapter, it is a quite bizarre coincidence that the two worst crashes caused by SPADs post-privatisation should have happened on one of only two lines in Britain fitted with ATP equipment as part of a BR experiment, and that on both occasions the equipment was not functioning. In the case of Southall this was a result of a failure to train drivers in its use and a general lack of interest on the part of Great Western, and a similar nonchalance was shown by Thames.

The fact that Thames did not have ATP, even though all the trackside was fitted and there was even space earmarked for the equipment in the Turbos, seems unbelievable. As we saw in the last chapter, BR's trial Automatic Train Protection programme had lost its way as a result of privatisation. Thames seems to have shown as little interest as Great Western in continuing with the pilot. The management buy-out team took over the franchise in October 1996 and within a few weeks the management executive of the company decided that ATP should not be fitted to its Thames trains. Following the Southall crash in early 1998 the company decided to reconsider this decision and commissioned a study from W.S. Atkins to establish the costs and benefits of installation. W.S. Atkins found that it would have cost £9m to fit, operate and maintain ATP between Paddington and Oxford. The study suggested that statistically it was probable that only one life would have been saved by fitting ATP, which meant that in terms of the standard value (which was then around £2.45m and is now £3.2m) ascribed to a life in the rail industry in the consideration of such schemes, it was too expensive, and Thames was happy to concur with this decision.

Clearly the Thames directors failed to consider the wider circumstances if an accident were to occur and the particular dangers of the Paddington throat. A subsequent analysis of the Atkins study performed for the Cullen inquiry by Det Norske Veritas found that it lacked robustness and had not sufficiently taken into account the possibility of a major catastrophe. Some of the figures, too, underestimated the benefits and exaggerated the costs, though not sufficiently to bring down the price to less than the £2.45m per life used by Railtrack. Indeed, Thames's decision to commission the W.S. Atkins study has all the hallmarks of a back-covering exercise to ensure that Thames could continue to eschew ATP despite Southall. Of course, Thames was unlucky that its driver should have made a disastrous mistake that cost thirty-one lives, despite having a fully functioning Automatic Warning System which he cancelled properly, but the company's failure to consider the wider implications was an inevitable consequence of the way that the industry was fragmented. Oddly, despite the flaws in the Atkins methodology, Cullen accepted Thames's argument for not fitting ATP, even though, as we saw in the last chapter, neighbouring Chiltern, an equally small company which operates the same type of trains, was prepared to spend the money because its directors realised what an enormous benefit the system represented above and beyond the narrow financial considerations. As we saw in the last chapter, essentially there were two ways of approaching the ATP issue: a 'can do' approach of trying to sort out the problems, or negatively, merely seeking excuses not to do the work because ATP was a hassle. Chiltern chose the former, Thames and Great Western the latter.

One of the factors that influenced Thames's decision not to fit ATP was that, at the time, the company expected the new Train Protection and Warning System (TPWS) to be fitted relatively soon. TPWS is an extension of the Automatic Warning System, explained in the previous chapter, which will stop most trains from going through red lights. It works through having a device about 350 metres in advance of a signal that will monitor the train's speed and ensure that it is not going too fast to stop at the signal if a red is showing. Because of the technical limitations of the system, trains travelling above 70mph may not be stopped in time to avoid a collision but they will be slowed down considerably.

After the Tory government effectively abandoned ATP in the run-up to privatisation, Sir George Young, the transport secretary, announced in 1995 that trials of TPWS would take place the following year and 'the aim is to start wider installation in 1997'.[25] Inevitably, the timetable slipped. The trials, on Thameslink, took longer to implement. Eventually, however, in early 1999, a report recommending the adoption of TPWS, found its way on to John Prescott's desk but he dithered for seven months until August 1999 before making a decision to implement the system across the network by the start of 2004. TPWS, then costed at £310m but now at least double that amount, would have prevented Ladbroke Grove (but only slowed down the Southall impact), but, of course, it would not have been fitted in time, even if Prescott had not prevaricated.

The government's delay over TPWS had a bizarre side effect that was to have a highly damaging consequence in the aftermath of the Hatfield accident. On the Saturday after the Ladbroke Grove crash, fearful of critical coverage of the government's role in the following days' papers, a high-level meeting, which included Tony Blair, John Prescott, Lord Macdonald and their respective press officers, decided to try to hijack the news agenda by letting it be known that the government intended to remove the safety role from Railtrack. The group had got wind of the fact that Prescott might be under the cosh for having hesitated over the implementation of TPWS and that the hacks would not be sophisticated enough to realise that, even had Prescott given an immediate go-ahead, the accident would not have been averted.

The briefing to the Sunday newspaper journalists suggested that taking away Railtrack's safety responsibilities was the recommendation of a report prepared by the Health and Safety Executive. In fact, the HSE report recommended no such thing, merely suggesting that the issue needed to be looked at. This was confirmed on the Monday in Parliament when Lord Macdonald merely said the government was 'minded' to make the move. The spinning, however, had done its trick, focusing press attention on Railtrack rather than Prescott, and it showed Railtrack just how dirty the politicians could play. Indeed, the knowledge that ministers were so ready to attack the industry to protect their own backs contributed to Railtrack's extremely conservative response in the aftermath of Hatfield. How could Railtrack executives take any risks when they knew that there was no 'air cover' – to use Gerald Corbett's term – from government? It was a disgraceful episode that continued to sour government relations with the industry, which had already been damaged by Prescott saying, from the accident site, that money was no object in ensuring safety on the railway. This is one of those knee-jerk responses which can never be challenged at the time but which are, in fact, a blatant lie. Prescott did not make it clear who would foot the bill when, in truth, safety measures always have to be paid for by government.

In the event, an inquiry was set up to decide how to restructure the safety role of Railtrack and it recommended that Railtrack's Safety and Standards Directorate should be hived off into a separate subsidiary,[26] Railway Safety, operating completely independently of Railtrack Line, the main business. However, the situation remains fluid, as in September 2001 the second part of the Cullen report recommended the setting up of a new investigation organisation to examine accidents, filling the same role as the Air Accident Investigations Branch in the aviation industry, as well as separating Railway Safety from Railtrack to form a new, independent Rail Industry Safety Body.

So, as with Southall, the question of the role of privatisation and fragmentation in the accident needs to be addressed. Would this accident have happened if BR had still run the railways? And again, the evidence is very strong that it would not. One can view the accident from the perspective that here were two utterly incompetent sets of management who, between them, got a rookie driver into an area with an appalling history of SPADs without proper training or appraisal. It took the involvement and failings of both companies to bring about this disaster because, had either of them done their job properly, the crash would never have happened. Both companies are fake constructs, bits of the railway hived off for reasons that had nothing to do with improving services or safety. Railtrack we know about already. Thames is a small train operator, originally a management buy-out which was later sold on, making the original managers millionaires. Such a small company clearly could not have the large-scale and well-resourced training programmes run by BR.

To suggest that the same set of circumstances would have come about under BR is fanciful. It is inconceivable that the whole fatal sequence of mistakes would have occurred under the unified structure: the failure to call signal sighting committees; the lack of response to Alison Forster's concerns; the inadequacy of the driver training programme; the failure to spot the flaw in the track layout; and the unwillingness to install ATP. An alternative scenario on any of these issues would have produced a completely different outcome. More importantly, in BR days there was a 'Fat Controller' or general manager who was responsible for every aspect of the railway including all engineering, civil, mechanical and signal and traffic, and who would have dealt with the concerns of the likes of Alison Forster.

Above all, there was the failure to follow recommendations of inquiries into incidents. The old railway culture – both BR and pre-nationalisation – was about learning from mistakes and trying to reduce the number of small ones so that there was less chance of having a big disaster. Railtrack's Great Western zone's culture of ignoring recommendations was, quite literally, a disaster waiting to happen, given that this was a deliberate failure to prevent the recurrence of the situations which had already put lives a risk. There is no doubt that this would not have happened in the tighter and more disiplined BR culture where, also, safety responsibilities did not end up with 'business development managers'.

Which brings us back to Hatfield. That was an accident which was such a direct result of privatisation and fragmentation that the case hardly needs to be made. The events leading up to it are analysed in the next chapter.

Hatfield: the accident that broke the railway

'The accident at Hatfield was not caused by a broken rail. It was caused by total mismanagement by Railtrack and its contractors. The broken rail was the result of complete incompetence by the management somewhere between Railtrack and the contractor, Balfour Beatty.' Those are the words of Chris Garnett, the chief executive of GNER, the company which ran the train that derailed at Hatfield. Indeed, Hatfield was the perfect example of an accident caused by the way that the railways had been fragmented. Broken railways, broken rail. There is a poetic neatness about it, but not for the families of the four men who were killed.

They were travelling on the 12.10 from King's Cross to Leeds, which came off the rails on a curve between Welham Green and Hatfield station at 115mph, the maximum speed allowed on that section of the line. (Actually, it was travelling at 117mph; and the locomotive was in the hands of a trainee driver who shouldn't have been at the controls because she hadn't completed enough weeks of her course. Neither of these facts had any bearing on the accident, but they are just two more examples of the sloppiness that seems to be all too common in this tale.)

The locomotive and the first two coaches stayed on the track but the other seven and the driving van trailer were derailed. The four unlucky men were in the buffet car, which, because it smashed into one of the stanchions supporting the overhead line electrical equipment, was the only coach that was severely damaged. Of the other 178 people on the train, seventy were injured, four seriously, and it was only the strength of the BR design of the modern Mark IV coaches which prevented a much higher death toll.

After the accident, following early speculation about a bomb or a broken axle, it quickly emerged that the cause of the derailment was a broken rail which was later revealed to have smashed into 300 pieces. Some 90 metres of line, in two sections, had totally disintegrated leaving, oddly, a mostly intact section of 44 metres in between. The line was closed for twenty-four days and the disruption caused by the panic about the condition of the track around the whole network was worse than anything previously encountered on Britain's railways and has been described in detail in chapter 1.

The fact that that piece of track was allowed to deteriorate into such a disastrous condition was the result of a series of decisions by people at two very different levels. In the months prior to the accident there were several errors concerning the maintenance of that part of the track, the failure of which resulted in the disaster. But while at first glance this was an accident caused by the immediate failings of the maintenance company and Railtrack, in fact its roots are to be found in the privatisation process described at length in this book. In the case of the Ladbroke Grove and Southall accidents, the interactions between privatisation and the causes of the accident were extremely complex; at Hatfield the part played by the fragmentation and sale of the railways is very clear. The whole ghastly tale of mismanagement, greed and incompetence that caused the Hatfield disaster was a result of the crazy structure for the railways created by John Major and his ministers, aided and abetted by civil servants and, worse, railway managers who should have known better. Hatfield was the epitome of the failings created by rail privatisation. It may also be privatisation's epitaph, given that Hatfield turned Railtrack from a profitable company into a financial wreck, forever waving the begging bowl at passing transport ministers.

At the time of writing, the legal processes have yet to reach the courts and therefore it is impossible to set out in detail the circumstances of the accident. The British Transport Police are investigating the possibility of a manslaughter charge against senior executives of the companies involved, but this is highly unlikely given the legal difficulties. As one of the investigators told the journalist Ian Jack, for corporate manslaughter you really need a piece of paper which says, 'Do not repair this track, we can't afford it. Yours sincerely, the Fat Controller.'[1] Instead, some poor hapless middle manager or foreman is likely to cop the blame and heavy fines will be imposed on any firms found guilty of breaches of the Health and Safety regulations.

One of the ways that the modern railway differs most markedly from BR is that the various organisations involved no longer cooperate readily with each other and the investigators in order to ascertain what happened. Indeed, the author of a report by Railway Safety, Railtrack's safety division, into the disaster was unable to get a clear picture of what happened and to reconcile conflicting accounts because twelve Railtrack employees and one former employee were advised by the company not to give oral evidence in case of a future prosecution. The report, leaked to the *Financial Times*,[2] suggests that problems with this section of the track stretched back to 1998, two years before the disaster. By November 1999, according to documents from Balfour Beatty Rail Maintenance leaked to the *Guardian*,[3] the company was pressing Railtrack to replace the track within the next six months. The Railway Safety report says that after this there was a complex interchange of memos and reports between the two companies, which suggests that while some managers at these two companies knew that there was a problem, the complexity of the decision-making process and considerations of cost resulted in nothing being done.

As with all these accidents, it is an accumulation of little mistakes that built up to cause a disaster. Before getting into a consideration of the broken rail and what caused it, there is an interesting side issue that may have contributed to the accident. There is evidence that it was not the 12.10 which actually broke the rail but that an earlier train had damaged it sufficiently for it to have snapped with wheels still able to pass over it without derailing. This evidence comes from the track circuit, a system which involves a small current being run through rails to alert signallers as to the location of a train. When the circuit is broken because of a split rail or some other impediment, the train effectively disappears off the signallers' panel and when it returns at the next track circuit, it comes on without its train describer – the unique set of numbers and letters which identifies every train. When this occurs an alarm sounds in the box to alert signallers. According to a signalling source, this alarm – a Non Description Alert (NDA) – sounded frequently in the King's Cross control centre, but because of a fault on another section of line, not the Hatfield one. On the day of the Hatfield crash four trains sounded NDAs before the one that derailed. However, because NDAs had become almost routine on the nearby North London Lines section, the signallers failed to take any action or even to alert more experienced managers and, instead, merely cancelled the alert. Another source sent me a leaked memo issued in the aftermath of Hatfield, which suggested that this may have been because of a relaxation in policy by Railtrack in relation to such NDAs and confirming that such self-rectifying faults should be examined by technicians and not merely ignored. Railtrack refused to comment on this matter but it illustrates how minor decisions relating to safety can lead to major incidents.

Although both Balfour Beatty and Railtrack knew for a long time that there was a problem with the track, neither clearly realised – at the right level of management – how bad it was or else a speed limit would have been imposed. Various people seemed to be aware that there was a problem which needed sorting out properly but either their appeals for action fell on deaf ears or they were not prepared to push hard enough to ensure the work was done. Most remarkably, while the track inspector, Andrew Preston, walked along the track every Tuesday afternoon to check its condition, he had not been told that the rail was so bad that it had been scheduled for replacement. The accident happened on a Tuesday morning and it may be that he would have spotted the break that afternoon, but we will never know. Week after week, his reports – the last dated 10 October, precisely a week before the disaster – reported nothing untoward about the track, and yet some of his managers were preparing schemes to rerail that section because of its poor condition. Preston told Railway Safety that he had never been trained about gauge corner cracking – the type of damage which had affected the rail – nor about how to spot it or assess its gravity.

But even if the hapless Preston had been properly trained, he would not have been able to see the damage. Rails are inspected by teams of labourers walking by the side of the track to check their condition. Busy lines like the East Coast Main Line are walked every week, often by the same person. There are four sets of track on this part of the railway, going from east to west, the down slow (conventionally, down tracks lead away from London, up tracks towards it), down fast, up fast and up slow. Balfour Beatty, responsible for the day-to-day maintenance through its contract with Railtrack, had got into bad habits, prompted by cost-cutting. The way that the railway was privatised meant that both Railtrack and its contractors had to reduce costs by 3 per cent per annum in order to retain the same level of profits. Instead of teams of four or six people, which would allow the vital look-outs at the front and back, the gang consisted of just two men. This meant they could not venture onto the six-foot – the gap between each set of lines – or the ten-foot – the gap between the down and up lines – because, even with a ten-foot width, it is simply too dangerous, given the prospect of two 115mph trains from different directions bearing down on these vulnerable track workers.[4] There are four sets of rails to check and the men walked on the cess (the railway's name for the trackside path, not a pit) alongside the track rather than risk their lives on the track. Moreover, according to the Railway Safety report, the track inspectors lacked clerical back-up, which suggests that their reports may not have been sufficiently monitored.

They went up one cess and down the other, but this did not give them a good view of all the rails. Indeed, as far as the Welham Green curve was concerned, they might as well have saved their blisters. On the bend the rails are canted – set at an angle – in order to reduce friction to a minimum. The cant meant that the top of the rail at the bend was not visible when the inspectors were walking in the nearer cess, and too far away to see it clearly when walking in the further one. The gradual deterioration as the crack – already noted in 1998 – dug its way into the rail, went unobserved. Even when a manager came to inspect the line in July 1999, he stayed in the cess but, because he knew what he was looking for, spotted cracking and suggested that replacement should be considered.

The rail was also checked with ultrasound, using a machine which is pushed by hand along the track and which beams sound down on to the line and back to record any cracks. Unfortunately, though, the equipment was not, in the term used by safety inspectors, 'fit for the purpose'. The machines could not measure the sort of crack – gauge corner cracking – which was propagating rapidly through the rail. The standards for these machines had been inherited by Railtrack from British Rail and not updated, even though there was growing evidence round the network of gauge corner cracking. Railtrack was 'slow in adopting best practice in ultrasonic inspection',[5] as a report into the broken rails problem later pointed out, largely because the company was simply not prepared to find the money to invest in modern equipment.

The inadequacy of the equipment meant that, although the track was tested by ultrasound every three months, the results were difficult to interpret. There was, moreover, no proper evaluation of the results and the rail was not rechecked when no reading was recorded. In November 1999 the test found that there was a 'loss of rail bottom' – in other words, the equipment was not able to get a measurement of the depth of the crack. In April 2000 that section was found to be untestable, and two months later there was, again, total 'loss of rail bottom'. Then on 5 October, just twelve days before the crash, the equipment again found 'loss of rail bottom'. Such readings should have prompted immediate attention.

Clearly, somebody should have rechecked that part of the line manually and, in the meantime, imposed a temporary speed restriction. Even if such checks had been undertaken, the day might not have been saved, however, because there are doubts as to whether this information would have found its way to managers. Investigators have found that there were serious gaps in the record-keeping and, moreover, the whole story reveals that the lines of accountability both within and between Balfour Beatty, Jarvis Fastline – which is responsible for renewals in that Railtrack zone – and Railtrack were so unclear that while certain managers were busy trying to replace the damaged rail, others knew nothing about the problem and the poor traction inspector on the ground had no idea of its state because no one had bothered to alert him.

There was a series of missed opportunities and a timetable of events which make painful reading. In 1998 Vernon Bullen, Balfour Beatty's area maintenance engineer, said he was aware of gauge corner cracking in the area. He recommended grinding for early in 1999 which never happened. In mid-1999 he proposed the rerailing of ten sites, with Welham Curve as top priority – rather than any time in the following year, the normal expectation for renewals – to Railtrack. However, Railtrack seems not to have understood the urgency of the situation and the scheme was sent back to Balfour for prioritising. In January 2000 Jarvis was asked to survey the up fast line but it examined the wrong line and only undertook the correct work three weeks later. In March 2000 Jarvis and Railtrack agreed to a rerailing schedule but, as we see below, the work was never carried out in time. Somehow the sense of urgency which built up at various times was lost in the bureaucracy and the interface between the three companies. A quote from the Railway Safety report perhaps explains why:

> Any item requiring to be done to a tighter timetable [than a year] i.e. outside the bounds of normal planning, would be flagged as an emergency because of its potential impact on maintenance costs or its effect on train performance resulting from a Temporary Speed Restriction, or both.

Furthermore, there were clear conflicts of interest between the three firms. As explained in chapter 5, maintenance was arbitrarily split at privatisation between renewal and maintenance companies. Under Railtrack's standard RT1a contracts, there was a set but arbitrary procedure about when 'maintenance' should be upgraded to 'renewal': any length of continuously welded rail that needs replacing which is longer than 600 feet has to be done by the renewal company – in this case Jarvis Fastline – rather than the maintenance firm, Balfour Beatty. The way that maintenance and renewals were separated was another bit of privatisation madness. The maintenance contracts are fixed price and therefore any work that can be passed on to Jarvis is good news for Balfour Beatty. Work by Jarvis is carried out on a job-by-job basis which means that the more work there is, the more it gets paid. Railtrack, meanwhile, is trying to ensure that the least amount necessary is done by Jarvis and that disruption to the network, which affects its performance payments, is minimised. As a former Railtrack manager quoted in the *Financial Times* related, the arguments between the three parties at times almost came to blows: 'It was a constant battle. . . . At some of those meetings with contractors, we nearly came to fisticuffs because we, at Railtrack, were having to deny them the access they required.'[6]

A Balfour Beatty inspection sheet dated 11 January 2000, leaked to the *Guardian*,[7] reported that 'gauge corner cracking' was 'showing bad' and said the rail needed replacing. After Railtrack had inspected the site in February, it was decided to replace the rail, but Welham Green was one of ten sites which needed rerailing. However, the request to do all the work was turned down by Railtrack's senior project manager for the North East zone, Amanda Henderson, because, according to the Railway Safety report, she said it was 'considered impossible to deliver without deleting half the existing track renewal programme'.

However, the Welham Green section was reckoned to be a priority. It was given P1 status, which means replace within a month but, amazingly, the Railway Safety report says that Ms Henderson did not understand this appellation. By March, however, the zone engineer was in a position to go the to Black Tower – Railtrack's ugly black headquarters next to Euston station – and put a business case to Asset Management for the cash and authorisation to carry out the work. This department keeps a check on cash flow and has to give permission for all major work on the network. Railtrack claimed to the *Guardian* that 'The cost of rerailing the track is never an issue where safety is concerned'[8] but this is not true. Requests are made by zone directors for replacement of rails and these have to be slotted into existing timetables of possession and to the budget. Risk assessments are made as in any safety-critical industry.

In this case, it was agreed to replace the rail, but then the request was passed on to Possession Management in the zone for the work to be scheduled. (When I explained this process to a senior executive of Amtrak, the US passenger railway, he said: 'You're kidding? If we have a rail that needs replacing, the chief engineer just orders the work to be done.') The job of the Possession Management is to work out the 'rules of the route', the schedule of when parts of the network can be closed – normally at weekends – in order for major repairs to be carried out. There are routine closures determined two years in advance with all the operators, both passenger and freight, but Railtrack tries to avoid having extra possessions – closures – because it has to pay compensation to the train operators for the disruption. However, Possession Management seemed to have grasped the urgency of the situation because it agreed to a special 27-hour closure of the line on 19 March in order to replace the dodgy rail.

The whole Hatfield tragedy and its appalling aftermath would not have occurred without another of those seemingly inconsequential little mistakes: there were three failed attempts to deliver the rails before they all reached the site and by then the lengthy possession had been lost. The first train – in one of those further complexities of fragmentation, it was operated by Jarvis but staffed by Railtrack – was late and then the second was the *wrong sort of train*: it could not unload the rails without fouling the overhead line equipment. At the third attempt, in early April, half the rails were dropped off and finally, on 28 April, the rest were delivered. Replacement was carried on neighbouring sites but Welham Green could not be done.

Possession Management, by this time none too pleased with the delay, refused to sanction another emergency closure, particularly as it was now the busier, summer timetable and disruption would have caused delays to more trains, incurring greater penalties. According to John Ware who made a BBC *Panorama* documentary on the crash, Jarvis was seeking five 8-hour possessions to do the work and this was not acceptable to Railtrack which offered only two, each for just 4 hours and 20 minutes. This was not, as has been presented, a question of money. The work could not be done in such a short period of time, as it takes an hour to turn the power on or off and this would simply not have left sufficient time for any rerailing to be carried out.

There was, though, another aspect which does involve money. The reluctance to close the line during the busy and lucrative summer period was clearly a result of financial pressures. Payments to Railtrack from the train operators under the performance regime are dependent on keeping the line open at all times, except during scheduled possessions. Moreover, this pressure may also have been felt by some individual managers as, according to an engineer,[9] 'You should never underestimate the influence of bonuses. Everyone's bonus was based on not going outside the agreed possessions. When a Railtrack zone beats its performance regime, then the zone directors get bonuses. It's done on a [four-week] period-by-period basis.' In the summer, contractors also found it more difficult to find sufficient skilled workers, such as welders, to carry out the work, and had to pay them more because of competition for their services from the construction industry.

Consequently, as a result of these pressures and a failure to understand the seriousness of the condition of the track, the work was rescheduled for November – two years after the cracks were first discovered and a month after the Hatfield disaster.

The biggest question, and one which will only be revealed by the court cases and the inquiry, is why no speed limit was imposed. It is routine to place temporary speed restrictions on damaged sections of track. There were literally dozens of people who must have realised that there was a rail in poor condition. Obviously, the failures of the inspection regime meant that no one quite knew the extent of the damage to the rail, but given that a decision had been taken that the rail needed to be replaced, the failure to impose a speed restriction is inexplicable.

Apart from the failings of the inspection process, how did the rail get into that state anyway? Of course 20-20 hindsight is an easy science. But the likelihood of a rail breaking was frighteningly predictable; if the accident hadn't happened at Hatfield, it would very probably have occurred on some other part of the network with similarly dramatic consequences.

Hatfield was the first accident caused by a broken rail since the Hither Green disaster on Guy Fawkes night in 1967. There, a break at the fishplate – the fitting which connects rails, now largely redundant because of continuous welded rails – led to a broken rail, causing a derailment at around 75 mph and killing forty-nine people in a crowded Sunday night train travelling into London from Hastings.[10] The Hither Green accident was caused by a phenomenon known as starcracking, which was allowed to propagate into the rail due to inadequate maintenance. Improved maintenance ensured that starcracking never caused another accident.

In the intervening years, under BR, rail maintenance standards had improved enormously, but with privatisation came immediate doubts about Railtrack's ability to keep the track in good condition because of the way that all work was done through contractors. In order to assess the impact of the creation of Railtrack on safety, Her Majesty's Railway Inspectorate (HMRI, part of the Health and Safety Executive) conducted its most comprehensive ever study into railway safety.[11]

The report specifically highlighted problems with the relationship between Railtrack and its contractors and the way in which the company ensured compliance with its safety case. In the words of the then deputy chief inspector, Vic Coleman, 'There were weaknesses in the way that Railtrack seeks to maintain health and safety,' some of which 'cause concern'.

The report pointed out an inherent weakness in the way that the contracts had been established. The outputs for Railtrack's maintenance contracts were very unspecific. They set out broad objectives such as ensuring the track met certain standards, rather than more specific aims such as that a set of points would be out of action for only a given amount of time per year. Therefore Railtrack needed very efficient monitoring and control systems, but the HMRI report found cases of contractors who did not have safety cases approved by Railtrack and 'many examples of contractors not meeting Railway Group Standards'.[12] According to a manager involved in setting up the contracts, 'The monitoring and auditing requirements were set out in meticulous detail in various documents. But, with possibly only one exception, none of the Railtrack zones did enough monitoring and made sure that work was carried out.' Here again money was at the root of the problem: 'We were under constant pressure from Norman Broadhurst [Railtrack's finance director] and the regulator to cut costs. They didn't give us the resources to carry out the checks. It became just a ticking box exercise.'[13]

The correct systems for selecting, managing and controlling contractors were also not being followed. While these matters may have appeared minor, the HSE was clearly very concerned. Coleman concluded that while Railtrack had made great efforts in putting in the right systems to manage its contractors, 'We were disappointed that greater progress has not been made.' While Railtrack assumed that the contractors were self-auditing, the HSE clearly did not trust them to do the work without extensive monitoring. That fundamental difference of approach seems never to have been satisfactorily resolved.

An accident to a freight train at Bexley in February 1997 highlighted the disparity between theory and practice in the way that this horde of new contractors on the railway were being controlled by Railtrack. The train, operated by English, Welsh and Scottish Railways, the main privatised freight company, was carrying old ballast from track renewal work when part of it derailed on a viaduct just after passing Bexley station. It was travelling at around 55mph, considerably faster than the 40mph which was the maximum permitted speed for freight on that line. Seven wagons were completely derailed, and six of them smashed through the small wall protecting the track and toppled eight metres onto the cars and yards underneath the viaduct, seriously injuring four people.

The train had not only been travelling too fast, but the track renewal contractor, Southern Track Renewals Company Ltd (owned by Balfour Beatty), had overloaded the wagons causing extra pressure on the rails. This would not have mattered had they been in good condition, but they were not. They had spread as a result of rotting timbers that were in a very poor state of repair. As the accident report[14] showed, the timbers had sunk deep into the ballast and there was evidence of botched repairs using bitumen and incorrectly fitted tie bars. Indeed, as the investigators discovered, the local track maintenance company, South East Infrastructure Maintenance Company Ltd (SEICML, again owned by Balfour Beatty) had long known about the appalling condition of the track. As far back as August 1995, a bridge examiner had reported finding serious decay in the timbers. Inexplicably, nothing was done and a consultant's report drawing up a replacement programme in December 1996 was also ignored. As the report puts it, 'Because of poor organisation and a breakdown in communication within SEICML, no one arranged for the work to be done.'[15] The local section manager again recommended, in February 1996, that the timbers 'needed renewing' but again nothing was done. Meanwhile, the weekly patrollers continued to report defects, stressing that the timbers were in 'very bad condition' and needed changing.[16]

As for the track renewal company, its managers clearly had no understanding of the relationship between weight and volume. The wagons

were originally used for transporting steel but if they are filled with a
dense material like ballast, they are grossly overloaded – some 30 per
cent according to the investigators.[17]

The most worrying aspect of the accident was the fact that it showed
Railtrack had failed to remedy the defects in its management of contractors identified in the 1996 HSE report, although it had introduced a new
system of controls and checks. As the report put it, 'The HSE accident
investigation found very little evidence of the new standards having been
implemented. Railtrack were unable to produce an audit plan for the
twelve months leading up to the accident.'[18] Again, money was at the
root of the failure: Railtrack had simply not budgeted for the cost of extra
controls since 'The resources available to the Railtrack Permanent Way
Engineer were insufficient to enable the end product checks to be done.'
In other words, Railtrack had never intended to ensure that its monitoring was improved.

As no one was killed, the Bexley accident and its aftermath attracted
little attention, even though a major disaster had only been avoided by
sheer luck – the wagons could easily have fallen on people, cars or even
buses. Moreover, because of prosecutions by the HSE, which resulted in
fines and costs of nearly £200,000 for the two firms (both, as we have
seen, owned by Balfour Beatty), the subsequent report was not published
until March 1999 which delayed its recommendations (or 'lessons', as the
report calls them, because clearly the HSE realised it was dealing with
companies whose managers needed to go back to school) being put into
effect.

Essentially, however, these 'lessons' merely reiterated what the 1996
HSE report had already recommended. The multiple failings which led to
the Hatfield crash demonstrated that these lessons had still not been
taken on board eighteen months after the publication of the Bexley
report. The failure of communication about the cracked rail at Hatfield
between Balfour Beatty and Railtrack and the fact that Railtrack
appeared unaware that Balfour Beatty's inspection teams were inade-
quately staffed, in clear breach of group standards, is a clear illustration
that little had changed.

Bexley was not the only accident involving sloppy practices by Balfour
Beatty which resulted in the company ending up at the wrong end of
heavy fines. Balfour Beatty is one of the biggest players in the 'Infraco'
market. It bought three of the thirteen Briscos originally put up for sale

by the government, seeing them as a bargain because of the guaranteed contracts they had with Railtrack. The company's recent record, however, is unenviable. Already, before taking up these contracts, Balfour Beatty had been responsible for the collapse of the Heathrow Express tunnel in 1994, leading to an amazing hole emerging in the middle of the airport into which a small office block collapsed. Fortunately, no one was killed but the firm was later fined £1.2m, then a record for Health and Safety at Work offences. The subsequent HSE enquiry found that 'The collapses could have been prevented but for a cultural mind-set which focused attention on the apparent economies and the need for production rather than the particular risk.' Then, just six months after the Bexley derailment, another freight train went off the rails at Rivenhall in Essex as a result of faulty working by the contractor. Again, Balfour Beatty was given a heavy – £500,000 – fine and an admonishment from the judge in Chelmsford Crown Court who said that the men working on the track were 'not properly monitored or supervised with the result that a serious risk to health and safety was created'.[19]

The 1999 annual audit of Railtrack by its own Safety and Standards Directorate (later to become Railway Safety) highlighted a key change that seems to have exacerbated the failings over the management of maintenance on the railway. Railtrack, on the advice of management consultants McKinsey, was implementing Project Destiny, based on the idea of targeting replacement of assets only when it was reckoned to be needed rather than at set time intervals. According to the audit, however, this 'just-in-time approach led to major shifts from track renewals to maintenance'. In other words, it was a 'patch and mend' rather than replace approach which resulted in 57 per cent of proposed renewals being either postponed for a year or put into maintenance. The Railway Safety report into the Hatfield accident confirmed the impact of this policy. The report quoted the Balfour Beatty manager who had been in charge of the East Coast Main Line, as warning that the rate of track renewal had been 'too low' for the previous two or three years as 'The strategy [was] inappropriate for the heavily trafficked and high-speed East Coast Main Line.'[20] The report attributed this to the recommendations by McKinsey.

Long before Hatfield, the problem of a rise in broken rails had already been identified as having the potential to cause a disaster by the Health and Safety Executive. With frightening prescience, in the press release accompanying the annual rail safety report, the chief inspector of the railways, Vic Coleman, said, 'We took a snapshot look at the state of the tracks at the end of June 1998. This showed us that track quality was getting worse . . . If this decline is not reversed it will have an effect on safety.'[21] His figures showed that rail breaks on the Railtrack infrastructure had risen from 2.75 to 3.31 per million train-miles in 1998/99.

The energetic new rail regulator, Tom Winsor, who took up the post in July 1999, was already on the case. Barely a month into the job, he had noted that an HSE report[22] recounted a sharp increase in broken rails, a 21 per cent rise to 937 in 1998/9 compared with 755 in 1997/8 and a Railtrack forecast of 600. One of Railtrack's licence conditions, which are policed by the regulator, is to ensure that its assets are managed properly and safely, and Winsor felt that the rise in broken rails was evidence that there might be a breach of licence. On 12 August 1999 he wrote to Gerald Corbett, Railtrack's chief executive, in tough terms, demanding more detailed information about rail breaks and, in particular, clarity about Railtrack's policy on what was the acceptable level of breaks. Winsor had spotted that in Railtrack's 1998 *Network Management Statement* – the annual report on its proposed investment strategy – the forecast number of broken rails for the next two years was 525 and 400. Yet in the 1999 statement those predictions had risen to 770 and 700. Now Railtrack's target was 600. In other words, Railtrack was accepting that a higher number of broken rails was going to occur, partly as a result of the higher volume of traffic, and seemed not to care.

Winsor also referred to a spat between the Health and Safety Executive and Railtrack over rail maintenance in the four-mile-long Severn Tunnel which seemed to be symptomatic of the company's attitude towards rail replacement and of its bellicose attitude towards the safety authorities. Historically, in this wet tunnel, which requires a continual pumping operation in order to remain usable, rails had been replaced every six years, about eight times more frequently than normal. No science had been called on, no textbooks consulted. It was just that the old BR engineers knew that the conditions required such frequent replacements or otherwise there would be broken rails. There had been none in the tunnel for many years.

Railtrack changed that. The local zone director decided to save 50 per cent of the costs by fitting a new type of rail that was thought to require replacement only every nine years. Suddenly, in a seven-month period there were four broken rails, all involving sections that were more than six years old, and it was only through good fortune that no major accident was caused.

That was bad enough. But even more amazing was Railtrack's attitude to the subsequent complaint about the Severn Tunnel by Her Majesty's Railway Inspectorate. In April 1999 the Inspectorate complained about the situation but Railtrack, not taking sufficient account of the consequences of a derailment and possible collision in the network's longest tunnel, said it was too difficult to replace the rails before October because of the disruption to the service and suggested 50mph restrictions with daily inspections instead. Infuriated, Vic Coleman, who had by then become chief inspector of the railways, took the very rare step of issuing a formal notice to require Railtrack to do the work, and, in the meantime, imposed a 20mph limit on the tunnel, causing prolonged delays on train services to and from Wales. Many trains had to be diverted via Gloucester, adding an hour on to journey times. In taking this action Coleman may well have prevented the Severn Tunnel from being the name that resonates through the rail industry in the way that Hatfield, sadly, now does.

Coleman even went on the radio to explain his actions, a rare move since the HSE is usually happier doing things behind the scenes with quiet words in the right people's ears. The rail regulator[23] joined in too, demanding a report from Gerald Corbett. Then, suddenly, like some backstreet car mechanic offered a fat tip, Railtrack found it could, after all, do the work, and promptly replaced the rails in June, four months ahead of schedule.

Coleman identified the key issue at the heart of the problem. Railtrack's Project Destiny was intended to ensure that assets were maintained and renewed when they became life-expired, rather than at set intervals of time. Therefore, for example, heavily used points should be replaced more often than those on less busy routes. This all sounds very reasonable except that this strategy was based on the obvious notion that Railtrack knew what its assets were and their state of wear. However, Railtrack – incredible as it seems – does not have an asset register. The company does not know what it owns or anything about the condition of its assets. The zones had some knowledge but each one worked on a different basis. As Tom Winsor later put it, 'There's nothing wrong with replacing your assets on the basis of condition, as long as you understand their condition.'[24] (Moreover, at the time of writing, in mid-2001,

Railtrack still does not have an asset register, although, at last, the rail regulator was in the process of changing Railtrack's licence in order to ensure the company produces one, probably by 2003.)

So Coleman was extremely concerned that Railtrack's lapse was not a one-off, but a systematic failure that led to cutting maintenance costs without sufficient information on which the company could base rational decisions on what to renew and what to leave. This was a clear example of how policy changes, which at board level sounded reasonable, created extra risks at the sharp end. The authors of a report into the broken rails situation were incredulous, recording that Railtrack 'does not keep central statistics'[25] and was therefore unable to plot trends about defects in its rails, even though contractors were required to maintain such records.

Like Coleman, Winsor, the rail regulator, was also worried that this type of event was evidence of a systemic failure rather than a one-off. Railtrack responded to his 12 August letter by arguing that the increase in breaks was a result of the rise in the number of trains on the network and partly of 'rail nearing the end of its life in high tonnage routes'.[26] Winsor was not satisfied, even when in subsequent correspondence Railtrack categorically rejected the suggestions that the backlog of track defects had built up through lack of maintenance. To sort the issue out Winsor commissioned a report from the US consultants, Transportation Technology Center Inc., a subsidiary of the American Association of Railroads, and its findings were critical of Railtrack's management of the network. There was one major problem with the TTCI report – it was published nearly a month after the four men were killed in the Hatfield disaster, having been completed on 25 October, just eight days after the accident. Winsor's attempt to rein back the damage caused by Project Destiny had, through no fault of his own, been too slow. Hatfield, according to one jaundiced train operator, 'was McKinsey's finest hour'. The TTCI report outlined several reasons for the increase in rail breaks, attributing it mainly to changed practices on Britain's railways or a failure to take account of the changing nature of their use. It found that the condition of the track had deteriorated dramatically in 1995 and 1996, and despite subsequent improvements, 'has not yet consistently reached the 1994 levels'.[27]

Railtrack's inspection methods were criticised, including the fact that in 1995 the company had mothballed BR's Ultrasonic Testing Train because it argued that 'hand testing' was more accurate, even though the train was much quicker. The TTCI report looked at the experience in Europe and found that much more sophisticated equipment was being used, with ultrasonic trains capable of covering 150 miles in a shift. The authors of the report said: 'All the comparison railways inspect primarily using inspection vehicles, with manual methods used mainly for verification tests and tests at special areas like switches and crossings.'[28] In other words, Britain was in the railway dark ages. Again, after Hatfield, Railtrack sought to make good its error, despatching Richard Middleton, who was hastily appointed technical director in the aftermath of Hatfield, having previously been commercial director, with a blank cheque to buy as much testing and grinding equipment as he felt necessary – a far cry from the penny-pinching days of the late 1990s when Railtrack's sole agenda was to cut costs.

The virtual abandonment of the rail grinding programme in the run-up to privatisation was another major factor in the deterioration of the quality of the track highlighted in the TTCI report. Rail grinding smooths off the top of the rail, preventing small cracks from spreading further into the rail. BR had rundown its rail grinding regime and by 1991/2 had just one machine working, operating some 120 shifts per year.[29] In the following two years, BR's last and Railtrack's first in charge of the infrastructure, there was no grinding at all. Throughout the period 1994/5 to 1998/9, Railtrack had that one machine back in operation, at a cost of just £1.1m per year, and it was only in 1999/2000, as part of Railtrack's belated attempt to reduce the number of broken rails, that more resources were beginning to be devoted to grinding rails, with a new machine doubling capacity and a further two being ordered.

This was, of course, too late to prevent the Hatfield disaster or the track deterioration which resulted in the post-accident chaos (described in chapter 1). According to an expert on rail damage, Stuart Grassie, rolling contact fatigue (of which gauge corner cracking is one type) was a growing phenomenon on many European railways. Ironically, the best research on the problem had actually been undertaken in Britain at Cambridge University and British Rail Research during the 1970s and 1980s. BR Research was privatised along with the rest of the industry and sold to AEA Technologies and much of its expertise was lost because the companies which took on the railways had no commitment to such research. This again was a gap left by privatisation since the importance of research and development was not taken into account by those who privatised the rail-way. (In contrast, in Japan, where the railways are also owned privately, rail research is funded by the government.) Belatedly, Railtrack, along with Corus and Schweerbau UK, had agreed to pick up the cost of some of this research before the Hatfield accident as the problems of broken rails became apparent, but as Dr Grassie put it, 'Regrettably the benefits of this work will come too late for the families of the four people who died at Hat-field . . . and perhaps also too late for Railtrack itself to benefit fully from maintaining its rails rather than simply replacing them.'[30]

According to Dr Grassie, the main way of preventing rolling contract fatigue is through regular grinding which was carried out in Europe at a far higher rate than in Britain. Rails always develop tiny cracks as trains pass along them, and these are generally ground out naturally as more trains pass over them or by treatment from grinding machines. The cracks initially are shallow and at a small angle towards the direction of travel. It is only when they turn down, after about 10mms, at right angles from the top of the rail, that they begin to pose a danger.

In another awful blunder Railtrack got round to grinding the rail that caused the Hatfield crash on 4/5 September, just five weeks before the accident. Unfortunately, it was, as Railtrack now concedes, quite possi-bly, 'the wrong treatment at the wrong time', because the cracks were, by then, too deep to be remedied by grinding (which, incidentally, is carried out by yet another contractor, Serco). The rail was, in fact, subjected to very heavy grinding that may well have weakened the already damaged rail even further, although the Railway Safety report was inconclusive on this question. It did, however, confirm the possibility that the heavier trains in use on the line since the completion of its refurbishment in 1989 could have weakened the rails over time.

Railtrack suggested to the TTCI researchers that the main cause of the rise in broken rails was the increase in the number of trains on the network and changes in rolling stock design which had unexpected consequences. Certainly, both of these explanations formed part of the story and con-tributed to the spread of gauge corner cracking. A Railtrack insider said:

> I'm convinced that it was a change in wheel profile initiated by BR which caused the outbreak of gauge corner cracking. However, the phenomenon had existed for a long time, as I recall there was a rail showing signs of it at Warrington in the 1970s and it had to be replaced.[31]

The intensity of use, particularly the rise in numbers of freight trains, involved sweating old assets and inevitably led to more breaks. There was an increase of some 1,200 passenger trains per day between 1996 and 2000 (a 7 per cent rise in services, which, because they were mostly long-distance trains, represented an 11 per cent rise in mileage)[32] and many additional freight services (as the amount of freight carried on rail grew 41 per cent in the first four years of privatisation[33]). Because of the way that the industry was structured, Railtrack had no incentive to ensure that the track could cope with this influx of new traffic, as its track access charges were largely fixed and train operators were allowed to provide 8 per cent additional services without paying any extra money to Railtrack.[34] There is much anecdotal evidence, too, that there are more wheel flats (a wheel that is out of shape after being damaged during braking or sliding) on the network than under BR, possibly because train operators reduced maintenance to cut costs after privatisation. While this is difficult to prove, the TTCI report noted that wheel flats might be a major contributor to rail damage, as flats place enormous stresses on the rails.

This was symptomatic of the fact that no one was in charge of the 'wheel-rail' interface (and indeed a high-level committee, the excitingly-named Wheel-Rail Interface Authority, was created to deal with this issue by the industry after the Hatfield crash). Under BR if a particular train or type of train was causing damage to the track, the engineer would quickly track it down and ensure that the operations manager sorted out the problem. But with three different companies involved in the wheel-rail interface – Railtrack, the operator and the rolling stock leasing company – there was no one to ensure that this key relationship was working safely. In the aftermath of the accident Gerald Corbett said that one of the causes was that no one was managing that interface. Dr Grassie's research supports this contention by highlighting a counter-intuitive reason for the increase in gauge corner cracking: 'RCF has become more prevalent not only because ever-greater loads are borne by the rails (and wheels) but also because wear has been greatly reduced, primarily as a result of more effective lubrication.' In other words, better lubrication prevented the wheels operating as a kind of huge polisher. This was precisely the sort of unexpected consequence of technological changes which might have been spotted in an integrated railway but had no hope of being discovered within the fragmented structure.

Tellingly, the TTCI report found that Railtrack estimated that 400–600 miles of track were affected by gauge corner cracking, although the 'full extent of the problem is not known',[35] as events following Hatfield proved only too clearly. At one site gauge corner cracks were emerging on rail just one year old, according to TTCI. If, as is clear, Railtrack had known about this problem for some time before Hatfield, and indeed instances were recorded as far back as the 1970s, why was the company not doing more to tackle it? The TTCI research backs up the suggestion that had the Hatfield disaster not happened, it is highly likely that the same kind of accident would have occurred elsewhere on the network with more or less disastrous consequences.

Professor Roderick Smith, who was quickly hired by Railtrack to investigate the problem of gauge corner cracking and the wider phenomenon, rolling contact fatigue, in the immediate aftermath of the disaster, is convinced that the abandonment of an extensive rail grinding programme is the key reason behind the spread of gauge corner cracking: 'No one knows why Railtrack abandoned its grinding programme. If the railway had been in tip top condition, it would have been possible to have a maintenance holiday for a few years. But the railway was not in tip top condition and therefore it was the stupidest thing they could do.'[36] While heavier loads, the extra trains, the increase in wheel flats and the standardisation of the wheel profile, which meant the same part of the rail tended to be used by every train, all contributed, Professor Smith says, 'It was the absence of grinding which was the key element.'

There was another possible cause of the deterioration of the quality of rails across the network. In its early years Railtrack simply did not buy enough new rail. The decline in orders for new rail had started as part of BR's rundown in preparation for privatisation and continued under Railtrack. Richard Hope, the veteran rail journalist, had obtained figures from British Steel for the Commons Transport sub-Committee showing that the rail replacement rate was just 0.8 per cent per year, implying that rails would have to last 125 years. To show the absurdity of this, Hope pointed out that had no rails ever been replaced since the railways were first built, the average rail life would have, at the time, been precisely 125 years. This compared with an average of forty years in the major railways of Europe such as the French, Italian and German systems. As the TTCI report concluded, 'Reduced rail purchases over the years have led to increasing rail age and a consequential increase in rail fatigue. That is, there has been a prolonged under-investment in rail.'[37]

Railtrack's explanation given to the Committee by David Rayner, the director of safety and standards,[38] was that BR had been 'living on its inventory' but, in fact, when Railtrack published its 1996 *Network Management Statement*,[39] setting out its investment plans, the same rate of rail replacement, just 250 kilometres per year over the next ten years, was forecast. This compared with a rate of 402 kilometres per year during the previous four years under British Rail. Railtrack explained in the NMS, rather unconvincingly, that it was able to achieve this reduction because of 'recent technical advances'.

Railtrack had inherited from British Rail the British habit of making do and had exacerbated the problem with its parsimonious approach and its adoption of McKinsey's recommendations. The TTCI authors noted that there was a higher tolerance of broken rails on the British railways than on other systems, and Railtrack had seemed happy to go along with this traditional acceptance of a high rate of rail breaks until 1999 when it began to increase its purchase of new rail. Moving away from this culture will be a slow process and the report warns, 'A substantial reduction in broken rails will likely take several years,'[40] not least because, according to the researchers, there were a staggering 25–30,000 track defects around the network, something like one for every mile of track. While rail breaks were counted because they were part of Railtrack's performance regime, defects – including cracks – were not a measured output. There was no incentive built into the system for Railtrack or the maintenance companies to keep the level of defects down, except the vague requirements of the contracts which stipulated that the track had to be maintained to an adequate standard. The number of broken rails was one of the targets Railtrack set its maintenance contractors, but surface cracks were not. And that is always a problem with a targeted outputs way of managing rather than a holistic standards approach – everyone goes for the targets and other factors are ignored, particularly when there is a lot of financial pressure. It was of little comfort to the relatives of the dead that in the six months prior to the Hatfield accident Railtrack, reacting to the increased pressure on the issue, had reduced the number of broken rails by 30 per cent. It was too little, too late.

Railtrack might have been able to cope with these pressures had there been a strong culture of engineering within the company. However, as

Corbett explained just before he was sacked, the structure of Railtrack created for privatisation marginalised the role of engineers:

> The way the maintenance was contracted out broke the engineering chain and, at the time, no one realised that. Under British Rail, the engineering function was very strong. There was a chain going right down to the local area engineer. The local engineer was in charge of the system and optimising the wheel-rail interface and the chain of command went up to the top engineer. But when maintenance was broken off, a load of engineers went into the maintenance companies and some stayed with Railtrack, but the interface stopped being an engineering interface. *It became a commercial interface*, with all the problems.[41] [my italics]

Railtrack's *de facto* head of engineering (though his title was actually head of asset management), Andy Doherty, was therefore not on the board and, amazingly, the area engineers did not report to him. They reported, instead, to infrastructure contract managers (ICMs) who were not engineers but commercial people, often from outside the industry. There was only a 'dotted line relationship' between the area engineers and Railtrack's head of engineering in HQ. In other words, these local engineers did not report into Railtrack's corporate engineering structure and there was no direct link between the two, an extraordinary anomaly. There was another complexity, too, which prevented quick and effective decisions from being made. The ICMs worked with their counterparts in the maintenance companies but, as a Railtrack insider put it,

> You would have another chain of command in the contractor, with all its different layers, and somewhere you would find an engineer, but that engineer, talking to Railtrack's engineer would be a terribly vague relationship. In BR, there would have been a direct chain from that person up to the top.[42]

Tony Roche, a career railwayman and President of the Institution of Mechanical Engineers, is convinced that Railtrack's focus on money detracted from its engineering role:

> There are a number of factors which make a successful operation or business. Money is always there . . . but for the railways, key issues are engineering and people. . . . Engineering was not understood because people didn't look at inputs – they didn't actually understand, from the risk assessment point of view, the importance of all things working properly.[43]

He feels that the huge number of interfaces between the various companies that once made up BR generated a 'culture of confrontation' rather
than cooperation.

Corbett told the Commons Transport sub-Committee inquiry that the
financial pressure from the regulator to reduce delays affected the whole
culture of the organisation and put the wrong priorities at the top of the
agenda. Corbett, who in his three years at the head of Railtrack had
begun to understand the flaws in the way the industry had been privatised, became convinced that the Hatfield accident was not only a managerial aberration but a result of structural weaknesses. He told the
sub-Committee, that he felt 'There is a conflict between performance and
safety.'[44] He went on to say that the fundamental question for the investigators in the Hatfield crash was to understand why a speed restrictions
had not been imposed and whether the decision had been influenced by
concerns about performance:

> I think we do have to understand whether or not there is not an issue at the
> front line in the maintenance contractors and within Railtrack . . . we do
> need to understand better on the front line what the impact of the drive for
> performance is . . . I think it harder to balance the safety/performance equa-
> tion if you have a set of external pressures on you that are focusing on one
> particular bit of it.[45]

Corbett pointed later to the sheer random nature of the regime: 'To
take, say, £20m costs out of the system is quite hard work, but to make it
out of the performance regime is relatively easier. But it is haphazard,
though, largely dependent on the weather.'[46] So the whole highly clever
regulatory regime is dependent on how much it rains and snows. Railtrack estimated that without Hatfield the flooding of the autumn of 2000
would, in any case, have cost the company £150–200m. This was against
the background of constant pressure from the regulator. According to
'Insider' the anonymous rail executive who writes a column in *Rail* magazine, Railtrack had been set an impossible task: 'Where the Regulator got
it 100 per cent wrong, was an insistence that overall costs were reduced
while network use was growing . . . The cut in permanent way staff is at
the heart of what went wrong [at Hatfield] and this was caused by the
cost reduction targets the regulator had said must be achieved.'[47]

Tom Winsor, the regulator, disagreed, which was hardly surprising
given that it was his performance regime that Corbett felt was at the root

of the potential conflict between safety and performance. Winsor argued that the two went hand in hand and that a punctual railway was a safe railway. While this is undoubtedly true, Winsor, with a mindset based on legal contracts and regulation, may have missed the wider point made by people like Roche and Corbett – that an emphasis on performance had infected the culture of the railways and its staff.

Not surprisingly, given his increasingly outspoken comments suggesting that the railways needed a completely new structure, Corbett also fell foul of his fellow directors. He had already offered to resign in the immediate aftermath of the Hatfield crash but after a late night board meeting, the directors asked him to continue. However, a month later and just a few days after he had made the remarks quoted above to the Transport sub-Committee, the non-executive directors (one of whom was Jenny Page, whose recent experience included running the Millennium Dome and being on the board of the ill-fated Equitable Life), organised a coup by persuading the ineffective and weak chairman, Sir Philip Beck, to sack Corbett. The finance director, Steven Marshall, also a man with little experience of the rail industry having joined Railtrack only a year previously from GrandMet (now Diageo), replaced him.

Corbett's departure, which his friends at the company say was also supported by Jonson Cox, just made things worse for Railtrack. Corbett was one of the railway's few class acts and, after a bad start, he had earned respect within the railways for standing up for the industry in the aftermath of Ladbroke Grove. On Corbett's departure Cox, the rookie director, was promoted to chief operating officer, leaving Britain's railways in the hands of two forty-three year olds with barely a year's railway experience between them. The appointment of another non-railway man, John Robinson, whose previous job had been as chairman of Smith & Nephew, a medical devices company, as chairman from July 2001 after a long search for candidates with more relevant experience, further added to the sense in the City, government and the rest of the industry that the company had lost its way, but Robinson made a good start by sacking Cox and publicly accepting responsibility for the Hatfield crash at the company's AGM. It was hardly surprising that in the months after Hatfield the City lost so much confidence in the company that its share price fell well below the original privatisation price of £3.90.

When Railtrack was first created there was a deliberate policy of having a minimal core with most of the work contracted out. Hatfield was payback time for that mistake and the company immediately set about transforming itself by strengthening its engineering function. In November, following Corbett's sacking, Richard Middleton, the sole engineer on the board, was made technical director after having been commercial director. But even this move was carried out with some reluctance. Initially, Marshall had originally suggested that Middleton reported to Cox, but Middleton baulked and threatened to walk out, leaving the new board even more bereft of railway savvy. In addition, another engineer, Andrew McNaughton, was appointed chief engineer – though not given a place on the board – in order, according to the Railtrack press release, to 'ensure that engineering is given proper priority by the company'. Despite this promise, even after the accident, only two of Railtrack's seven executive directors had extensive rail experience – Middleton and Chris Leah, the safety and environment director.

It is clear that Railtrack and the industry will change radically as a result of Hatfield. It has been virtually bankrupted by the accident and its aftermath, and it is not an exaggeration to say that the accident completely wrecked the Tories' model of privatisation by highlighting its fundamental flaws. As we saw in chapter 1, Hatfield and the following six months brought the company to its knees. Indeed, despite massive injections of government cash, Railtrack will never be the same again. Hatfield buried Railtrack's gung-ho 'maximise profits for the shareholder' approach, which had already been changing under Corbett, once and for all – at the cost, however, of four lives.

CHAPTER 10

The price of privatisation: a dysfunctional railway

Privatisation and fragmentation has created a dysfunctional railway. The underlying problem with rail privatisation is that it was not carried out for the benefit of the railway or its users. It was undertaken for ideological and financial reasons with little consideration of the outcome for rail passengers, particularly in the long term. Such a radical experiment, the restructuring of a long-established industry in a completely unprecedented way, inevitably led to many unintended consequences, most of them undesirable.

Of course there have been some benefits from privatisation and these, along with all the negative consequences, are assessed in this chapter. But before getting into the nitty-gritty of this analysis, it is worth considering a wider point about the whole way that the railways now operate. Instead of an integrated operation run through a hierarchical structure, the essential *modus operandi* is one of competition and relationships governed by contract.

THE CULTURE OF RAILWAY

Possibly the most important but least tangible change brought about by privatisation is the transformation of the culture of the rail industry, the way people within it work together. This cultural change underpins many of the damaging consequences of privatisation outlined in this chapter. As with every privatisation, there are far fewer people working in the industry, particularly on the track. According to evidence given to the Cullen inquiry on Ladbroke Grove by Professor Christopher Baldry, head of the department of management and organisation at Stirling University, the railway workforce had fallen from 159,000 in 1992/3 to

92,000 in 1996/7. The rate of decline is exaggerated because the newer figure only includes main contractors and not sub-contractors, but these statistics are a clear indication of the trend. According to evidence provided by the RMT union to the Commons Transport sub-Committee,[1] the number of permanently employed maintenance workers had fallen from '31,000 in 1994 to between 15,000 and 19,000' by the end of 2000. Chris Leah, Railtrack's safety director, told the House of Commons Transport sub-Committee that of the 18,000 staff working for the British Rail Infrastructure Companies at privatisation, there were now about 12,000 left, though, because some tasks were being done by other staff, the real decrease was around 3,500.[2] Professor Baldry describes this process as 'work intensification', a smaller number of people coping with a larger volume of traffic in the network. As he told the inquiry, the view of the contractors was that 'The only way we can survive is by reducing our costs in line with Railtrack's reducing their contract prices so more and more mechanisation, and fewer and fewer people, is the name of the game.'[3]

Secondly, the whole culture of the way that the railways were run was changed by contracting out the work. There were no longer railwaymen who knew every bit of their patch of track and saw themselves as part of the industry, but a new generation of railway navvies, touring round Britain with their sometimes faked PTS (Personal Track Safety) cards from job to job. The RMT research found that there were 84,000 people, working for more than 2,000 companies, who were qualified to work on the track. These casual workers felt no allegiance to the railway or, indeed, their colleagues from other firms. This most cooperative of industries, traditionally operated on military lines because of the need for safety, routine and integration, was now maintained by a ragbag of individuals, some excellent, some hopeless, but few with any real understanding of their role in keeping the trains running.

Professor Baldry, who spoke to many track workers for research carried out for the trades union, described to the Cullen inquiry how the culture of trust and cooperation turned into one of deliberately stimulated antagonism:

> We were given on several occasions evidence that if track workers from Scotland had been sent down to York, for example, to work on a bit of track that was unfamiliar to them, they find themselves working with other employees

from a different contractor. Their instinct is to ask the local people about the nature of the track. The local people may have been told by their employer 'Don't talk to these persons because they are employed by the opposition.' In other words, there are actual obstacles put in the way of this pooling of both site knowledge and hazards knowledge.[4]

A seminar held as part of the Cullen inquiry highlighted this change in culture:

> Privatisation has created a big cultural change. There is now little inter-linking of culture from one company to another. There has been a loss of comradeship between drivers, signalmen, cleaners etc. There is no longer a sense of working together. Questions of delays and attribution of blame strengthen the divide. This has led to a lack of confidence in others. No one is encouraged to discuss someone else's problem, or volunteers, or shares information. There has been a loss of learning and this leads to poor communication.[5]

There is a safety consequence of this: the railway is dependent on the sharing of information about dangers and risks.

A track worker, 'Bert', described the casualisation of the railway labour force to the union paper, *RMT News*[6] in 1998. Although he had worked for the railways for forty years, he was now entirely casual. Once a job is finished, he has to move on: '[The private companies] expect you to travel round the company like nomads.' Companies like Balfour Beatty that had taken over the contracts had closed workshops and sacked apprentices, he added.

Professor Baldry highlighted this aspect of the way that the rail community had been broken up, telling the Cullen inquiry:

> But, more worryingly, it used to be the case that signallers would probably know the personnel that were appearing in the stretch of track under their jurisdiction and when track maintenance was done on a more geographical basis. Now they have people requesting possession of track and they have no real idea of what their competence is or what their track awareness is or what their knowledge of the track layout is.[7]

Professor Baldry added that staff trying to enforce safety regulations sometimes faced hostility: 'It has been reported to us that safety representatives can be threatened with physical violence if this is way out in a remote rural situation.'[8]

Given the number of firms working on the railway, it is also remarkably easy for newcomers to obtain a job on the railways and find themselves in a safety-critical position. A couple of months after the Hatfield crash, a colour-blind *Mirror* reporter, David Pilditch, took a two-day training course to obtain his PTS certificate and was offered a shift on the East Coast Main Line in Nottinghamshire. His colour-blindness, a safety critical problem, was never discovered. Because he arrived early, he was given the job of site access manager, checking the safety qualifications of the rest of the gang of 200 workers and giving a safety briefing prepared by his boss, even though he had never worked on the railways before.[9] At least he gave the safety briefing. Testimony to the Cullen inquiry seminar showed that 'In other companies, safety briefings had been discarded.'[10]

Managers have, obviously, been most affected by the new culture. The Cullen inquiry seminar reported that: 'There has been a fairly widespread loss of confidence [by junior staff] in local and middle management. . . . Local managers appear to be more concerned with budgetary requirements, and new management structures appear to have been created to cope with performance and financial penalties.'[11] Amazingly, staff are sometimes banned from talking to their colleagues in other companies on the same site and, instead, have to go through an off-site manager.

THE SAFETY OF THE RAILWAY

While the evidence of the last three chapters suggests strongly that rail privatisation has made the railways less safe, not all the statistics support this thesis. In particular, analysis of minor incidents demonstrates a falling rate. The key indicator is 'significant train incidents per million train miles', which includes a vast array of incidents ranging from major train collisions to broken windscreens on a locomotive. This has been in steady decline for a long time. The HMRI statistics[12] show a rate of 1.01 in 1975, falling to 0.42 by 1990, and after a small rise pre-privatisation, to 0.26 in 1999/2000.

Other evidence, such as broken rails and signals passed at danger, suggest a more mixed picture. The causes of the increase in broken rails were analysed in the previous chapter. The trend in SPADs was not so clear cut but had been a matter of concern to HMRI. Between 1995 and 1998 there had been a steady reduction in the number of SPADs and the total was 596 in 1997/8 compared with 771 in 1994/5, Railtrack's first year of separate existence. However, HMRI statistics[13] show that in the first half of 1998 the number had started to grow and it remained largely stable until the middle of 1999. Then the greater awareness by drivers and the action taken by the railway industry following the Ladbroke Grove disaster led to a reduction. Worryingly, however, even after the disaster the number of *serious* SPADs,[14] remained stubbornly level at just over 200 per year, with the majority of the reduction in the overall total being accounted for by very short technical overruns, which are mostly caused by wheel slippage or minor misjudgements by the driver.

So what can explain this apparent paradox – a series of major accidents caused by the failings of privatisation and yet a reduction in the number of minor incidents which, superficially, creates the impression of a safer railway? First, there is a widespread suspicion within the industry that the level of reporting of incidents has gone down. Given the fragmented and competitive nature of the railways, there is little incentive for workers to report incidents, especially as staff do not have the same public sector ethos they were imbued with at BR. Although this was a problem with BR, it is likely to have worsened. According to the Ladbroke Grove inquiry seminar, 'Staff are frightened of reporting slight incidents of a non-serious nature, as they get pulled in by their supervisor, asked to fill out a form and sometimes get disciplined. There is also the reluctance to "shop" a colleague.'[15]

Secondly, the reduction in minor incidents – some of which have serious consequences, such as people on platforms being hit by slam doors that are opened while the train is still moving – is part of a long-term trend that stretches back almost as far as the creation of the railways. The trend line therefore merely confirms that the railways have continued their long-term improvement in safety that was underway under BR. This is hardly surprising. Improved technology, a much more conservative approach to safety following the 1988 Clapham disaster, the scrapping of most slam door trains, the replacement of level crossings with bridges or tunnels, and the fitting of central locking devices on InterCity trains[16] all contributed towards a safer environment. Incidents involving track workers also went down, as they were now all provided with such basic safety aids as fluorescent jackets and better-organised lookouts. There were also fewer of them, as we have seen, therefore reducing the overall exposure to danger. It would, in fact, be very shocking if this extremely long-term trend towards a reduction in minor incidents had been completely reversed by privatisation.

The argument that the railways have become safer under privatisation does not, therefore, hold water. A reduction in a few minor incidents is no compensation for the major accidents that have been caused by the fragmentation and privatisation. The evidence of the last three chapters is clear. In each case the way the industry was broken up contributed to the accident. At Southall, the key factors include the botched reorganisation of the maintenance depot, the lack of clarity about reporting faults to 'control' and the complete lack of interest in implementing the Automatic Train Protection pilot programme; at Ladbroke Grove the main issues were Railtrack's failure to address the SPAD problem (a point reinforced by the comments made above from the inquiry seminar about the difficulties of coordinating the different players in the industry) and driver training; and at Hatfield, the main elements were the very structure of Railtrack, which meant it was far too weak on engineering, and the way it was forced to contract out maintenance through very badly drafted contracts.

As a former Railtrack manager, who is still working in the industry and therefore must remain anonymous, put it,

> Safety will always be more difficult to manage in the fragmented railway than under BR. It has to be controlled through cumbersome safety cases and group standards that are always open to interpretation whether they concern maintenance or driver training. Moreover, Railtrack does not have the authority to use its powers to enforce the standards it is supposed to check.[17]

There is an even more worrying aspect of the damage done to the railways by these accidents and the role of privatisation in them: their effect on public perception. There will always be some rail crashes, particularly on a crowded network like Britain's, which is one of the most intensively used in the world. The accident at Great Heck in February 2001 demonstrated this universal truth – who could ever have predicted that a Land Rover slipping off a main road would result in Britain's fastest ever rail collision and cause ten deaths? Under British Rail this was broadly accepted. There were occasional accidents, invariably caused by human error or technical failure, which were the subject of an inquiry, held within weeks without the presence of any lawyers, that made recommendations to ensure the same type of errors were not repeated. Now, however, public tolerance of major accidents has been greatly reduced. Part of this was happening before privatisation. Lawyers first became involved in a major way at the 1989 Clapham inquiry and all subsequent major investigations. Media coverage of railway accidents has always been extensive but the advent of satellite television with news channels that give blanket 24-hour coverage and tabloid newspapers with a sensationalist approach have heightened public interest. The fact that most major accidents have happened around London within easy reach of TV studios has been a further factor in the disproportionately extensive coverage of railway accidents, a phenomenon that can be described as catastrophe pornography.

And then add in privatisation. One of the first questions that reporters will always ask is whether there has been a conflict between profit and safety.[18] The answer is, of course, that there is always a trade-off between the two, as some safety measures are clearly not worth paying for in terms of the number of lives it is estimated they might save. The process called cost-benefit analysis (which was mentioned in chapter 7) aims to evaluate safety projects by dividing the cost of an improvement by the number of lives the change is expected to save. The government's guideline figure is around £1.15m per life saved (or, in the jargon, Value per Prevented Fatality, VPF). In other words, if a scheme costs more than this, it is not implemented and vice-versa. On the railways this is increased by a factor of 2.8 for investment that would prevent multiple fatality incidents, giving a VPF of something like £3.2m. In contrast, because so little money is available for safety schemes on the highways, according to Professor Andrew Evans of the Transport Studies Unit at University College, an expert on the statistics of railway safety, the equivalent figure for accident prevention measures on the roads is around £100,000. In other words, over thirty times more is spent per life saved on the railways than on the roads, which, incidentally, kill 3,500 people per year. Equivalent sums spent on road safety,[19] or indeed kidney machines or even other types of railway safety schemes,[20] would save many more lives.

And it gets worse. Because the industry is being run privately and the public is suspicious of the motives of the rail companies, this traditional cost-benefit approach is about to be thrown away, wrecking the finances of the railways and absorbing incredible amounts of public money for schemes of very marginal value. This was clearly set out in a press statement that accompanied the publication of the report in March 2001 by Professor Uff and Lord Cullen on train protection systems. The report recommends the installation of the European Train Control System that will prevent trains from going through red lights by the year 2010. While the aim is laudable, the installation of the cheaper Train Protection and Warning System due to be completed by the end of 2003 will prevent something like 70 per cent of accidents caused by signals passed at danger (SPADs) and will reduce the speed of impact for the others. Therefore, using the report's figures, ETCS is predicted to save two or three lives per year[21] at a cost of some £2–3bn – which, assuming a life of thirty years for the system, means something like a £30m VPF.

In a remarkable passage in the press statement, which demonstrates both the failure of privatisation and the way that it has distorted railway economics, the two authors effectively argue that spending on rail safety should not be tested against any normal criteria of value for money:

> At the time of privatisation, it was foreseen that the railway industry would itself promote and fund major safety improvements through the regulation system. It is now accepted that the bulk of the cost of the next generation of train protection systems will be met by public funding. Accordingly, the need to justify expenditure on the basis of cost benefit analysis has largely been overtaken by decisions made by government, in conjunction with the Health and Safety Commission. *We have not, therefore, been concerned with establishing the economic justification of the new train protection systems,* but rather with ensuring that the relevant issues have been addressed with adequate transparency and that, where alternative courses are open, the one which is in the wider public interest should be adopted.[22] (my italics)

In other words, bugger the cost, the taxpayer is coughing up and so it does not matter. Railtrack's chief executive, Gerald Corbett, had, in fact, said in the aftermath of the Ladbroke Grove accident that the company was willing to pay for an ATP-type system, but only provided it was given enough funding by the government.

What is more bizarre is that the public interest is considered by these two not-so-wise men to be represented by the accident victims. In a passage in the joint inquiry report they say, 'The interests of the public are represented most closely by HMRI and the Regulatory bodies, and in this Joint Inquiry, *by the Passengers' Group*'[23] (my italics). This is quite simply nonsense. The Passengers' Group (formed by survivors and relatives of the victims of the accidents) is, by definition, a very narrow interest representing a small number of people who have had a particularly awful experience of the railway. This does not make their views more valid in representing the public interest than, say, the Rail Passengers' Council, the Department of Local Government, Transport and the Regions, the House of Commons Transport sub-Committee or the Health and Safety Executive. Survivors and relatives are clearly always going to be demanding a totally safe railway, something that is an economic and practical nonsense. Indeed, this approach is, as Professor Evans put it, 'Alice in Wonderland'[24] economics which, at some time, will return to haunt ministers because decisions about railway investment will be completely distorted towards safety measures. He points out that the careful cost-benefit analysis approach used for many years 'has not been produced by out-of-this-world economists, but are our best estimate of the preferences of the public, who actually pay for and benefit from the safety measures'.[25] Moreover, since the taxpayer is footing the bill, the industry has little reason to resist this process foisted upon it and, indeed, as Evans points out, 'Quite a lot to gain, notably a reduced risk of the adverse publicity that surrounds high-profile accidents.'

Professor Evans reckoned that a generous estimate of the benefits of the ETCS system would be £100m in terms of lives saved (at £3m per life), which meant that some £1,900m, assuming the cheaper level of construction cost (£2bn) is achieved, would be wasted.[26] He argued that the whole project of renewing the railways was being put at risk by this emphasis on expensive and unnecessary safety features:

> Once in a generation, the purse strings [of the Treasury] have been loosened and the industry has been offered serious investment funding. One such occasion was the 1955 Modernisation Plan, another was the 1998 Transport White Paper, and the subsequent ten-year plan . . . Apart from the non-availability of £2,000m for something more beneficial, the most serious cost could be that the industry and its associated public bodies get the reputation of not being able to make sensible decisions with public money.[27]

Another example of the way that politically-driven safety decisions distorted investment patterns in the industry was the investment of several million pounds (the exact amount is, as yet, unknown) on fitting cup and cones, a device to minimise damage in crashes to old Mark 1 trains which have a very strong chassis and a weak superstructure. At the Cowden and Clapham accidents this design had caused extra casualties as the chassis of one vehicle smashed into the seating of another, and the Health and Safety Executive had got very exercised about this. It decided to require the train operators still running these old trains to fit a cup and cone system designed to stop the chassis from riding up into the body of other coaches in the event of a collision. However, the old carriages were due to be scrapped anyway,[28] as John Prescott had announced that they should be phased out by the end of 2004. This left a small hiatus of two years during which some Mark 1 stock would still be running and the HSE decided to require these trains to be fitted with the cup and cone device. In fact, the chance of one of the remaining couple of hundred Mark 1 trains being involved in a major accident with another Mark 1, the only time the device would come into play before they were eventually scrapped two years later, was miniscule. There is no doubt that, in terms of allocation of resources, the money would much better have been spent on virtually anything else on the railway. Again, the structure of the railways meant that there was no Fat Controller to lobby the politicians about such distorted priorities. The SRA should have stood up to such excesses but failed to do so, constrained by its position as a creature of government.

The post-Ladbroke Grove changes involving the separation of Railtrack's Safety and Standards Directorate into a separate subsidiary, Railway Safety, may make it even more difficult for railway managers to make rational decisions about safety. It outsources both Railtrack's costs and risks and means that there is no one to make a rational decision between them. If safety is a product supplied free by someone else, then it is bound to be over-ordered. The disaster scene statements put out by politicians like John Prescott at Ladbroke Grove about no penny being scrimped in order to ensure absolute safety are pure political guff. There is always a trade-off between cost and safety and rightly so. Because of the spate of accidents and the changes within the industry, the balance has swung far too far towards the latter. While this is partly a consequence of the fragmentation of the industry, it is also part of a wider societal move towards risk-aversion prompted by the compensation culture and disproportionate media interest in accidents.

Rail is the safest form of transport. Indeed, the commonly used statistics even tend to understate the relative safety of the railway because of the way they are compiled.[29] The public's mistrust of rail safety is completely irrational but the railways' unique selling point on safety has been put at risk by privatisation. Yet, because of the lack of public trust in a privatised environment, the industry is going to be saddled with enormous costs for safety improvements whose benefit will be, at best, marginal. The worst aspect of all this is that, as the aftermath of Hatfield showed, we now have a paranoid railway in which decisions over safety are likely to be so conservative that performance and capacity will be diminished in the pursuit of illusory safety objectives. The slightest potential risk will lead to train cancellations or delays, further reducing the attractiveness of the safest form of transport in relation to other methods of travel. While this process had started before privatisation, the fragmentation of the industry together with the recent disasters has hastened it. Indeed, the railways may well find it very difficult to return to pre-Hatfield levels of performance because of this risk-aversion. We may, therefore, end up with a railway that statistically looks safer but causes more risk to society as a whole because fewer people use it and choose, instead, more dangerous forms of travel.

THE PERFORMANCE OF THE RAILWAY

What about all the other promises made during the privatisation process? Adrian Shooter, the managing director of Chiltern Railways, a well-respected railwayman with twenty-six years of BR experience behind him, argues that privatisation resulted in a number of improvements to the way the railways were run. In a list provided to me, he cites a dozen 'positives since privatisation'. Several of these are nebulous or marginal but in sum they amount to: passenger growth; good services from several operators; more investment; new stations and car parks and upgraded stations; better measurement of outputs, in particular the passenger's charter; and better information through the National Rail Enquiry Service, improved platform technology and the internet. There is, too, the advantage of some financial stability as franchise payments are guaranteed for the term of the contract, ranging from seven to, now, possibly twenty years. Shooter sums it up by saying that it is easier to 'make a real difference and deliver change and investment now that we are in the private sector'.

Certainly, the growth figure has been impressive. Between 1996 and 2000 there was a 30 per cent increase in usage, a growth rate of about 5 per cent per year. Much of this was centred around the London commuter market, but the former InterCity companies have also been successful in attracting extra passengers. Most analysts[30] argue that much of this growth, particularly in the London commuter market, is simply a result of the buoyant economy. Three other factors have played a role. First, the continuing rise in road congestion and the rise in fuel costs – both as a result of tax rises and, later, as the world price of oil went up – has pushed more people onto the railways. Secondly, the price controls on certain types of tickets – the rise in seasons and savers was to be capped at the rate of inflation (RPI) for three years and one per cent below for the following four years – introduced as part of privatisation, along with some excellent marketing initiatives to sell off-peak tickets very cheaply, have undoubtedly attracted passengers on to the railways. Thirdly, improved access to ticket purchase through the internet and telephone sales and better information through the National Rail Enquiry Service and Railtrack's website has made it easier to get on to the railway. The trainline.com, for example, reckons that between a third and a half of its ticket purchasers would not have used the railway without its service.[31] Other possible reasons for the growth include better revenue protection, as barriers were installed in several busy, previously open, stations, and, ironically, the massive publicity given to the industry by the controversy over privatisation.

Despite all these theories, the extent of growth was somewhat inexplicable and it was certainly unexpected. The train operators had mostly bid for the franchises on the basis of a modest amount of growth over seven years – for example, GNER had planned for 18 per cent over that period when, in fact, passenger numbers increased by 21 per cent in three years – and while the extra income was vital in keeping these companies profitable, the pressure of all these extra passengers on the network made it much more difficult for the operators and Railtrack to run a punctual service.

Hatfield, of course, completely disrupted this growth, although the London commuter companies, with their captive markets, had regained virtually all their passengers within three months, but the losses sustained by the long-distance operators had not been fully regained by the spring of 2001, despite a crop of marketing initiatives.

Leaving aside the Hatfield mayhem, it is questionable how much of the growth was down to privatisation. The marketing initiatives were impressive but BR, too, had become quite innovative, introducing the supersaver and running promotions with Kellogg's, Boots and Lever Bros, for example, and having one of the best ad campaigns of the early 1990s, the endearing 'relax' InterCity campaign. Moreover, while some price-capping has helped attract passengers, the conventional wisdom that ticket price rises have been below the rate of inflation is questioned by the country's foremost expert on fares and timetables, Barry Doe. He says, 'Overall fares rises have most certainly not been below inflation.'[32] He has calculated that savers went up by 14 per cent in the first five years of privatisation, compared with inflation of 15 per cent. Doe points out that some other fares have gone up well beyond the rate of inflation. For example, on InterCity lines supersavers, 'where they have not been abolished, have risen between 20 and 30 per cent (between 1996 and January 2001) but open returns have fared worst of all – Anglia and GNER are up 20 per cent, First Great Western and Midland Mainline 30 per cent and Virgin 70 per cent.' Virgin, in particular, tried to exploit captive business markets with a series of increases on heavily used routes which have pushed fares up to levels comparable with those of competing airlines. The open return from London to Manchester was raised a further £14 in May 2001 because of the post-Hatfield losses, bringing it to £164 compared with £96 five years earlier under BR – a rise of 71 per cent compared with inflation of 15 per cent. On the other hand, there are some very good deals on offer at off-peak times if booked in advance, such as £13 return fares from London to Liverpool or Manchester.

In other words, the argument that privatisation has kept fares down is only partly true. BR had long been forced to raise fares above the rate of inflation, partly to pay for investment but mostly in order to price off demand.[33] Certainly, had BR survived, that policy would have continued and therefore prices are below what they would have been without privatisation, but they are still going up above the rate of inflation and remain the highest in Europe.[34]

The other unequivocal claim for privatisation, stressed by its supporters, is the increase in investment, with the highlight being the new trains for Virgin's two franchises, West Coast and CrossCountry. However, here, too, the result is by no means an unequivocal success (see chapter 11 for a full analysis of investment under privatisation).

Shooter is right to argue that privatisation has delivered some innovations and it is easier in the private sector to make a difference. His Chiltern line was the first to order new rolling stock post-privatisation and it also entered into a partnership with Railtrack to reinstate double track for a section of line, thereby increasing capacity. There have been other examples, such as new services – Rugby–Gatwick, London–Hull and Chelmsford–Basingstoke – and new stations such as Warwick Parkway (but actually reopenings and the number of new stations decreased because of the complexity of the structure of the railway – see chapter 11).

The National Rail Enquiry Service replaced the shambolic localised BR system and has become Britain's most used telephone number with over 81m calls in the year to the end of March 2001 (of which 72m were answered). Its success is one case where clear and tight regulation paid off. At first the service could not cope with demand and did not meet the standard set by the regulator, John Swift, who imposed fines of £350,000 on train operators because the target of answering 90 per cent of calls was not being achieved. Subsequently, operators increased capacity and the target has mostly been met or, where it has not, the companies were let off the hook because the volume of calls exceeded the regulator's stipulation.

Shooter is right to say that it can be easier to get things done quickly in the privatised railway, but only provided that not too many players are involved and that there is a financial case. When Railtrack was approached by a cycling campaign to provide more stands for cycle parking, its head of major stations replied that

> Railtrack is remitted by the Rail Regulator to increase commercial income for industry benefit. Every £1 of income received at major stations contributes towards reducing track access charges to train operating companies and thus provides long-term benefits to the rail industry. Therefore cycle facilities will not be placed in areas better used for other customer facilities which provide a better economic return.[35]

Quite apart from the fact that this statement is not strictly accurate, as three-quarters of Railtrack income from property is not regulated and therefore can simply go to shareholders, it is a small example which neatly illustrates the incompatibility of having a profit-maximising firm at the heart of an industry that has major social responsibilities.

The introduction of the passenger's charter, which provides figures to allow passengers to judge the punctuality and reliability of the railways, together with the performance regime which gives companies a financial incentive to reduce delays and cancellations, is another undoubted benefit of the new structure. The figures[36] show that in the first full year of privatisation, 1997/8, punctuality improved from 89.5 per cent in BR's final full year, 1995/6, to 92.5 per cent. However, as ever, the figures do not tell the entire truth. Companies were able to declare 'void days' when disruption was so bad that they were not included in these figures. Virgin declared around forty-five void days per year, which severely distorted the figure.[37]

Much of this was down to Railtrack rather than the operators. According to the company, there were 2.8m minutes delay attributable to Railtrack in 1997/8 compared with 6.8m two years previously, a reduction of 58 per cent. It would be churlish to suggest that this did not represent progress. However, the reality was not as good as the figures might indicate. Booz Allen Hamilton, appointed by the regulator to assess Railtrack's performance, reported that part of the improvement in the figures was a result of better fault attribution procedures by Railtrack, as three-quarters of unattributed faults were assumed to be Railtrack's responsibility.[38] The more faults for which Railtrack managed to identify a culprit, the fewer ended up with the company. Therefore it is not surprising that Booz Allen Hamilton found that the overall passenger's charter statistics suggested that industry performance in 1995/6 was worse than before privatisation, in 1993/4.[39] Indeed, the overall number of delay minutes in the industry as a whole remained the same over the subsequent two years, 1997/8 and 1998/9. And, of course, delays soared to record levels after Hatfield and remained high even nine months later.

Nevertheless, despite such caveats, the performance of the railway, and in particular that of Railtrack, immediately after privatisation was a good achievement given the upheavals in the industry. It remains a source of some mystery to this day, even to many industry insiders who talk about it with awe. One senior manager put it down mostly to the weather: 'We had relatively mild weather and the train operators had not got round to sacking anyone yet.'[40] Indeed, this confirms the view expressed by Gerald Corbett in the previous chapter that weather is a key determinant of payments under the performance regime, which, to a great extent, is a wager on meteorological conditions.

A junior controller with a London commuter operator gave a revealing explanation for the brief period of improvement, explaining that the old culture of the railway survived for a couple of years after privatisation:

THE PRICE OF PRIVATISATION

> At first, we all worked together under the old rules, just as if we were all with the same company. We knew that there were these contracts but we ignored them. Then as more new people came in to the industry and started applying the letter of the contracts, things deteriorated and services suffered as a result.[41]

The increase in the number of trains was partly responsible for the downturn in performance. The extra services which resulted from the sweating of assets created problems for Railtrack, especially as it did not receive extra income because of what has been called 'the financial architecture of the railway' (see chapter 5). Railtrack calculated that for every extra 1 per cent of services, delays went up by 2.5 per cent as the network filled up. The company complained that it had no incentive to invest in providing for these extra trains, but as one sharp commentator put it, 'As the company has gained a reputation for under-investing in its assets, there is no guarantee that it would have spent more if its revenue increased.'[42] The excuse that these additional services caused much of the downturn in performance was not, however, universally accepted. According to the consultants Booz Allen Hamilton, who studied performance on individual routes, those which experienced the greatest rise in traffic were not necessarily the ones where delays increased. As Booz Allen Hamilton put it, 'There seems to be limited correlation between improved performance and traffic growth or density, suggesting that other differences such as in management (both internally and of contractors) may be responsible.'[43]

While a few train operators have developed a reputation for good customer care, most have barely matched BR's standards. Indeed, one of the most amazing failings of privatisation has been that the oft-repeated promises that the private sector would treat its customers much better than BR have been largely unfulfilled. In an assessment of customer service after privatisation, Roger Ford, the highly regarded rail journalist, attempted to set out all the 'soft' improvements to service to passengers.[44] It proved to be a short list and, indeed, some of the customer-friendly innovations made by BR had been scrapped:

> When InterCity introduced the claret-jacketed customer-help teams, they chose personable, outgoing younger men and women who would watch for passengers looking lost and ask if help was needed. Post privatisation, Virgin got rid both of 'help' staff and the information booth on the ramp to the platform. GNER staffed the platform with 'old railway' 'blokes' who stood around in pairs

waiting to be approached. Not only that, they were dressed in dark suits, which is an excellent way of blending into the forecourt at a mainline station.

Ford's trawl for improvements became desperate and he had to include a new on-train magazine for Anglia first-class passengers, travelling cleaners on Cardiff–Manchester trains and better provision for cyclists on Scotrail; and finally, after really thorough research, he discovered that First Great Western now had a 'safer and more robust vestibule litter bin in each coach'. The only really worthwhile commitment was First North Western's promise to staff all stations from fifteen minutes before the first train to fifteen minutes after the last one had left. Ford attributes the paucity of initiatives on customer care to the fact that most of the franchisees are bus companies who have, traditionally, paid little regard to the needs of their customers.

As people's expectations, raised by the promises made during the privatisation process, had not been met, the number of complaints soared, reaching the million mark for the first time in 1998/9, over half of which were about lateness or cancellations. The inability of the private companies to provide good customer care may have been unexpected, but is not really surprising. The way that the franchises were structured meant that cost-cutting had to be the first imperative to make up for the rapidly declining rate of subsidy. Therefore the number of staff employed by the twenty-five operators fell from 43,000 in March 1996 to 38,100 two years later, but rose slightly to 39,300 by March 2000,[45] as operators realised the importance of staff in providing a good service and in collecting revenue. The operators, most of whom were bus companies, had not realised the difference between the two industries, notably the contrasting markets for which they catered. Despite that slight improvement, it was amazing that the majority of the privatised companies were so little interested in collecting revenue that many trains were left unstaffed and few stations had barriers installed. Revenue loss was still reckoned to be 2–3 per cent across the network as a whole, with much higher rates on some suburban flows.

Not all these staff are doing anything useful. All train operators have large cohorts of people checking on the fault attribution system to ensure that they minimise the penalty payments they have to make to Railtrack. A manager in one of the larger operators[46] said he had thirty people employed solely in this activity, and the *Financial Times*, in an attempt to count what it called this 'army of arguers', suggested that on a very con-servative basis there were at least 300 staff engaged in this Kafkaesque activity.[47] As the rail manager put it, 'Fault attribution has become an industry in its own right.' Centrally, the number of people employed in the rail bureaucracy has risen sharply since the start of privatisation, recreating a kind of virtual BR HQ. The rail regulator now has a comple-ment of 125 and the Strategic Rail Authority nearly 400.

Even the much vaunted encouragement of innovation from privatisa-tion cannot be taken as a given. The Ladbroke Grove seminar reported, 'A key problem is the large number of different organisations that often had to be contacted in order to effect a solution. It is more difficult, therefore, to be pro-active. Communications take longer and are less effective.'[48] Again, this has safety implications, as shown in chapter 8 with the role that the complexity of the industry played in the failure to tackle the repeated SPADs in the Paddington throat prior to the disaster.

The list of positives from privatisation is therefore a thin one, particu-larly when set against the cost of the upheaval that some estimates put as high as £600m,[49] let alone the chaos following Hatfield. Moreover, many of the perceived advantages of privatisation have a downside. For exam-ple, the idea of stimulating competition by having twenty-five operators is superficially attractive because of the hope that it will lead to lower fares. However, the introduction of an ethos of competition rather than cooperation has led to a greater reluctance for connecting trains to be held when they are operated by a different firm. Why should company A hold up its trains, causing a deterioration in its passenger charter figures and possibly even a financial loss under the performance regime, just to help a few customers of company B? While trains are occasionally held despite this, there is undoubtedly far less cooperation on this matter than there used to be under BR.

Other perceived benefits of privatisation were probably going to happen anyway. As we have seen, BR in its last days was enjoying some-thing of a golden age thanks to a mix of good leadership and the right emphasis on commercial considerations. Better information systems and improved telephone booking may well have been introduced. There had long been a programme of station reopenings and, in fact, they slowed down after privatisation from an average of fourteen per year to eight.[50]

It is doubtful, however, that there would have been quite as many additional services and, as mentioned above, there would have been higher fare rises in order to squeeze out what was perceived as excess demand. Another benefit is the creation of a regulator to give greater public accountability, something that was sadly lacking in BR's day. There is, too, plenty of extra money coming in for investment, but even that is not unequivocally positive, as the analysis in the next chapter shows. But the price for these gains has been extremely high and that it is why the final chapter suggests that reintegration is the key to recreating a coherent and functional railway.

A BANKRUPT RAILWAY

Privatisation was supposed to liberate the railways from dependence on government finance and Treasury meddling, and, as a corollary, reduce the amounts of taxpayers' money going into the industry. To say that it has failed on both counts is an understatement. Passenger numbers had, pre-Hatfield, almost reached an all-time high and yet the railways are in a state of near-bankruptcy.

Privatisation was a costly exercise. The total cost, including the amounts paid out by bidders and other purchasers, is reckoned to be at least £1bn.[51] For the taxpayer the cost was £600m which merely includes the obvious spending such as fees for consultants and lawyers, redundancies and administration and makes no estimate of secondary effects on such things as train performance, safety and efficiency.

Privatisation came at a time when the rail industry had already been squeezed of resources for a long time and the need to make economies in order to make parts of the industry profitable meant that there was intense pressure on what was, contrary to conventional wisdom, an already lean industry. As 'Insider' in *Rail* magazine put it,[52] under privatisation, 'year on year, we have sought to win more mileage from less rolling stock, more paths from less infrastructure and more passengers with a lower ratio of staff. . . . The availability of resources has been cut to the point where there are no more belts and braces available when rail operations are disrupted.' It was hardly surprising that this sweating of assets resulted in a financial crisis which had already shown signs of emerging before the Hatfield accident.

In order to smooth the passage of privatisation and ensure that there were sufficient numbers of bidders, the amount of subsidy was nearly doubled from £1.1bn to £2.16bn when Railtrack was hived off at the

beginning of the 1994/5 financial year. The precise figures for the period
1994/6 are difficult to determine because the government disguised the
real costs of privatisation by throwing in the capital receipts from asset
sales and because, at first, the extra subsidy merely went to create quasi-
profits for Railtrack, the train operators and the rolling stock companies,
which, since they were all still state-owned, were simply returned to the
Exchequer. However, when the franchises and Railtrack went into the
private sector the subsidy remained at nearly £2bn, much higher than BR
had ever received. The plan was that the subsidy would then decline,
slowly at first, but rather faster in the middle and later years of the franchises, the majority of which ended in 2003/4.

Yet, the doubling of the headline figure for subsidy was not quite as
generous as it looked. As a study[53] by the Railway Forum showed, the
proceeds from sales reduced the headline figure by some £300m per year
and tax paid by the railway companies amounted to another £100 annually. The Forum concluded that subsidy had really risen 25 per cent,
rather than doubled. While there are a lot of complicating factors, too
detailed to go into here, the Forum's basic argument was that far from
benefiting from a Treasury bonanza, the railways hardly did better than
when they were state-owned. And since the subsidy was planned to go
down in subsequent years, the railways were not being treated as well as
the headline figures suggested. After all, cutting subsidy had been one of
the Treasury's principal aims, so it always seemed unlikely that privatisation was going to be generously funded. In fact, the Treasury merely
made sure that the path to privatisation was smoothed with a bit of extra
money that then quickly declined.

Labour, hidebound by its promise of keeping to Tory spending plans,
failed to understand that privatisation had not even provided much extra
funding to the railways and rashly allowed the cuts in subsidy to proceed,
reducing support for the railways from £1.85bn to £1.2bn (in real terms)
in the four years from 1997/8. The subsidy decline looked good on paper
for the bean counters, but in practice it was unsustainable. Inevitably,
some train operators got into financial difficulties as the declining subsidy levels proved unworkable for those who had made over-optimistic
bids.

The train companies had been fortunate in that the railways were
enjoying an unprecedented boom, thanks largely to the buoyant
economy, but those who ran a lot of lightly loaded trains in rural areas

lost money. They had been caught up in the bidding war at the end of the franchising process in late 1996 and early 1997 when suddenly the City, which had initially been wary of rail privatisation, was keen to get in on the act. It was a minor railway bubble that was to prove costly, not so much to the companies themselves as to the taxpayer. For franchisees covering these areas, fares from passengers represent only a small proportion of their income, most of which is made up of subsidy from the government and the Passenger Transport Executives in the major conurbations such as West Yorkshire, Greater Manchester and Merseyside. These franchisees had gambled on the notion that they could reduce costs dramatically, but once in control they discovered that BR had been run more efficiently than expected. In desperation they tried the obvious tactics of cutting back on station staff and even drivers, but to no avail. One, First North Western, even got into trouble with the Office of Passenger Rail Franchising for having cut back too many staff.

MTL, which ran the Merseyrail and Regional Railways North East (Northern Spirit) franchises, had to be bailed out in February 2000 with their franchises being handed over to yet another bus operator, Arriva. The rescue, of course, came at a price, and Arriva received £208m in subsidy for the year 2001/2 to run Northern Spirit, £55m more than MTL had been slated to receive. The extra subsidy did not ensure a good service. Arriva found itself with a shortage of drivers in the summer of 2001 and had to cut 100 daily services from its schedule. Similarly, Prism, which had won four franchises, was forced to allow them to be taken over by National Express Group because of sharp losses on their two rural lines, Wales & West and Cardiff Valleys. FirstGroup would have also handed in its Regional Railways North West franchise (First North Western), which was losing money, had it not been for the fact that it also ran two highly profitable ones, Great Western and Great Eastern which the company would also have been forced to give up. Eventually, when the Strategic Rail Authority started redrawing the franchise map, FirstGroup managed to buy its way out of most of its losses for £37m.

As TAS, a business monitoring organisation that researches railway company finances, pointed out, 'It is clear that some bidders in the first round took too much risk and, as a result, heavy losses are being incurred.'[54] But it is the taxpayer who has largely had to make up for the shortfall. The railway cannot be allowed to stop and therefore these regional franchises have been bailed out. According to TAS, extra subsidy paid to Arriva and NEG for rescuing these franchises will amount to '£650m by 2003/4 – just to secure existing levels of service'.[55]

This demonstrates a harsh truth for the Labour government. The train companies had taken a one-way bet. Some were highly profitable, like Stagecoach which ran the South West Trains franchise that made a pre-tax profit of £40m in 1999/2000, and there was no mechanism to reclaim the money, while others that got into trouble had to be rescued, even though theoretically there was no extra money available. In other words, the fat cats got fatter while the thin ones had to be fed at taxpayers' expense. No wonder John Prescott seethed in private and harrumphed loudly in public whenever the train companies were mentioned.

TAS found that all but nine of the twenty-five train operators had declining profits or increasing losses in the financial year 1999/2000, the year before the Hatfield crash, showing that the railway system was already in a parlous financial state before that disaster. Moreover, seven companies were making a loss, principally those working with poorly-loaded trains and highly dependent on the (declining) subsidy. In addition, Anglia and Virgin Cross Country were also loss-making, the latter because it had been dogged by performance problems as its whole fleet was reaching the end of its useful life and was due to be replaced in 2002/3.

On top of this already parlous state of affairs came the Hatfield disaster and its aftermath, which sent the economics of the railway into free fall. The former InterCity operators were hit worst by the speed restrictions which crippled the railway and sent swathes of passengers back on to the roads. They had achieved a 16.5 per cent increase in revenue in the four weeks prior to the Hatfield disaster compared with 1999, but suddenly they found themselves losing a large proportion of their customers. In the month after the disaster, revenue went down by 37.5 per cent,[56] which, given that the operators had expected the growth to continue, meant that expected income had reduced by over a half. Stagecoach, which owns half of Virgin Trains, reported that instead of an expected £15m surplus from its rail operations for that year, it had now budgeted for a £25m loss. And the internet selling operation thetrainline.com, owned jointly by Virgin and Stagecoach, had also lost £10m.

Commuter networks did not fare so badly, broadly retaining the same number of passengers who are, mostly, a captive market. There was no shortage of anecdotal reports on the radio and TV of people simply giving up their jobs rather than face the nightmare of commuting by train; but since the economy was still booming, the South East train operators were largely protected from the effects of the Hatfield aftermath. The regional operators lost vast numbers of passengers, but since their principal form of income is subsidy, this did not have such a large effect on their overall economic performance. Indeed, they may well have profited out of the affair because of the compensation arrangements, yet another unintended consequence of the privatised structure.

The compensation issue again highlighted the anomalies and weaknesses of the privatised structure, with some companies receiving nothing like the amount they had lost and others getting more. As a result of its contractual obligations to train operators, Railtrack was having to fork out vast sums of money – estimated at £400m – to compensate the train operators who, in turn, had to reimburse many users for part or all of their ticket price. For example, Silverlink, one of the worst affected companies, announced on 22 March[57] that its season ticket holders were entitled to seventy-one days of free travel and refunds because of post-Hatfield disruption. Other commuter networks which managed to get through with fewer cancellations actually did quite well because the compensation they received from Railtrack for delays and cancellations exceeded their payments to passengers. Their poor commuters, with no alternative way of getting to work, had to keep suffering the delays caused by the crawling trains.

Railtrack's payments to the train operators are assessed on a different basis to the compensation paid by operators to their passengers, and therefore some operators made a net profit. This was particularly true of the sparsely used regional operators, many of whom received far more in compensation payments from Railtrack than they paid out to passengers. Other companies, particularly the former InterCity operators, lost out heavily because Railtrack's compensation payments were restricted,[58] and Virgin even prepared to sue Railtrack for loss of revenue,[59] but in the event the threat of legal action was bought off with an extra £15m.

Overall, in monetary terms the operators lost £63m revenue (7 per cent) in the final three months of 2000 compared with the previous year, a financial disaster for businesses which were already in a precarious position because of the long-term loss of subsidy and which had expected, instead, a *growth* in income of around £140m.[60]

Railtrack, too, started off relatively well under privatisation, which was hardly surprising given that its agenda was initially purely a profit-maximising one. As we saw in chapter 5, for a while it was a City darling whose share price reached over four times the value at flotation by the end of 1998. It seemed that the company could do no wrong. Profits rose to over £400m per year in 1997/8 and seemed set to stay there, with dividends rising a little every year. There was some embarrassment, however, when a few days after the Ladbroke Grove disaster, the company announced record profits for the first six months of the 1999/2000 financial year of £236m and, by the time the full year figures were announced, an 'exceptional item' of £61m due to a technical revision of future renewals expenditure, explained very opaquely in the annual accounts,[61] had been found and ensured that the full year pre-tax profits fell to £360m.

During all this time, Railtrack was involved in a lengthy and at times very acrimonious public dispute with the regulator, Tom Winsor. Railtrack's income is largely made up of access charges paid by the train operators, and their level is set by the regulator in five-yearly reviews. The first of these 'control periods' was scheduled to run out at the end of March 2001 and there were intense negotiations between the regulator and Railtrack over the charges to be set for the second control period, 2001–6. Winsor's temporary predecessor, Chris Bolt, angered by Railtrack's failure to invest sufficiently (see next chapter), had suggested that Railtrack should be treated as a boring utility, implying that access charges should be cut.

Gerald Corbett, Railtrack's chief executive, cannily realised that Railtrack's best chance of boosting its profits was to ensure that the company had a good outcome to the regulatory review. Railtrack could not expand in the way of conventional companies because it could not create extra train paths where they were needed and, moreover, even if it could, it would not receive much extra money for them. Therefore he set up a regulation department at Railtrack which employed twenty-five people to do battle with Winsor. As a Railtrack insider put it, 'Railtrack realised that the best way to make money was not so much to cut costs but to win the regulatory argument and to convince everyone that the railway needed to grow and Railtrack needed to be set up to grow. Boosting revenue by pushing for a better deal from the regulator became one of our main focuses.'[62] This demonstrates again how trying to create a 'free market' situation in an industry like the railways merely leads to perverse incentives and unintended consequences. Railtrack's PR machine went into action arguing that Railtrack needed a strong balance sheet and very healthy profits in order to raise the capital to pay for new investment in the railway. And the strategy worked a treat.

Chris Bolt had announced in December 1998 that he felt Railtrack's rate of return was too high for the risks it undertook and suggested that the company should earn a rate of return of 5–6 per cent on what is known as its Regulatory Asset Base, the estimated value of its assets and the amount on which the company can expect to earn a return. This, incidentally, is a ridiculously arbitrary figure bearing no relation to any calculation of the actual value of the railway, such as the cost of its construction minus depreciation, or the possible income it could generate. Such estimates were impossible to make and instead a way had to be worked out to ascribe a value to the asset base that could generate sufficient income for Railtrack to pay for its renewal and maintenance. Bolt suggested that it should be the value of the company at the end of the first day's trading after flotation, which would have put its worth at £2.54bn. Railtrack had wanted the relevant date to be 1 May 1997, the day of the general election which resulted in Labour's victory, and as shares had risen to £6.52 by then, this implied a Regulatory Asset Base of £4bn. Railtrack's rather convoluted argument was that since Labour's opposition to privatisation had reduced its share price in the aftermath of the flotation, the election day was a fairer estimate of the company's worth. Bolt brushed this argument aside but Railtrack persevered, increasing its required figure to £6.86bn.

For the next two years there was a permanent state of war between the regulator and the company. Winsor, who took over from Bolt in the summer of 1999, seemed to be following an even more aggressive line than his predecessor towards Railtrack, and there were regular acrimonious exchanges between Winsor and Corbett in the press over the regulatory review, the West Coast Main Line, train delays, broken rails and other issues. But a preliminary announcement by Winsor at the end of 1999 suggested he was taking a more lenient view than Bolt on how much to allow Railtrack to charge for access. And so it proved. By the time he announced the final terms of the review a week after the Hatfield crash, Railtrack had got pretty much what it wanted. Railtrack was able to earn not just the 5–6 per cent envisaged by Bolt, or even the 7–7.5 per cent suggested in

Winsor's own interim statement, but a generous 8 per cent. The suggested asset base was increased to an equally bountiful £5.5bn, over double Bolt's initial suggestion. Moreover, the company was only made to assume annual efficiency savings of 3.1 per cent per year, right at the bottom of the 3 to 5 per cent range. Taken together, Railtrack's revenue in the first year of its second control period went up a staggering 35 per cent, and 5 per cent per year in real terms for the next four years. Christmas had come early. And all this extra money was to be paid by taxpayers, not the train operators who, in any case, were subsidised already. On every criterion, Winsor had made life easier for Railtrack. Bolt's tough line had been abandoned. Railtrack executives were so delighted that they withdrew previous threats to challenge whatever Winsor came up with and accepted the new terms. As one put it, 'We got a billion a year more out of the Exchequer and no other regulated industry had done anything like that.'[63]

The City, too, was surprised by Winsor's generosity. An analyst from Commerzbank[64] commented, 'This is breathtakingly generous. A complete capitulation by the Regulator. With every revision, it has got easier and easier for the company. Railtrack is having its cake, eating it, and having more served up with cream on top by Winsor.'

In fact, Winsor had been faced with an terrible dilemma that merely demonstrated the impossibility of trying to run a complex commercial business like the railways through regulation. He is under a duty 'not to make it unduly difficult' for Railtrack to finance its activities. If he were seen to cave in to Corbett's aggression by giving Railtrack large amounts of extra money, largely from the taxpayer, he would be accused of being a poodle. On the other hand, if he squeezed Railtrack, as Bolt had implied he would, then the company would claim it was his fault that there was insufficient money to deliver the investment plans which the railway desperately needed. The weapons Winsor had were also not as powerful as might first appear. His biggest stick is the ability to take away Railtrack's licence to run the railway, but this would stop the trains dead in their tracks – it is, effectively, an unworkable nuclear option. He does have powers to fine the company but this, too, is double-edged, because Railtrack can claim that he is merely taking away funds that would otherwise be used for investment.

It was hardly surprising, therefore, that Winsor erred on the side of giving Railtrack the money the company claimed it needed for investment. But it was to no avail. Within weeks of his decision, as the effects of

the Hatfield disaster emerged, it was clear that Railtrack would never be
in a position to make that investment because Hatfield and its aftermath
completely wrecked the finances of the company and meant the City
would never again have faith in what had previously been a favourite
among investment fund managers. All Winsor's lengthy and careful calculations during the review had come to nought. The events in the aftermath of Hatfield demonstrated the unfairness of the economic structure
of the railways. While the train operators were protected by compensation payments, Railtrack was left fully exposed to risks, which, in turn,
had to be paid for by taxpayers.

Railtrack was brought to its knees by the Hatfield crisis. At first it was
relatively gung-ho about its ability to cope with the financial consequences. Having first estimated the cost of the crisis at £200m and then
£400m, the company announced on 15 January that the total cost was
expected to be £600m. Of that, two-thirds was to go to the train operators as compensation for the delays caused by Railtrack's inability to run
the network, and £180m was for rerailing around 450 miles of track
affected by gauge corner cracking. The remaining £20m was for the
damage caused by flooding that was not covered by insurance. Railtrack
said that this exceptional charge would be made on its 2000/1 accounts
and 'would be entirely borne by Railtrack's shareholders'.

Inevitably, this was a conservative estimate and the line about shareholders footing the bill was pure bunkum. The figure kept on rising and
its executives quickly accepted privately that the eventual bill would be at
least £1bn. By Easter 2001 there were estimates that it would even reach
£1.5bn and reports that Railtrack would eventually be taken over by a
construction group.[65] As the *Daily Telegraph* city editor commented,
'Just think of all those shareholders losing their shirts. Except they
won't. . . . If Railtrack were ruined, does anyone think the train service
would be any better? The very idea helps explain why the shares fell only
25 to 968p yesterday.'[66] Instead, Railtrack went cap in hand to the government seeking a bail out, demonstrating that it was not the shareholders who would take the hit, but the poor old taxpayer. Railtrack wanted
£1.5bn of subsidy for investment that had been due to be paid from
2006, as part of the regulator's next control period, to be advanced early
in order to ensure its survival. It warned that without such help, its debts
would rise fourfold to £8bn within two years, threatening its ability to
borrow money to keep the rail network going. Already, ambitious plans

for enhancements – improvements in capacity – had been put on ice. Steven Marshall, Railtrack's chief executive, told a conference at the end of January that the events since Hatfield meant there was no money to invest: 'The end result of recent problems is that Railtrack is in no position to commit to any new enhancement.'[67]

Since the Labour government eschewed more radical options, such as taking Railtrack back into public ownership or transforming the company into a non-profit making trust, there was little option but to give in to Railtrack's demands. As part of a clearing the decks exercise in the run-up to the general election announcement, the government gave Railtrack its £1.5bn early in return for the company agreeing not to pay any 'exceptional or special dividends to shareholders over the next five years' and limiting dividend growth to that of earnings. The company also agreed to appoint a non-executive director, after consultation with the government, who would represent the public interest.[68] Advancing the money early to Railtrack cost the taxpayer around £300m and, in addition, the company was also to be reimbursed for being forced to cut freight charges by 50 per cent, a concession worth around £80m per year.

The City, which had been amazingly sanguine and slow to catch on to Railtrack's parlous position because there had always been the expectation that the government would bail out the company, suddenly realised that it had been backing a pup. The City hates the prospect of government interference and investors began to pull the plug once they realised the implications of the dividend controls and the appointment of the so-called government director. Moreover, Railtrack also gave up much of its enhancement role, which was now to be undertaken by specially created companies, and therefore it could no longer be considered to be a growth stock. After the announcement on 2 April, Railtrack shares plummeted, at one time hitting 430p, barely above the 390p at which the company had been floated five years previously. Then, in early June, after an analyst estimated that Railtrack's shares were worth only 58p, the price collapsed completely, falling to 300p and seemed set to remain under the flotation price of 390p because of the abandonment of the growth agenda. It was a humiliation for the company and many commentators perceived it as the beginning of the end of Railtrack as an independent private entity. Even conservative City commentators like Anthony Hilton in the *Evening Standard* suggested that Railtrack should be taken back into public ownership:

The effect of the [share price] slide is to lay bare the reality that the company cannot finance its needs on its own or raise sufficient new capital in the City. . . . Things are reaching the point where the quickest and least painful solution might be renationalisation and the company could then be run formally on a not-for-profit basis and financed by bonds.[69]

The bail-out highlighted the bizarre – and seemingly unworkable – financial and administrative structure of the rail industry. The regulator, Tom Winsor, was busy handing out government money to rescue a near-bankrupt private company which would have to be paid out of the budget of another organisation, the Strategic Rail Authority. Moreover, within a couple of months Railtrack came back for more, another £2bn. Winsor rejected this arguing that it was time for Railtrack 'to put away the begging bowl, and stop spending valuable management time hawking themselves unwanted round Whitehall and knuckle down to getting train services back to a sustainable level of reliability and quality.'[70]

The collapse of Railtrack also put into question the whole basis for the much-vaunted ten-year plan for the railways that the government announced in the summer of 2000 (discussed in the next chapter). The money was supposed to fund a massive investment programme but Railtrack's mistakes over Hatfield meant that the company needs all this cash merely to stay afloat. Insiders in the SRA were furious that the funds had been handed over to Railtrack without any proper controls, and they felt that the company had simply become a bottomless pit, absorbing all the extra resources the government had set aside for the development of the rail network.

CHAPTER 11

The pot of gold:
will we get a better railway?

The one Big Promise of rail privatisation was that it would herald a new age of investment that would transform the railways into a mode of transport fit for the twenty-first century. The key argument of the supporters of privatisation was that government, faced with the competing demands of basic services such as health and education, would never provide enough for transport and, in particular, for the railways. The private sector, on the other hand, would be eager investors in this newly opened up industry.

It was a juicy prospect. I remember an old BR press officer, transferred in both body and soul to Railtrack, trying to convince me, just after privatisation, that Railtrack's ten-year £10bn investment plan was an unprecedented bonanza which would never have happened under the straitjacket of British Rail. In fact, a billion per year was pretty modest by historic standards and grossly inadequate for anything other than patching up the railway. Under pressure, the old lag agreed that it was not that much money, but it was great because, 'The Treasury would never have allowed us to plan in advance in that way.'

That was true. The traditional short-termism of the Treasury had been one of British Rail's undoings. However, as we shall see in this chapter, much of Railtrack's investment programme comes straight out of the government's coffers and yet, because it is supposedly being spent by a private company, the usual short time-frame of the government has been extended. As Bob Horton, Railtrack's first chairman, put it,[1]

I realise that Railtrack gets a high proportion of its income from the Treasury but it would have been unable to get that money if it had not been privatised. Privatisation means that you can sign up to long-term contracts rather than

being subject to annualised Treasury accounting. Privatisation has broken
the Treasury logjam, forcing the Treasury to guarantee long-term funding.

This is wonderfully convoluted logic: the railway was privatised because
it was not getting enough public money and it can now get that money
because it is in the private sector, even though the taxpayer is still footing
the bill.

One of the cornerstones of the argument for privatising the railways
was that BR suffered from gross under-investment. In fact, BR had an
active investment programme, which, though always insufficient – 'twas
ever thus – was comparable with the level of the early years of privatisation and, indeed, would have exceeded it had the money spent on the
sell-off been diverted into railway hardware. For example, the BR Rail
Plan for 1989,[2] which covered schemes for the following five years listed
thirty-three infrastructure projects for Network SouthEast, InterCity and
Regional Railways which had already been authorised, worth nearly
£1.1bn. Approval for another sixty, costing £650m had been sought.
These covered only infrastructure and the plans for rolling stock were
even more impressive. Over those five years, BR planned to buy 2,267
coaches but, of course, these plans may not have all received Treasury
approval and, in the event, they were disrupted by the preparations for
privatisation which resulted in a near three-year hiatus in rolling stock
orders from 1994 to 1996. Sure, there never was enough money and the
trauma of the 1950s Modernisation Programme still dominated the Treasury's view of the railway, but, as we shall see, nor is there enough money
under privatisation. The key flaw in the old structure was the Treasury's
obsession with controlling the requirement for cash, which makes no
sense in a long-term business like the railways that is so dependent on
the performance of the economy. So when BR started doing badly in the
recession that began in 1989, because its income dropped and property
sales dried up while the investment rate could not be slowed immediately, the cash requirement shot up, allowing the Treasury to argue that
the whole organisation was incompetent and needed privatising. As an
old BR sweat put it, 'The fact that costs were being controlled quite effectively counted for naught.'[3]

Of the main categories of investment – track and signalling, rolling
stock and stations – Railtrack initially made much play of the last. The
company promised to spend a billion pounds on stations in its first five

years and it publicised its station regeneration programme widely in the media, with little panels showing how many had been improved. Much of the work, though, was cosmetic and not done to a good standard. Moreover, stations were easy; improving them did not involve stopping the trains – and the improvements are immediately and obviously visible to the public. Stations were a relatively painless way to invest in the railway and, while some money went on a coat of paint at those on minor rural lines, the bulk of the spending was on big projects at major stations where redevelopment offered, as the jargon put it, 'new rental opportunities'.

The emphasis on station regeneration was a mistake. It was a distortion of Railtrack's spending which reinforced public criticism that it was a property company rather than a transport infrastructure operator, a perception Railtrack was quite happy to foster, particularly in the City. Moreover, it concentrated resources on a facet of the railway that was most irrelevant to travellers. Of course, having a shiny station with a warm waiting room is pleasant and should be a fundamental part of the service, but really passengers want the trains to be running frequently, quickly and on time above any other considerations. And that requires lots of spending on behind-the-scenes schemes like track renewal and, in particular, signalling; such matters have much less public relations appeal and therefore Railtrack paid little attention to them.

It was rolling stock that absorbed the bulk of the early investment, and for good reason. The fact that there had been a three-year hiatus which needed to be made up meant there was a backlog and, furthermore, it was a part of the industry that the private sector, with long experience of leasing, could easily understand. The first order for trains came soon after privatisation when Chiltern signed up for what eventually became thirty vehicles for £25m. Other orders quickly followed in what proved to be a bonanza for the manufacturers. There was the backlog created by the hiatus to clear and some franchises had been granted for more than the standard seven years on the basis that new trains would be obtained. John Prideaux, the first chairman of Angel Trains, one of the three privatised rolling stock companies, reckons that coaches were ordered in the first three years of privatisation at nearly double the rate of BR's purchases in its last days.[4] By the time of writing, summer 2001, there had been £3,500m worth of orders for new rolling stock in the first five years of privatisation, representing a total of 3,683 vehicles.

Nevertheless, rolling stock would have been the easiest type of investment to obtain from the private sector, and off the government's balance sheet, without going through the wholesale sell-off of British Rail. Trains are a clear, discrete product that can easily be leased, as is commonplace with many other forms of transport, ranging from company cars to Boeing 747s. It is a simple matter to work out a rate of return and to show a clear investment case for the suppliers. In opposition John Prescott had even suggested that railway coaches could be leased from private companies. Indeed, London Underground, while remaining in the public sector, leased its new trains for the Northern Line from the manufacturers, Alstom, under a private finance initiative deal which meant that the company was responsible for ensuring that sufficient trains were available for every scheduled service.

The claims that rolling stock orders have increased as a result of privatisation are therefore somewhat spurious, especially as there had been the hiatus in orders because of the privatisation process. The increase, moreover, was not as remarkable as the figures suggest. An analysis[5] by Roger Ford of *Modern Railways* suggests that, in the four-year period before the hiatus, BR was ordering around thirty vehicles per month and that included an order for £150m worth of vehicles announced by transport minister Roger Freeman as a bribe just before the 1992 election. The rate of purchase went up to around forty-nine per month in the period from March 1997 to May 2001. However, if the three-year gap is added into that period, the rate is around the same before and after privatisation, which demonstrates privatisation has not seen a step change in the rate of investment in rolling stock but is merely making up for the backlog.

There was also a major hiccup with all this new rolling stock. Despite the plethora of orders, the trains took a long time to be put into service and literally hundreds of fully built trains were stuck in sidings for several months and even, in some cases, years. Most of the delays were caused by the failure of the manufacturers to get their new designs through Railtrack's extremely onerous safety case procedures. Railtrack's principal fear was electrical interference. There was evidence from the introduction of the cross-Channel Eurostar trains that rogue electrical currents emanating from them could affect the track circuits that indicate to signallers the location of a train. The main fear was that such currents could cause a red signal to go green, as had happened (because of a wiring error) in the 1988 Clapham disaster. Railtrack's lack of knowledge about its assets added to the problem, as it did not know what types of track circuits were operating on different parts of the network.

A second problem was that, as trains tend nowadays to be used widely across the system rather than on just one line, the new designs had to be built to specifications which would allow them to go everywhere on the network. When manufacturers approached Railtrack to ask about the maximum possible specifications of their trains, not only was the company unable to provide that information, but it even asked for money to find out the precise size of its own tunnels and platforms. The use of slightly smaller trains has not gone unnoticed by passengers who complain of the lack of room. Moreover, with space at such a premium, facilities for extra luggage and, in particular, bicycles, have disappeared.

Railtrack has no incentive to let the new trains onto the track, so it pursued a policy of 'prove your train is safe', which is virtually impossible. As a result, new trains sat in sidings or in factory yards while the manufacturers scrabbled about trying to pass the safety case procedure. Here again, much of the problem had its roots in the way the industry had been structured after privatisation. Although, clearly, the issue of electro-magnetic interference had to be considered, there was an element of over-reaction on the part of Railtrack, which had taken over the setting of standards upon the demise of BR. During this process, the tolerances were raised in the belief that there should be a gradual rise in safety standards. However, as one rail engineer put it,

> This can lead to ridiculous situations. For example, if the railway has been built to ensure there is a 30mm gap between platforms and trains, then there is nothing to be gained by increasing that to 50mm. Yet that is what happened with electrical interference. They raised the tolerances even though there has never been an accident caused by this type of electrical interference.

In fact, even if there was interference, this was intermittent, with signals returning to red very quickly.

Nevertheless, this tiny perceived risk was to lead to massive delays, sometimes of up to two years, for the introduction of the new rolling stock. For example, Connex South Eastern was supposed to start introducing new trains by April 1999 but did not manage to do so until two years later. The London, Tilbury and Southend services out of Fenchurch Street were being operated by thirty-five year old trains well into 2001 while the whole new fleet, which should have been introduced in 1999, was standing idle. The manufacturers were not totally blameless in this process. They should have taken more care to ensure that the safety case procedures had been addressed and, moreover, many of their new trains, such as those for Fenchurch Street and the 175s for First North Western were so unreliable that operators had to send entire fleets back for design changes.

There was, however, a deep irony about these delays. The trains that were to be replaced were far more dangerous than the new ones that were sitting in the sidings. Not only were they much less crashworthy, as was demonstrated in accidents like the Cowden head-on collision where five died in 1994 and the Cannon Street buffer crash which killed two in 1991, where older stock was involved, but they actually emitted much higher levels of electrical interference than the new trains. They were only allowed to remain in use because of 'grandfather rights', the dispensation given to older trains without which the whole railway system would have ground to a halt.

This was another case where the needs of the railway and its passengers were not considered in a coherent way, nor was risk assessed sensibly. It could again be described as the 'absence of a Fat Controller' syndrome. An integrated and inter-dependent system like the railways needs to have clear leadership from the top to resolve the differing interests of the various components that make up the network. In the days of BR this was provided by the chairman who, backed by the board, was able to make decisions that might have impacted adversely on some departments but, overall, would benefit the travelling public. In this instance, the chairman would have been able to assess the relevant risks and insist that the new trains should be introduced, taking the responsibility onto himself. The fragmented structure of the railway means that no one can now take such decisions; this inevitably leads to a far more cautious approach, whatever the objective assessment of the risks involved. The privatisation has led to a warped sense of priorities on safety. There is an obsession with certain trivial risks, while other more serious matters are being allowed to slip.

Railtrack's record for investment in stations and the infrastructure seems, on the face of it, impressive in comparison with the past but, as is inevitably the case with these big numbers, closer examination reveals a more mixed picture. The original plan of £10bn in ten years jumped successively as the Network Management Statement (NMS) – the company's annual document setting out its plans to maintain and improve the network – was published each spring. The sum went up from £10bn in 1997, to £17bn, £27bn and £52bn in subsequent years. The initial statements were thin affairs – 'a disgrace', according to John Swift, the first rail regulator. There was no detail and no ambition, with statements like 'A number of third parties . . . have made proposals for new stations.'[6] To further confuse the issue, each annual statement differed completely in format from its predecessor, making it very difficult to see precisely what Railtrack had achieved in the past year and how its aspirations and commitments were changing.

However, as the statements got thicker, the proportion of firm commitments to be paid for by Railtrack got smaller and the NMS was largely perceived as a wish list, with funding to be provided by government, rather than a clear set of commitments by Railtrack. For example, the 1998 NMS identified fifteen bottlenecks but at the time of writing, the summer of 2001, action has been taken to tackle only two of them – Leeds station, the only project to be finished, and the massive, unfinished West Coast Main Line (see below). The others, such as the East Coast Main Line and Coventry–Birmingham and London–Brighton, remain on the drawing board (or merely on a sketchpad somewhere in the Black Tower) with no firm date for committing any money. By the time the massive *NMS 2000/1* was published in the spring of 2000, listing £52bn worth of investment on the railways, Railtrack had become quite open about the fact that the funding would have to come from elsewhere. It had become apparent that the NMS merely set out aspirations for the railway that were increasingly dependent on government subsidy for their realisation. In any case, as we saw in the previous chapter, the aftermath of Hatfield led to a moratorium by Railtrack on starting work on any enhancements to the network.

Railtrack's performance comfortably exceeded the very modest targets that had been set by the first regulator, John Swift. In the complex system of finances in the privatised network, the regulator sets out what should be Railtrack's level of investment in the five-year control period (explained in the previous chapter). The regulator does this by setting the access charges and making assumptions about Railtrack's other income (e.g. freight and property sales and rentals) and its efficiency savings. He then makes an assumption about what Railtrack will be able to spend on investment. The big problem was that Railtrack was not set any output targets when it was privatised, only expenditure targets. Spending money is easy and Railtrack became good at it, but the effectiveness of that expenditure left a lot to be desired.

A major flaw in this system was that the regulator had no powers to make Railtrack invest. The thinness of the Network Management Statements was no accident. Railtrack did not want to invest in the railway – it wanted to maximise profits. As one of the managers from those early days put it,

> We perceived our job was to manage Railtrack's assets in such a way that we maximised the profit. As harsh as that. That's what all the bosses at the time – Bob Horton [the first chairman], John Edmonds [the chief executive], Norman Broadhurst [the finance director] – thought. Looking back, it was mad.[7]

Swift quickly realised that his calculations for the first control period – 1996–2001 – had been too generous towards Railtrack. Moreover, as he put it, Railtrack had 'got greedy', by concentrating on its share price rather than on improving and expanding the network: 'Its investment programme was still largely determined by renewal rather than enhancement.'[8] In other words, the company was not trying to make improvements to the rail system because of fears that it would not receive a proper rate of return.[9] Profits were being put before improvements.

Swift responded by imposing a new licence condition on the company, requiring Railtrack to ensure that it maintained, renewed and enhanced the network in a 'timely, economic and efficient manner'. Since this was the whole *raison d'etre* of the company, it seems incredible that this had not been written into its licence conditions at the outset. The reason for the omission, however, is obvious. To have imposed such obligations on Railtrack would have made the company less saleable. Swift was rather regretful about forcing through the change, having hoped that Railtrack would have behaved more responsibly anyway. Fat chance. The narrow-mindedness of its early directors ensured that Swift was forced into making the change. As he put it, 'Train operators told me that Railtrack was simply not responding to their plans for investment. They were getting fed up because Railtrack was only interested in its shareholders.'[10] Swift added that had Railtrack behaved differently to its customers and developed innovative schemes in conjunction with the operators and the government, then the new condition would not have been necessary. In the event, Swift also used the new condition to impose requirements on Railtrack to improve its performance in terms of delays, and this eventually led to Railtrack being fined £10m by his successor, Tom Winsor.

On paper Railtrack's investment performance looked good. Swift had calculated that the company should have been able to spend some £4bn on renewals in 1996/2001 and in the event Railtrack exceeded that target by £1.5bn. It was able to borrow money for this because of its high profits and share price. The overall headline figures on investment were also impressive. Railtrack invested over £2.5bn in 2000/1, compared with just £740m in 1995/6, the last year before privatisation. That does not include maintenance, which fell slightly in that period from £730m to £676m.

Of the £2.5bn spent in 2000/1, £500m was for the Channel Tunnel Rail Link, which is separate from the rest of the rail network. The rest was split between £700m of enhancements – principally the West Coast Main Line project – and renewals, £1.35bn.

However, the public perception of the railways was that they were not steadily improving. Quite the reverse. While, overall, the industry's figures did get somewhat better in the immediate aftermath of privatisation, this improvement had disappeared by the time of the Hatfield accident. Indeed, by then the performance was rapidly deteriorating, as witnessed by the terrible passenger's charter figures for the period immediately before Hatfield, which showed 'a clear downturn in performance on a network suffering from real capacity and reliability problems'.[11] Yet, as the investment figures quoted above show, there is no doubting that Railtrack was actually pouring more money into the system.

The answer to this paradox is that Railtrack was not getting value for money because of the convoluted way the railway had been broken up. Put simply, Railtrack had to spend a lot more than BR just to get the same result. Railtrack's increased spending on renewals was partly a result of rising and uncontrolled costs. As we have seen, Railtrack was not only forced to contract out maintenance and renewals, but to separate out the two in a way that had never been done on the railway before. This not only increased safety risks, but sent the cost of the work soaring. The maintenance contracts were fixed-price and what is called 'closed book' – in other words, they were for a fixed amount of money no matter

how much work was actually carried out and Railtrack had no right to
question how much money was being spent and what it was being used
for. Railtrack, therefore, had no clear idea of what the costs were or how
much profit the contractor was making. And there was no clear basis on
which to make decisions on whether to improve maintenance on a piece
of track or replace it. Indeed, as we saw in chapter 9, there was an underlying incentive for the maintenance contractor to pass on jobs to
renewals because the maintenance company received no more cash for
doing more work, while the renewals contractor did. This not only led to
delays, but also prevented Railtrack from having any control over its
spending. As a frustrated Railtrack insider put it,

> You cannot manage maintenance and renewal as separate things. The main-
> tenance contractors would do as little as possible because they were driven by
> profit. You have to manage the whole-life costs. The renewals in the first five
> years will, by definition, have been spent badly because we had no idea of the
> economics of maintenance.[12]

The concept of a fixed-price contract for maintenance work was disastrous, especially as there were good profits at the beginning of the mostly
five-year contracts, but these tailed off towards the end, putting even
more pressure on cost-cutting. However, the fixed-price concept had
been essential to ensure that the companies could be privatised. If they
had had an open-ended duty to maintain sections of the railway, it would
not have been possible to privatise them. The breakneck speed at which
the government set about privatising meant that these companies were
sold without a track record and therefore no one knew how profitable the
contracts would be.

A further difficulty facing Railtrack in spending its money efficiently
was that, as we saw earlier, it does not have a register listing its assets and
their condition. This might seem like a mere oversight on the part of the
company but, in fact, the reason was yet another demonstration of the
cynicism of those who planned and implemented the privatisation. Had
an asset register – normally an absolutely basic requirement of any sale –
been drawn up before privatisation, it would never have been possible to
sell Railtrack. The register would have been such a damning assessment
of the company's liabilities and the terrible state of Britain's under-
invested railways that it would have been impossible to prepare an
attractive prospectus.

Another reason for the failure of Railtrack's spending to make the expected impact on the network was that it became geared to the performance regime rather than the needs of passengers. Railtrack did jolly well financially, receiving £250m from the performance regime in the first three years, half of which was passed on to contractors; and Booz Allen Hamilton, the consultants, found that Railtrack renewed 50 per cent more rail than expected, but 20 per cent less ballast and fewer sleepers. 'It is possible that this reallocation of the renewals budget between track assets has been driven by a desire to maximise financial benefits under the performance regime.'[13] This, as the consultants pointed out, was because rail replacement shows an immediate improvement in performance while ballast and sleepers have more impact over the long term.

The consultants also found that, despite the extra money going into the system, 'Overall it appears that the physical programmes have, in aggregate, been below those which were envisaged . . . It is likely that there has been a decline in the underlying quality of the network assets as a whole.'[14] Moreover, much money simply went to managers and bureaucracy, which perhaps explains the lack of effectiveness of all this extra spending: 'Project management overheads have proved to be very high, *physical works representing less than 50 per cent of project expenditure* within the station backlog programme'[15] (my italics). No wonder passengers did not notice any improvement.

If Railtrack's money did not seem to be going very far in terms of its maintenance and renewals, the situation was even worse on its largest project, the refurbishment of the West Coast Main Line.

WEST COAST ROUTE MODERNISATION

Investment in major projects has been one of the surprise failures of rail privatisation. The private sector has been a reluctant investor in the railways, apart from rolling stock, but even where money has been available, it has been impossible to spend it in a coherent and cost-effective way. Even optimists about privatisation such as George Muir, director general of the Association of Train Operating Companies, admit that 'Investment in large scale projects has proved difficult under the privatised structure of the industry.'[16] One Railtrack insider was more blunt: 'The complexity is a structural issue. The railway has not been privatised in a way that facilitates or enables capacity enhancement.'[17]

Railtrack's biggest project, the modernisation of the West Coast Main Line (WCML), illustrates many of the problems of investing in the railway under a privatised structure: the difficult legacy from BR; escalating costs; conflicts between different users; difficulty of managing contractors; enormous compensation claims for disruption; lack of coordination; Railtrack's difficulty in dealing with the competing demands of operators; and so on. It is hardly surprising that no other major project has even got off the ground in the first five years of privatisation, with plans for other major lines, such as the East Coast and Great Western, bogged down by delays and the absence of a clear vision.

In 1966, the electrification of the London–Liverpool/Manchester section of the WCML had been the high point of the post-war railway modernisation programme. Passenger numbers boomed above expectations and the term 'sparks effect' was coined to explain the public's reaction to the brand new electrified service that was later extended to Glasgow. The success should, of course, have led to an investment boom on the railways, as happened in several other European countries, but successive British governments, influenced by a transport ministry that was always in hock to the road lobby and a Treasury deeply sceptical of rail investment after the Modernisation Plan debacle, failed to follow up this initiative. This failure, in turn, sowed the seeds of the eventual disastrous privatisation.

As the WCML began to show signs of age, BR made two attempts to improve the service on what is Britain's key route. First, in the mid-1980s, the tilting Advanced Passenger Train was developed with the aim of a four-hour journey time between London and Glasgow, but even though the train briefly entered service (a bad mistake as passengers reported that the tilt made them feel sick, earning the train the moniker of the 'vomit comet'), the train was cancelled because of teething problems. Ironically, these problems were on the point of being solved, but the government lost confidence in the technology and, as a result, Britain lost the chance of leading the world in tilting train technology

Then, at the end of the 1980s, BR tried again. This time the solution was a conventional high-speed train – InterCity 250 – combined with progressive infrastructure upgrades that would gradually enable its 155mph top speed to be exploited. An order for the new trains had actually been put out to tender when, in 1992, the recession persuaded the Treasury that the project was over-ambitious and it ordered cancellation.

Instead, BR drew up a more modest scheme to replace the power supply, signalling and some track on the WCML, which would have cost £800m.

But privatisation intervened and BR's scheme went into abeyance. When franchising started in 1995, the government could not afford to let the WCML modernisation drift on. The trains and the track were quite literally falling apart, with breakdowns and delays increasing. Privatisation had been sold on the basis of bringing in new investment to the railways and therefore it had to provide the answer to the long-deferred modernisation of the WCML. The newly created Railtrack commissioned a £5m study on the future of the WCML from a consortium of consultants which assessed a number of options ranging from 'patch and mend' to complete refurbishment to allow much faster trains.

The best financial option was the Core Investment Programme (CIP). By introducing new signalling concepts based on computers and radio, lineside signalling equipment could be eliminated and it was thought this would make great savings. The key feature of the system was to be the 'moving block' signalling system, a revolutionary concept that had only ever previously been used on simpler railways such as metro systems and dedicated high-speed lines. Conventional signalling divides the track up into sections, or 'blocks', typically a kilometre long. Safety is ensured by allowing only one train at a time into a section. With moving block, each train has an 'envelope' in front and behind which protects it from collisions through radio signalling directly into the cab. There are no lineside signals, which saves enormous sums on maintenance, and, in theory, the system would have allowed more trains to run. The consultants, mainly from outside the railway industry, had claimed that the computer technology and the associated digital radio was available off the shelf in other industries.

Prompted by Brian Mellitt, the director of engineering and production, Railtrack decided to go for this ambitious idea. The resulting maintenance savings were supposed to pay for the £1.35bn CIP that would bring the West Coast line up to modern standards. Virgin won the Inter-City West Coast franchise in February 1997 on the basis of the CIP and negotiated a further £600m upgrade which would allow it to run twelve trains an hour in and out of Euston, with a 140mph top speed south of Crewe from 2005. It was an exciting prospect, turning the WCML into Britain's best rail line, and the total cost was reckoned to be around £2.2bn.

But then the complexities began to emerge. The agreement had to gain approval from the regulator who was concerned about capacity for other passenger operators and the rail freight companies. His acceptance of the scheme was conditional on Railtrack providing forty-two extra paths on the slow lines from 2005. That was to prove extremely difficult to achieve.

In addition to problems over the number of train paths and the signalling, there was an overall lack of commitment from Railtrack to the project. According to insiders, the scheme just seemed to be drifting along even though it was supposed to be completed, in two stages, by 2002 and 2005. Virgin, which also had its share of management problems, brought in Chris Green, the former managing director of InterCity, to run its two franchises. His immediate task was to rescue Virgin's passenger franchises that had been going downhill fast, but he also needed to gain control of the renewal project that was foundering.

Green pushed hard to get Railtrack to take the project seriously. 'They don't seem to see themselves as committed by the people who signed the contracts,' one Virgin insider commented.[18] The main contract to overhaul and renew the overhead electrification had still not been signed after the initial bids had come in at twice Railtrack's expected figure of £400 million. There was uncertainty about the scale of track renewal and major capacity issues, such as four tracking bottlenecks, were unresolved. And the issue of the forty-two extra paths also remained unresolved, which soon brought about another crisis for Railtrack when the failure resulted in the rail regulator issuing an enforcement order to get the information by March 2000, together with costings for the extra infrastructure work and train timetables.

As an insider put it,

> The trouble with the West Coast project was that Railtrack charged off and did a deal with Virgin without any thought for what the other users wanted and before any discussion was had with them, let alone how it would work to the timetable. No one had realised the complexity of dealing with so many people.[19]

Meanwhile, it soon became apparent that there were no off-the-shelf systems available for what was extremely complex, safety-critical signalling equipment. Mellitt's desire to use the most modern technology had proved over-ambitious The contract had been awarded to Alstom who were now warning that the signalling system would not be available until 2007/8, three years after the West Coast modernisation was supposed to be completed. Railtrack was forced into a humiliating retreat. In November 1999 it announced that the moving block was now considered too expensive. Instead, it would switch to a system using cab signalling, involving the installation of sophisticated radio systems, but would also retain much outside equipment. Therefore, the maintenance savings predicated on having no lineside equipment, which underpinned the whole project, disappeared. (Ironically, Mellitt, in his previous post as director of engineering at London Underground, had also specified a moving block system for the Jubilee Line Extension but it had to be sidelined and then scrapped at the eleventh hour at great expense.)

Worse, the existing signalling was becoming time-expired and would have to be patched up while a new signal system was installed, which resulted in the cost estimates soaring. The extra costs created by the privatised structure, such as huge compensation payments to train operators when work on the tracks disrupts services and the need for every party involved to make a profit, also came into play. Overnight, the cost of the West Coast modernisation more than doubled, to £5.8billion. What had started out as an £800m upgrade for BR and become a £2.2bn Railtrack project had now transformed into a near £6bn behemoth. Even worse was to come. When Railtrack was given its £1.5bn bail-out in April 2001 as a result of the crisis brought about by the Hatfield accident (explained in the previous chapter), the company also slipped out the fact that costs on the project had gone up a further £500m, bringing the total to £6.3bn.

Even with hindsight, the detail of how this progressive increase in costs happened is rather baffling. The two main categories for which costs rose most steeply were signalling and control, where the increase went from the original £485m for the moving block system to £1,900m for its less sophisticated replacement, and 'remodelling track lay-outs', which jumped from £640m to £1,800m. In contrast, electrification renewal merely doubled from £285m to £580m and 'track and structures renewal' rose from £570m to £780m. There was, also, the extra £1,000m cost of providing extra capacity and a few other minor increases. How could Railtrack have not realised that the costs were increasing in this way? The only explanation is that, as Railtrack insiders later admitted, the project had simply drifted, with no one taking responsibility.

Even the £6.3bn estimate was by no means fixed. When Railtrack announced its disastrous preliminary results in May 2001, it admitted that the cost may rise further and the 2005 deadline could be pushed back, putting the whole project in jeopardy. There seemed, in fact, no end to the capacity of the West Coast scheme to absorb more and more money.

The comparison with the costs of the parallel East Coast Main Line, refurbished in the late 1980s under BR, is illuminating. Authorised in 1984 and complete in 1990, British Rail's East Coast Main Line electrification cost £306million (at 1984 prices which translates to £540million today) and was delivered on time and on budget. The East Coast investment covered around 350 miles of main-line electrification with installation of overhead cable, some resignalling with state-of-the-art electronic equipment and new fibre optic communications. It was done rather on the cheap, as witnessed by the delays when wind brings down the cables. Nevertheless, in contrast, the electrification renewal alone – power supplies and new overhead cables – for the 400-mile WCML costs around the same as the complete East Coast project under BR a decade or so earlier. Admittedly, the ECML did not require track renewal and rather than track remodelling the layout was simplified, but the enormous cost difference is still difficult to explain. Aside from the signalling, where, as we have seen, Railtrack was having to repair and renew conventional lineside equipment as well as installing an in-cab radio system, the big increases came in track and remodelling. Here the hidden inflator is what Railtrack calls 'programme level risks', which, in English, largely means payments to train operators for disruption to services when stations or tracks are closed for work – something which BR never had to consider as a direct cost. It is unclear just how much of the WCML's costs are actually compensation – which is really a financial transfer between rail companies that should never be included in investment totals – but of the extra £500m added to the cost in April 2001, £300m was for compensation. In a way, the maddest thing is that, as one Railtrack insider commented, 'We have to pay compensation to the operators to get on their tracks to give them a better service. There's no logic to that.'[20]

Then there are the extra costs of having to do work in small overnight bites, rather than long possessions. New safety regulations mean that it can take an hour simply to switch off the electricity so that work can start. With an hour setting up and closing down, productivity from a four-hour, night-time possession will be low, even with high-performance track laying machinery. However, train operators with access contracts and profit targets to meet will not allow longer closures. Railtrack is seeking to close parts of the WCML for four weeks to speed up the refurbishment but the operators are fighting the proposal. Under BR it was possible to close lines and divert trains on to other tracks. For example, Manchester trains were run into Paddington during the original electrification of the West Coast. Now that would be impossible. Great Western and Thames who operate out of Paddington would complain about the disruption and their lost revenue. Virgin, who run the Manchester trains, would argue that its passengers – and therefore its income – would be affected too badly by a closure.

Thirdly, there are regulatory issues. After Railtrack has drawn up a scheme, it has to be sure that the needs of all the potential users – the various freight and passenger operators – have been met. In practice, this is almost impossible. There are so many players with competing demands that, within the context of a growing railway it is impossible to satisfy them all, as the example of the WCML improvement shows. This imposes costs in several ways. Schemes have to be drawn up with options to satisfy different criteria; time is wasted as ideas are circulated around the various operators; the regulator may then intervene, forcing Railtrack to include certain features; and the ultimate scheme may therefore end up being a Rolls-Royce where a Mini was needed. All these delays and decision-making complexities result in extra costs. This is not Railtrack's fault but a feature of the fragmented system. There is no one in charge who can ensure that a speedy decision is taken. The whole regulatory framework, which is a necessary feature of a railway operated by thirty passenger and freight companies, imposes a considerable cost burden on the industry.

Finally, there are the extra costs caused by having several companies involved, all of whom have to 'make a turn' on every project. Railtrack, too, has to try to be profitable at every stage and this means that it charges for every piece of work that it does, even if that does not make long-term economic sense. For example, the company will charge potential freight users for an assessment of whether it would be possible to run their trains, even though eventually Railtrack would make money on the extra access charges.

Railtrack also adds in management and supervisory costs for all work undertaken on the network. It is, therefore, not only on the West Coast that costs have soared since privatisation. The price of virtually every scheme, big or small, has gone up as a result of the increased complexity of the railway. In an analysis of ten projects, half before and half after privatisation, Roger Ford calculated that in real terms Railtrack has to spend 2.5 times more money than BR to get the same result.[21]

Railtrack's second biggest project on the existing network, Thameslink 2000, also suffered from cost escalation and delay. The scheme is intended to increase capacity on the heavily used north–south cross-London link opened up in the 1980s. At privatisation in 1996 Railtrack, after much lobbying of ministers, was effectively given £200m to fund the improvement as the equivalent amount of debt was written off. The scheme was seen as an important flagship project for the company, which was keen to show the City that it could improve the rail network and therefore increase its income through access charges. Originally priced at £225m at Railtrack flotation, by February 2000 the cost had risen to £850m (at 1995 prices) and will undoubtedly top £1bn. The completion date, which had gradually crept up to 2003, is now thought to be 2007 or 2008 at the earliest and, after the Hatfield debacle, Railtrack was considering whether to withdraw from the construction side of the project, which would involve paying back some of the government funding.

Even small schemes are affected by what could be called 'Railtrack inflation' and this is particularly noticeable when it comes to the construction of new or reopened stations. For example, a new station at Kidlington near Oxford has appeared in Oxfordshire County Council's local transport plan for a number of years at steadily rising prices, starting with £500,000 in 1994 and reaching £1.3m in 1999. According to a spokesman for the Railway Development Society, there are several reasons why station costs are rising faster than inflation:

> In the days of British Rail, there was less need to show all ancillary costs against a particular project as they were subsumed into the general accounts. Nowadays, the functions of design, construction and project management are divided amongst a number of private companies, each of which needs to be run profitably. Enhanced safety requirements during the construction phase add to the cost, as do new directives for the provision of access for wheelchair users and other facilities for the disabled, required by the Disability Discrimination Act 1995. Higher expectations of quality for the built environment means that cheap, concrete structures and rolled hardcore for car parks can no longer be contemplated.

BR also used to have the advantage of a Parliamentary Bill each year to allow developments, whereas Railtrack has to go through the lengthy Transport and Works Act process which, inevitably, is expensive. Therefore not all the extra costs can be attributed to privatisation and fragmentation, but it is clear that under the new system it is much harder to get value for money and that the considerable amount of public funds going into the railways do not stretch as far as under BR.

Railtrack's problem of escalating costs applied to freight, too. For example, Railtrack's estimate for a proposed reopening of a line from Stirling to Alloa via Dunfermline went up from £8m to £25–35m within a year. The difficulty facing those proposing such enhancements to the network was that they have no alternative. As Tony Berkeley, chairman of the Railfreight Group put it:

> The problem is that there is no way of checking Railtrack's prices, or whether a particular item is necessary at all. I certainly have my doubts, based on the experience of the costs of level crossings where, for crossings on freight lines, they appear to find it necessary to inflate the estimate by ten times.[22]

The Passenger Transport Executives which support a wide range of rail projects also found costs soaring. As a former BR director told me,

> The Passenger Transport Executives in regional conurbations such as Manchester and Leeds used to get all their schemes done by BR and they suddenly found that they were costing three and a half times more. Railtrack was putting up the price to make a profit, and then there is the cost of all the interfaces between customers, contractors, and sub-contractors which all add overhead.

The massive increase in costs on the West Coast project sent Railtrack into a nosedive from which it has failed to recover. Although the regulator effectively agreed to fund the extra cost of the investment from the public purse, the uncovering of this cost overrun marked the start of Railtrack's financial and managerial decline, which was, of course, exacerbated by Hatfield. The cost rise was deeply embarrassing not only for Railtrack but also for the Labour government which was so wedded to the notion that the private sector was more efficient at managing its costs. Labour had, indeed, predicated its whole controversial Private Public Partnership scheme for the London Underground on this notion, and ministers frequently referred to the huge cost overruns on the Jubilee

Line Extension which were, in fact, much more modest than that for the WCML – the bill merely doubled from £1.7bn in 1992 to around £3.5bn on completion, partly because of the abandonment of the moving block signalling and also because the collapse of a tunnel being built for the Heathrow Express in October 1994 led to concerns over building methods which resulted in delays to the construction of the JLE. And note that the WCML modernisation whose cost has nearly tripled is nowhere near complete, so there is plenty of scope for extra rises and, in fairness to the JLE, it is an elegant underground line with world-class architecture at its stations.

The way that costs escalated on the West Coast was not a unique case of a project spiralling out of control, but, as we have seen, was rooted in the new structure of the industry. One reason for this systematic cost escalation is that the way the industry has been structured means there is less control over costs than under BR. Again, the East Coast electrification project in the 1980s is a good comparator. It only just slipped through the government's project assessment procedure and, as a result, there was much cheeseparing which affected the reliability of the service. The trains, for example, had constant air-conditioning problems, the locomotives had high failure rates and, most important, the overhead catenary was not robust and tended to fall over whenever the wind was slightly higher than expected. In contrast, parts of the current West Coast project will be gold plated because of the lack of discipline over costs and the absence of accountability. There is no one to stop such overspending.

Moreover, since it is politically and probably contractually impossible for the government to leave a private sector scheme half finished by pulling the financial plug, the risks to the public purse have greatly increased. As a former senior BR executive put it, 'Without the government being there in the way it was under BR, there are no controls over such projects. Who is doing the evaluation of that £6.3bn to see whether it is worthwhile?'[23] Indeed, there are railway executives who consider that the second tranche of West Coast work, which will increase line speed to 140mph at a cost of £4bn, is not worth the extra cost, but there is no Fat Controller to call a halt and Railtrack has no interest in curtailing a process that is a guaranteed moneyspinner, given the fact that the regulator has an obligation to ensure that Railtrack can fund its investment.

The key point is that while the railway may be in private hands, with investors making a profit, *the risks to the taxpayer have not been eliminated.* This has been demonstrated several times since privatisation. We have already seen that the franchises which got into trouble because of the over-optimism of the bidders were rescued by the Strategic Rail Authority with extra money for the new franchisees. And, as noted above, Railtrack's cost overruns on the West Coast Main Line have also resulted in extra costs for the taxpayer rather than the company. And then there was the veritable scandal of the dividend Railtrack paid to its shareholders on the day that it announced losses of £534m after taking into account the stunning £733m cost of Hatfield and its aftermath.

It should be noted that Railtrack had done really badly that year even before considering Hatfield. Its pre-tax profits before exceptional items like Hatfield were taken into account had halved from £421m to £199m and yet its priority was to maintain dividends to shareholders at the same level per share as in the previous year at a cost of £140m in order to maintain 'access to the capital markets'[24] for future investment schemes. Taxpayers were paying dearly for that continued access – which was notional, anyway, given the wrecked state of Railtrack's finances – and virtually any other way of funding the rail industry would have been cheaper, as will be discussed in chapter 12. By then, Railtrack's share price had plummeted to the point where the company was worth only around £2.5bn. Yet the government was planning to pump just under £15bn into the company over the next five years and had already, as we have seen, advanced a £1.5bn grant in order to keep it afloat. Clearly, Railtrack executives, who did have the grace to forego bonuses (though, oddly, they did this voluntarily, suggesting that despite record losses, lousy train performance and palpable safety failures, the terms of their contracts were so generous that they would have been entitled to these extra payments anyway), reckoned the company was fireproof. Labour ministers, in the midst of an election campaign, had already said they had no intention of renationalising the company and therefore could not really criticise the scandalous dividend payments because of the inevitable rejoinder: 'Why don't you do something about it?'

It is just worth savouring this little episode as possibly the best example of the crazy contortions which had been made in order to try to mould the railways into a conventional capitalist construct: a firm which has lost £733m totally through its own mismanagement and incompetence, and has just received £1.5bn of government grant, insists on paying its shareholders their dividends because otherwise it would be in even worse trouble. So, if losing £733m is not bad enough, in what circumstances would the brave, risk-taking capitalists who own this maimed company actually forego their dividends? If the Forth Bridge collapsed through Railtrack's failings? Or if trains were crashing because of broken rails every week? Or exactly what? The balance of risk between shareholders on the one hand, and taxpayers and rail passengers on the other, seemed, to say the least, to be slightly out of kilter.

Yet, while the risk has not been privatised, the opportunity for scrutiny has been reduced. Under BR, spending an extra £3.5bn or so on something like the West Coast scheme would have at least prompted a Parliamentary debate. Now, apart from the valiant efforts of the powerless House of Commons Transport sub-Committee, chaired by the redoubtable Gwynneth Dunwoody, such decisions are considered to be commercial matters to be settled between private companies and a semi-independent regulator, with only scant scrutiny by Parliament through the National Audit Office's examination of the SRA's accounts.

It does not take an Hercule Poirot to detect that perhaps Railtrack is aware of the strength of its position in relation to such cost rises. Railtrack is a monopoly supplier of railway infrastructure and, like all monopolies, it is able to charge prices that allow the company to make excessive profits. It is worth noting, too, that while there was constant pressure on Railtrack's contractors and on the train operators to reduce costs and cut staff, Railtrack had almost the same number of people on its books in 2001 as it did at privatisation – around 11,200.

A little statistic tucked into Railtrack's 1999/2000 annual report offers possibly the most telling clue as to why the company's investment has been so badly directed and inefficient. The report reveals that Railtrack spent just £1m on research and development during that year, half the paltry total for the previous year. In a company with a turnover of £4bn, that seems scarcely credible, but highlights the short-term nature of its concerns.

The spiralling cost of investment was to spur the Strategic Rail Authority to try to break Railtrack's monopoly power by creating Special Purpose Vehicles – i.e. consortia set up specifically to build improvement schemes on the railways – but, as we see below, it was a scheme that would prove to be fraught with difficulty.

THE FAILURE OF THE STRATEGIC RAIL AUTHORITY

The Labour government's response to the failings of rail privatisation was to create the Strategic Rail Authority to coordinate investment and planning in the industry. As we saw in chapter 6, it was long in gestation as John Prescott had not pushed sufficiently hard to obtain an early legislative slot, but it was created in shadow form in early 1999 and Sir Alastair Morton was appointed as its chairman, even though it did not officially come into being until February 2001.

Labour ministers made a big political investment in the SRA. They repeatedly said it would be the vehicle for bringing order into the fragmented rail industry but this was patently over-ambitious. With the industry owned by so many different players pulling in different directions, such a task proved, not surprisingly, impossible.

The SRA took over the functions of OPRAF on franchising, but had the added responsibility of trying to coordinate investment in the industry in a strategic way. Sir Alastair immediately tried to reassure the industry that he would not try to run it from Whitehall. He stressed that he was not seeking 'command and control' of the industry but instead to 'lever in resources and skills' from the private sector into the industry through 'partnerships'.

It was a muddled agenda that soon became bogged down in the realities of an uncoordinated and fragmented industry. Sir Alastair's stated aim was to maximise 'investment, investment, investment', as he put it, into the industry and, realising that Railtrack was never going to be able to supply all that was needed, he tried to get the train operators to put forward schemes to improve the railway. As an inducement, the successful bidders were to be offered twenty-year franchises, as opposed to the mostly seven-year deals in the first round of franchising. This was predicated on the idea that it would provide the stability the operators needed in order to be confident enough to make substantial investments.

But Sir Alastair's strategy seemed to be based on a false premise. Train operating companies (TOCs) are bizarre constructs which actually own no assets – they lease trains, rent stations and are given a contract to operate services by the government. Therefore, what can they invest in?

Sure, they can order more coaches, but it is actually the rolling stock companies which take the risk and provide the capital; they can invest in station improvements but as Railtrack owns the buildings, there is limited scope; or they can invest to improve the track and infrastructure but this is highly complex[25] and, again, ultimately Railtrack's responsibility.

This strategy therefore led to TOCs submitting all kinds of outlandish bids which, in turn, resulted in the complete paralysis of the refranchising process. The bidders, mostly those who had already won a franchise but with a few newcomers such as Serco, Group 4 and foreign railways (ironically, all of which are state-owned, such as the Dutch, French and Swiss), came forward with all kinds of expensive schemes for new lines between London and the North, tunnels under London, double decker trains and rebuilt stations. But who was going to pay for all this? By asking bidders to come up with their ideas, Sir Alastair had misunderstood the relationship between the private and public sectors. Private companies want Christmas every week and they acted as if there were an infinite amount of money available. Yet the bulk of these schemes would have to be funded by the taxpayer because such schemes are never commercially viable.

There is a more fundamental question about this whole strategy: why should these bidders know better than government? Franchisees are in reality only transient contractors who do not have a long-term interest in the railway. Even if they have a twenty-year deal, it can be rescinded by the SRA should they not perform properly. Moreover, most of the bidders were bus companies with little imagination or experience of working in an expanding industry. Despite widespread criticisms and pressure from within the industry, Sir Alastair refused to set out clear proposals for where he wanted to take the railways. Instead, he sat back while the bidders tried to outdo each other in the scale and imagination of their schemes, without much concern about the cost. To make matters worse, the SRA failed even to clarify the precise boundaries of the franchise areas until well into the franchise process. At first, the SRA had announced that it wanted fewer franchises in order to simply the rail network, but eventually it only managed to reduce the overall number to around twenty-three.[26] The highly cerebral Sir Alastair, and his chief executive, Mike Grant, were finding it very difficult to make decisions, much to the frustration of franchise bidders, the government and Railtrack, all of whom wanted some certainty about what was happening on the railways.

The Treasury was not amused. The mandarins felt that Sir Alastair was not doing his sums and as one commented at a meeting, 'He likes big numbers but doesn't seem to care whether they are black or red.'[27] The Treasury started to give Sir Alastair and his crew a hard time by blocking the signing of franchise agreements. Sir Alastair had, at first, promised to get the eighteen franchises which ran out in 2003/4 re-let by the end of 2001 and managed to get his first deal announced in the summer of 2000, the relatively easy decision to allow Chiltern to remain with the John Laing group. A couple of other deals, including booting Connex out of the large SouthCentral commuter franchise and retaining Stagecoach for South West Trains, followed, but at the time of writing, almost a year after the Chiltern announcement, no final contract, even the simple Chiltern proposition, had actually been signed because the Treasury wanted to see a firmer basis for the SRA's decision-making.

Even where franchises were let, there was a sense of unreality and hype surrounding the whole process. For example, when in April 2001 the SRA announced that Stagecoach would retain the lucrative South West Trains franchise, no financial details were offered, except that this was a £1.7bn deal to improve services. But only two months earlier, in February, the company had issued a press release setting out a £3.5bn vision for the SWT franchise; this had apparently been reduced to half that total by the time SRA announced its decision.[28] Stagecoach explained, rather unconvincingly, that this discrepancy represented the difference between aspirations and firm commitments. But even the basis of the £1.7bn was unclear. Stagecoach is receiving around £50m per year in subsidy for the existing franchise that runs out in early 2003 and was therefore unlikely to accept any reduction. Therefore the government was paying a large amount of subsidy in order to ensure that the franchisee invested lots of money. While that is very welcome, it can hardly be called 'private investment'. A big rolling stock order was announced by SWT soon afterwards but this was a requirement of the bidding process since there was a legal requirement to replace the old trains, Mark 1 stock.

Other franchises were stalled because of the SRA's lack of clarity over what it wanted. Several franchise processes were delayed, most notably the loss-making Central which was halted in February 2001 when the SRA said that the two remaining bids were not good enough, infuriating the two companies concerned, National Express and Group 4 who had

spent hundreds of thousands on their bids. In fact, this masked an interesting row that highlighted the problems over prioritising investment in
the industry. The local Passenger Transport Executive, Centro (not the
same as Central, which is the franchise area), wanted to retain many of
the services which it had funded in the past, but the SRA wanted to use
some of those train paths for longer distance services. Sir Alastair even
publicly criticised the local PTE and its director general, Rob Donald, for
being parochial in a speech in Birmingham in March 2001 that attracted
widespread criticism. Such petulance did not help the pace of the franchise process. Following the 2001 general election and the replacement
of John Prescott by Stephen Byers, the whole franchise process was put
on hold, including the notion of twenty-year deals. Instead, Byers sought
to get two-year extensions in order to obtain quick gains for passengers.

The SRA spent much of the two years of its shadow existence mulling
over its strategic plan. Originally, this was supposed to have been published within a few months of the creation of the organisation, but the
timetable kept slipping. There was a succession of excuses. Sir Alastair
felt it would be inappropriate to publish the plan until the government
had published its own ten-year transport plan (see below) but even when
this was issued in the summer of 2000, there were still further delays, as
Sir Alastair now wanted the results of the regulator's five yearly review of
Railtrack's access charges.

Far from setting the agenda, therefore, the SRA seemed to be chasing
everyone else's ideas. Yet without a plan the SRA was busy trying to let
out the franchises. It was a topsy-turvy way of doing things as the bidders
were desperate for a clear statement of what the SRA – and therefore the
government – wanted from a particular franchise to enable investment
plans to be developed. Railtrack was faced with trying to cost and
develop investment schemes for every hare-brained idea that any bidder
suggested on the back of an envelope. On a railway with limited capacity
this inevitably led to conflicts between different operators, both freight
and passengers, using the same lines. With the SRA unwilling to use its
strategic role to sort out such issues, Railtrak was left in an impossible situation. As a Railtrack insider put it, 'Railtrack can only respond to different demands by offering the lowest common denominator. No one has
the power to impose what to do in terms of the railway. Trying to please
all parties is impossible. Franchise propositions should have been clear
about what investment was needed, and then offered out to bidders.'[29]

The SRA's problem was that its task was more difficult than that of its predecessor, OPRAF, when it had let out the initial franchises in 1996/7. Then there was only one criterion – the cheapest bid won. Now, the SRA was trying to let out franchises for a growing railway by maximising the amount of investment. But it also wanted to reward the past efforts of good franchisees, improve standards for passengers and, where possible, increase the number of services. But if two competing bids offered very different types of improvements, making comparisons between the two was very difficult.

This was the problem that caused the refranchising of East Coast Main Line to develop into an almighty fiasco that highlighted the flaws in the SRA's 'let's try all flavours' approach. The incumbent, Sea Containers, which operated under the name Great North Eastern Railway and had a pretty good reputation, saw tilting trains – which it had mooted for the first franchise but which had never materialised – as the solution to the overcrowding on the line, as they would allow services to go faster. Virgin, its rival, wanted instead to put extra diesel engines on the trains in addition to the electric locomotives to speed up acceleration and, crucially, suggested around 100 miles of new parallel, high-speed line to improve capacity.

The SRA was paralysed. It did not know what to do because it had not developed a way of comparing such disparate proposals. After some hesitation it commissioned a study into the proposal for a new line and tried to get the two companies to put in bids that were on a comparable basis.

The SRA got into even hotter water when it decided to go with the Sea Containers bid even though its internal advisers suggested that Virgin was the best proposition, a view with which many neutrals in the industry, sceptical about the advantages of tilting trains on a relatively straight track, concurred. A letter, sent anonymously (but reliably) from within the SRA, suggested that while the Virgin offer was better on technical and financial grounds, Sir Alastair had recommended to the government that the Sea Containers bid should be accepted. The anonymous writer warned that if the award of the franchise went ahead, Virgin would be able to overturn the decision at a judicial review.

The issue was further confused by a vicious public spat between Railtrack and the SRA over the costs of upgrading the line. In February 2001 the SRA seemed to discover that the cost of the proposed upgrade was £3.4bn rather than the original estimate of £1.9billion, and possibly much more as the details of the scheme were worked up. This was not due to Railtrack's incompetence or inefficiency but was principally related to the perceived risks of the project, which always add considerably to privately funded schemes. However, rather than quietly having it out with Railtrack, the SRA went public, pulling the franchise process, arguing that Railtrack was trying to exploit its monopoly position by increasing the costs. The company responded by saying that it wanted a clear franchise proposition from the SRA so that it could know what investment plans would be needed.

Accusations of duplicity and double-dealing were thrown about by both organisations and the episode degenerated into farce, infuriating ministers and the Treasury. Railtrack responded with a press release that said the cost increases were 'not unusual for a project at this early stage'[30] and eventually the SRA seemed to accept this view. After a three-week delay, peace broke out, rather unconvincingly. The row, however, hardly reinforced public and, more importantly, City confidence in the ability of the railway to handle major investment projects and the SRA's understanding of the private sector.

In fact, the SRA's battle with Railtrack over the East Coast was part of a wider war between the two organisations over how improvements to the railway were to be brought about. Sir Alastair had long been highly critical of Railtrack's inefficiencies and its lack of discipline over costs, which, as we have seen, was a perfectly reasonable accusation. His preferred solution was the creation of Special Purpose Vehicles. These would be consortia of investors and engineering companies who would carry out improvements to the rail network and, probably, sell on the scheme to Railtrack to operate. The advantage was that this would create extra sources of capital for the railways but the disadvantage, as Railtrack was quick to point out with much justification, was that it would lead to further complexity on an already highly fragmented network. The plan was strongly opposed by Gerald Corbett when he was chief executive, as he argued that to design and deliver major projects separate from the day-to-day management of the railway was a very complex process. Moreover, a Special Purpose Vehicle would face all the difficulties already experienced by Railtrack on the West Coast Main Line: making decisions about precisely how to improve the infrastructure right down to the detail of where every signal should be placed; accommodating the various rival train operators; sorting out temporary line closures; liasing with the maintenance and renewal companies; and so on.

In July 2001 the government finally announced its decision on the ECML. Or rather it didn't. Byers instead said the twenty-year franchise decision would be put on ice and that Sea Containers would be granted a two-year extension, provided it offered more passenger benefits. The East Coast saga was part of a bad habit which the SRA seemed to have got into. The organisation was be structurally incapable of making decisions or meeting deadlines. The promise to let out the eighteen franchises that terminated in 2003/4 by the end of 2001 was clearly not going to be met and, indeed, by June 2001 no deal had even been signed. In the *Strategic Agenda* published in February 2001 the SRA admitted that some of the new franchises would not start much before April 2003, both because of its slowness at negotiating and because it is unable to force incumbents to hand over the tail end of their lucrative franchises to their successors. As we have seen, the publication of the document itself had been delayed several times, and when it eventually appeared it was testimony to the failings of the SRA.

The industry had been looking to the SRA to set the agenda and produce a vision for the railways, detailing precisely what it wanted from each franchise area. Indeed, Steven Marshall, the chief executive of Railtrack, even asked the SRA to be a 'benign dictatorship', making clear the parameters it was setting for the railway. Instead, the *Agenda* was a sparse document, providing a brief *tour d'horizon* of the state of the railways and a list of potential projects, with no prioritisation, all interspersed with the thoughts of chairman Morton. Nor was there any attempt to address the big questions such as 'What are the railways for?' or 'On what markets should they focus?' A former executive of the SRA said: 'Alastair rejected any attempt to set out a clear plan. He just didn't see it as our job. The whole basis of the refranchising exercise was based on investment ideas, rather than on what was feasible. You end up with batty ideas.'[31]

Indeed, the Strategic Rail Authority's approach to investment, together with the much hyped promises of privatisation, created a fantasy about the potential for an improved railway without proper consideration of the realities of railway finance and the government's ability to pay for what Railtrack executives like to call 'a world class railway'. Even with the most generous settlement from the rail regulator, Railtrack was never going to be in a position to fund much more than £6–8bn worth of enhancements in the five-year period from April 2001. Yet the implication of the SRA's behaviour was that everything was possible since it steadfastly refused to prioritise between the many options being suggested or to set a realistic agenda, defining the kind of railway it wanted to see and even, as a wider consideration, what type of journeys it wanted to encourage. With some £1.5bn of subsidies for services to allocate each year, the SRA could encourage InterCity travel through targeting investment on the main lines, or it could make it easier for commuters by investing in their services. But there was no such debate. Nor was there any discussion of how safety factors were distorting investment priorities, as discussed in chapter 10.

The SRA should, as one wag put it, have been called R because it had no strategy and no authority. Indeed, its failure during the first two years was not only an embarrassment to Sir Alastair, the man who had successfully bludgeoned through the Channel Tunnel project in the face of hostile bankers and rapacious contractors, but also to the government which had invested its hopes for the railways in the organisation.

It was, though, not his fault alone, but also a demonstration of the difficulty of bringing any coherence to the fragmented rail network. The root of the state of semi-paralysis was in the failure of the Labour government to set out any clear aspirations for the railways and, inevitably, also the constant meddling of the Treasury – which had never gone away – over investment plans. In private Sir Alastair complained constantly of Treasury interference. Moreover, a secretary of state with more determination and a more strategic sense than John Prescott would have been able to drive through some of these projects more quickly. Instead, ministers seemed to think that the mere creation of the SRA would solve the problems caused by the fragmentation of the railways. Inevitably, it failed. The government's other weapon in this fight, the ten-year plan, also got into difficulties as a result of the intractability of a dysfunctional railway.

THE GOLDEN RULE OF RAILWAY ECONOMICS

As mentioned in chapter 6, the government strategy for transport was an ambitious sounding £180bn ten-year investment plan. This was equally divided between roads, rail and local transport and aimed to 'tackle congestion by improving all types of transport – rail and road, public and private – in ways that increase choice'.[32]

As ever, the headline figures were more impressive than the detail, especially as all the figures included estimates of inflation, which made them look higher. Of the £60bn promised for the railways, for example, £34bn was expected to be provided by the private sector and therefore could not possibly be quantified accurately by the government or even included as a firm commitment, given the uncertainty in the industry after Hatfield. Indeed, this was highlighted by Sir Alastair Morton in evidence to the Commons Transport sub-Committee just before the 2001 general election when he accepted that the £8bn that was supposed to come from Railtrack for enhancements to the railway would not be forthcoming following Railtrack's post-Hatfield decision to back away from funding major projects and to concentrate on its core business of maintaining the existing infrastructure. This, he said, left 'a fair old hole'[33] in the plans.

The hopes invested in the private sector were based on an over-optimistic view of what they could get out of the railways and disguised the fact that most of the money had to be underpinned by government subsidy or grant. The emphasis on private investment masked the fact that the railways simply do not offer a commercial rate of return. In other words, the increase in ticket office revenue from extra investment is not enough to service the debt and provide a reasonable rate of profit for the investor.

Over £10bn of the £60bn was already earmarked for the West Coast Main Line, the Channel Tunnel Rail Link, Thameslink and safety concerns such as the introduction of Train Protection Warning System (see chapter 8) and the European Train Control System, with most of that money having to come out of the public purse.

Another £14.3bn was simply the annual subsidy paid to the train companies. Worryingly, this was set rather arbitrarily at between £1.3bn and £1.6bn per year, which, as it included an estimate for inflation, represented no significant growth and never equalled the levels attained in the early years of privatisation under the Tories when the railways received £1.8bn per year at 1997/8 prices. All this meant that there was not really any extra money for new schemes. The plan was really a consolidation of what had already been announced, rather than a brave new deal for the railways.

Despite these caveats, there was some good news. Investment paid for by the Exchequer was scheduled to rise rapidly, particularly in the early to middle years of the ten-year plan when it would leap from £1.6bn in 2001/2 to £4bn in 2005/6 but this railway boom would soon end as the figure for the last year of the decade is planned to be £2.5bn. But, as we have seen, there is little evidence that this money will be spent effectively. Ministers, even the incredibly on-message Lord Macdonald,[34] admitted as much, but seemed to believe that the SRA could improve the situation, though there was precious little evidence to indicate that this was the case.

Indeed, for all the money going into the industry in the name of investment, passengers will reap few benefits over the next few years. The most visible improvement will be the new rolling stock currently sitting in the sidings and, most spectacularly, the trains for both of Virgin's franchises, West Coast and CrossCountry. The first phase of the West Coast line will also be finished, but otherwise there will be few major improvements that will make a perceptible difference to everyday journeys. There will be the first phase of the Channel Tunnel Rail Link, due for completion in October 2003, which will speed up Eurostar journeys by fifteen minutes, but the second phase will take another four years. Otherwise, there will be precious little for the second Labour government to point to when election time comes around again. Sunderland will be connected to the Newcastle metro system under a £90m scheme but all the rest, such as Thameslink 2000 (which Railtrack is threatening to pull out of), the East Coast, and schemes to break bottlenecks remain largely on the drawing board.

To be fair to Railtrack, the SRA and government, the industry was not structured for growth and massive injections of investment. As Booz Allen Hamilton put it, 'Railtrack has no effective incentive to enhance and develop the network in an entrepreneurial manner.'[35]

As we have seen, the railway was privatised on the notion that the industry would gradually decline and require only patching and mending. Now it is being seen as a major component of the nation's infrastructure, which requires investment, but the complexity of the structure is proving an insuperable barrier.

The railway's need for investment is, in fact, almost infinite but there is a harsh reality at the core of railway economics which could be characterised as its golden rule: as more people are attracted on to the railway, more subsidy will be needed. The recent demands for more railway investment has been stimulated by the fact that the number of passengers grew by 30 per cent in the five years up to the Hatfield crash. While it was possible to accommodate much of this growth on existing assets, there is a limit as to how many people can be crammed into a particular train or how many services can be run on a particular line. Once that point has been reached – which it clearly has on many routes – and every last drop of sweat has been extracted from the assets, this golden rule of the railways comes into play. Whether it is more rolling stock, extra train paths, better signalling to increase throughput, faster trains, longer trains, more stations, extended platforms or whatever, the investment required will never earn a commercial rate of return. That fundamental truth of railway economics is at the root of the investment crisis in the industry. Worse, as the West Coast project – where phase one was relatively cost-effective but phase two is astronomically expensive – suggests, there may even be diminishing rates of return as more investment is required and technological thresholds have to be crossed.

The government seems to have cottoned onto this basic truth. In a paper published just before the 2001 general election the Railway Forum[36] points out that the ambition of the ten-year plan is incredibly limited, merely restoring public sector investment levels in the railway to those of 1993/4 and is based on a conservative estimate of passenger growth on the railways – 50 per cent in ten years. In other words, the Forum argues that the government is making no attempt to bring about a major modal shift in favour of rail, but is merely providing enough to patch up the railways.

As I write this, the French are celebrating the opening of the TGV Méditerranée with a massive firework display in Avignon. The trains have become a symbol of modern France, a constant source of embarrassment to Britain which is connected to the system via a branch line to Waterloo on which the trains are forced to slow to half their normal line speed of 186mph. The British media are asking why we have not got the same sort of service here. The answer is that, thirty years ago, the government was hooked on a roads agenda from which successive administrations have barely been weaned and during that time, since the Modernisation Plan, there has been an entrenched reluctance to invest in rail. To achieve something similar in the next couple of decades, the government would have to commit itself to an expensive programme, which, though superficially not cost-effective, would ultimately form part of a national modernisation agenda whose value is incalculable. Nobody has ever questioned the value of the motorway network which was not subject to the same rigorous cost-benefit analysis as the railways. Spending on roads has always been seen as investment, whereas support for the railways has been perceived as subsidy.

The fundamental question on investment is not how to convince the private sector, and in particular Railtrack, to invest huge sums, since there is no commercial basis for such investment. Instead, the government should recognise the centrality of its role in this process by deciding precisely how much it will pay in investment grants or underwrite indirectly through the franchising process. If it wants a railway fit for the twenty-first century, it will have to pay for it.

The more mundane issue is that the government must be realistic about how much investment the industry can deliver efficiently without costs going through the roof because of overheating and skills shortages. There is no doubt, however, that to achieve effective investment requires a more coherent structure, an issue which is discussed in the final chapter.

CHAPTER 12

Putting the pieces back together

That privatisation would be a failure was widely predicted. But the extent of that failure has surprised even such vociferous critics as myself. Not only did it cause the total breakdown of the railway after the Hatfield accident and lead to three major accidents in as many years, but privatisation has delivered none of the objectives forecast by its supporters: stimulating competition, reducing subsidy, attracting investment free of the constraints of the Public Sector Borrowing Requirement, breaking the power of the unions or providing a better service for passengers through greater commercial nous.

Just to recap briefly on each of these, drawing together the themes of the last two chapters, the very concept of on-rail competition was dumped in the bottom drawer by the first regulator, John Swift, who quickly recognised that the idea of having competing services on the same track was ludicrous. He also realised that the whole franchising process would be wrecked by unfettered access to the network. His 'moderation of competition' regulations spelt the end of the Tory dream of red trains competing against green ones.

Rather than being reduced, subsidy was greatly increased to smooth the path of privatisation, and the attempt to cut it back to pre-privatisation levels and below, as set out in the first franchise agreements, failed simply because large swathes of the railway cannot function without a high degree of government support, even though passenger numbers have been rising. The sharp reductions in subsidy in the latter parts of the franchise agreements were based on over-optimistic assumptions about the ability of the privatised operators to cut costs. Instead, several companies had to be bailed out at the taxpayers' expense, and, under the refranchising process, operators will receive more money than predicted.

The railways are inherently unprofitable and fragmentation into smaller, *soi-disant* profitable companies can only worsen this fundamental problem. Indeed, the break-up exacerbated the situation, since each entrant needs to make a profit and that is why the amount of subsidy was doubled at privatisation. As ever, Mrs Thatcher's instincts about the impossibility of privatising a loss-making business, instilled in her father's grocer's shop, were correct.

Worse, subsidy is about to rise dramatically because of the privatised railway's inability to deliver cost-effective enhancement projects. Railtrack, post-Hatfield, has become virtually a quango, gorging itself on huge amounts of taxpayers' lolly. Lord Berkeley of the Railfreight Group calculated[1] that around 70 per cent of Railtrack's £15bn income in its second five-year control period, 2001–6, would come from the taxpayer. Given that this calculation was made before the £1.5bn bail out, the possible payment of the extra £2bn requested by the company, and the collapse in its share price, it is an underestimate. In addition, Railtrack will receive specific grants for the West Coast Main Line upgrade, the Channel Tunnel Rail Link and the installation of TPWS, which, depending on the progress of these schemes, will add around £1.5bn per year to its income from the Exchequer. In other words, Railtrack will receive over £3bn per year from taxpayers. Moreover, a few hundred million per year of subsidy – a precise calculation is virtually impossible – will go to the rolling stock companies and the train operators. At a conservative estimate, then, subsidy to the railways during this period will be at least £3.5bn per year, more than twice the amount British Rail ever received.

As we saw in chapter 10, the doubling of subsidy in the early days of privatisation, was somewhat counterbalanced by the income from sales and other savings. This is no longer the case and there is no expectation that subsidy levels can be reined back. The money which the government is now pouring into the railways is unprecedented since the days of the Modernisation Plan but, as we have seen, we are not necessarily getting good value for it. As one old BR man put it, 'Any fool can spend money, but it is more difficult to spend it wisely.'[2] This is well demonstrated by the West Coast Main Line upgrade. The costs of the second part, increasing line speed from 125mph to 140mph, are so out of control that in a rational world, someone would call a halt or at least demand a review. But in the devolved railway, there is no one to do so. Virgin has a contract for the upgrade with Railtrack – devised incidentally by the present regulator, Tom Winsor, in a previous incarnation – which would have to pay massive damages if it pulled out. So Railtrack is forced to ask Winsor for more cash to pay for the upgrade and he is virtually obliged to cough up, as he is under a duty to ensure Railtrack can reasonably carry out its investment plans. Therefore the project proceeds, at ever increasing cost, with no Parliamentary scrutiny (except *post facto* through the National Audit Office and the Public Accounts Committee) and a self-generated momentum.

The economics of the new railway are not only Byzantine, but extremely expensive for the taxpayer. No one wants to take decisions in the railways. Government has devolved the authority to private companies who, in turn, are paralysed by the failure of ministers to give them a clear direction. There is a pretence that decisions can be taken in the private sector but since so much government money is involved, they never can. Moreover, the Strategic Rail Authority is itself incapable of making decisions because it has run out of money, thanks to Tom Winsor's bailout of Railtrack and the escalating costs of the big schemes. The ten-year plan is unlikely to be met without massive injections of extra government cash.

The Treasury is not amused. But it only has itself to blame for having cooked up such a crazy scheme to try to get government out of the railway business. It has put pressure on the Strategic Rail Authority to bring the situation back under control and, indeed, there are fears that it may block any significant new investment schemes. The Treasury's discomfiture is very funny – for people who never use the railways.

Which brings us to investment. As we saw in the last chapter, the headline figures mask a complex situation where the cost of schemes has soared, boosting the sums of money being spent but with little result in terms of improvement to the railway. The belated discovery by those who privatised the railway that the network is inherently unprofitable meant that any hopes for a privately led investment revolution in the railways would be stillborn. In fact, as Railtrack's chief executive Steven Marshall has admitted,[3] there are no commercial projects on the railway. All investment on the railway has to be mostly – and now, after the collapse of Railtrack's share price, often entirely – funded by the taxpayer. The private sector is a simple beast whose only food is profit. Sure, private companies are often – but by no

means always – more efficient than public corporations but these effi-
ciencies are offset by the fact that they have to borrow money at higher
rates. The notion that these savings will always exceed the extra costs
of private borrowing is an interesting theory but should not be treated
as gospel. Yet, somehow, in the UK it has been. In particular, this quite
technical issue has got caught up in political ideology – theology
really – with both Labour and the Tories now on the same side, arguing
that the advantages of the private sector *always* outweigh those of the
public sector.

The rigidity in the UK over definitions of the Public Sector Borrowing
Requirement has helped to intensify the debate and has been used by
those in favour of using only the private sector whatever the economic
realities. This has, in turn, led to the ridiculous situation over the Public
Private Partnership for the London Underground in which common
sense and a rational exposition of the alternatives has been obscured by a
monumental political row. A few Treasury mandarins, supported by the
chancellor, Gordon Brown, have lined up against the rest of the political,
economic and transport *cognoscenti* supported by the media and large
swathes of the public.

Because the railway is governed by contracts, the inter-relationship
between the different players is financial. And here the system has
come totally unstuck. It is impossible to get the incentives right. For
example, one of Railtrack's main problems has been the significant
increase in traffic on the network. Yet not only does the company
receive no extra reward for most of those additional trains, but they
impose significant extra costs on Railtrack. The regulator tried to
address this problem in his access charge review, but could not do so
because that would have created another set of wrong messages.
Winsor's task is, quite simply, impossible. To explain: if the cost of Railtrack's access charges for putting on an extra service to meet demand
were very high, then train operators would be reluctant to do so and the
new passengers seeking to use the service would be crammed in to the
same number of trains or carriages. However, if the cost remains low,
poor Railtrack has no reward for its extra work. That conundrum is
quite simply insoluble.

Another example of the system's tendency to create perverse incentives is the setting of performance targets for punctuality, which
encourages train operators to have lax timetables in order to meet their

passenger's charter requirements. Considerable extra time has been added into timetables between, for example, London and Reading, and London and Watford, where the outward journey takes several minutes less than the return to the capital. Therefore, far from encouraging better performance, the incentives actually make matters worse. There are plenty of other similar examples which demonstrate that the failings of the privatised railway are structural and not just a matter of bad luck or happenstance. Every company within the railways is simply trying to maximise profits in its little domain, screwing the largest possible profit out of its contracts in return for doing the least possible work, rather than thinking of the broader social objectives of the railway.

This all highlights the fact that the most obvious failing of privatisation has been economic: selling the railways was an attempt to square the circle that was doomed from the outset. Steve Robson, the Treasury guru who was the architect of the structure, used to talk about 'risk-shedding' – passing the economic risks to the private sector. In fact, this has proved impossible. The costs of Railtrack's massive overspending on major schemes, its post-Hatfield debacle and the losses by the over-optimistic franchisees have all been met by the taxpayer. The risk has not been shed for the simple reason that the railways cannot be allowed to go bankrupt and both franchisees and Railtrack know this. In that sense, the railways have never really been privatised; instead, various parts have been contracted out.

Far from breaking the power of the unions, privatisation has actually strengthened them. The wages of train drivers, who nearly all belong to ASLEF, have soared with some now getting close to £30,000 per year, as they have the option of going to better-paying rivals and they are a small, well-organised group of workers whose ability to stop the trains in a dispute is absolute. The much larger RMT is also in a good bargaining position, as witnessed by the threatened strike of the summer of 2001 when the train operators were forced to cave in when the unions insisted that guards should have primary responsibility for safety on trains and that there should be no further introduction of driver-only trains. The reason for the train companies' hasty retreat was that, in the event of a strike, they not only lose a day's revenue – with a significant impact on profits, given the low margins of most operators – but they also become liable to performance regime payments to the SRA as their contracts do not consider industrial action to be a *force majeure* that would get them off the hook.

Possibly the most surprising failing of privatisation has been the absence of the improved customer care which was promised so often during the sell-off process. In terms of performance on reliability and punctuality, there was little improvement even before the Hatfield disaster. All those commercial disciplines and incentives and the hundreds of delay attribution clerks have done little to make life better for the average traveller. Moreover, passengers have, in fact, been treated very little differently than under British Rail. There has been the occasional improvement but, also, there has been deterioration under some operators, particularly when they have become stretched for cash. The improvements include the generally excellent National Rail Enquiry Service, some very cheap fares for long-distance travel at unpopular times, and the odd inspired initiative such as Connex's idea of turning ticket offices into supermarkets at small stations. But the comparison should not be with a static, unchanging BR but with one which was developing and improving, as demonstrated in chapter 3, and which itself would have introduced some initiatives.

There is another key aspect of privatisation which has surprised even its critics – though at least one, Peter Rayner, a former BR manager, was particularly vociferous about the issue in the run-up to privatisation:[4] the way in which safety has been compromised. As the three chapters on the major post-privatisation accidents show, the fragmentation of the industry and the shift from a cooperative culture to an antagonistic one governed by legally-binding contracts, usually enforced by financial penalties, has increased the likelihood of major accidents occurring. The railway used to have a very good collective memory which ensured that the lessons from mistakes were learnt across the industry. The key sentence in Lord Cullen's generally pedestrian and unincisive report into the Ladbroke Grove disaster was his comment on Thames's failure to warn trainee drivers about the dangers of Signals Passed at Danger: 'There can be no doubt that the corporate memory of Thames Trains was weak in that it failed to take note of these early warnings [about previous SPADs].'[5] With twenty-five train operators, a dozen maintenance contractors and a panoply of other organisations involved in the railway, that key safety element has been lost. No matter how many regulators and regulations, commercial contracts and legally binding requirements, the simple unity of purpose of the integrated BR, run by a knowledgeable Fat Controller, cannot be recaptured. This was well demonstrated by the fact that twelve Railtrack employees were told not to cooperate with the internal investigation into the Hatfield accident for fear of compromising the company's legal situation.[6] Since the purpose of such investigations is to prevent similar accidents, this is hardly reassuring for passengers. Safety has also been compromised by an over-emphasis on the commercial aims of the rail companies at the cost of safety. Gerald Corbett's demise as Railtrack's chief executive can be traced back to his admission of this possible conflict at the Commons Transport sub-Committee just a couple of weeks before his sacking.

Safety has been compromised because of the fragmentation of the network and this is the most powerful argument for some measure of reintegration. It is mistaken to compare the rail industry with other transport systems like aviation, where different companies happily co-exist, because on the railways every train and every movement is constantly controlled by a signalling system. Moreover, the movement of trains is highly circumscribed given their need to stay on the track and, as those silly people who wanted there to be open access to the network quickly discovered, there are very few passing places. What they did to the rail industry was not, as has been suggested, merely splitting it into various vaguely interlinked businesses, as is the case with aviation. The industry was split to its very core. It is rather like trying to run a restaurant with the chefs working for one company, the waiters for another and the washer-uppers for a third, all linked through a complex set of contracts and financial relationships overlaid with the threat of fines for inedible food or bad service.

Just to add to the depressing picture, the safety concerns have made the economic equation even worse. The public does not, with some justification, trust the privatised railway and therefore demands ever more safety systems, paid for out of taxpayers' pockets because there is no conceivable rate of return on very expensive safety measures which are, in any case, of very marginal value.

To sum up: the privatisation of BR was an attempt to inject capitalist methods and structures into an industry that is simply not able to adapt them to its needs. In time it will be seen as a crazy experiment led by ideological politicians and supported by equally messianic civil servants. In

the meantime, we all suffer the consequences of the naivety and arro-
gance of those who created this dreadful structure, and we have to work
towards a way out of the mess, unaided by those who created it or perpetuate it.

The most important lesson to be learnt from this depressing story is
that there are limits to privatisation. It seems incredible that, as I write
this, a new Labour government has been re-elected with more privatisation as its Big Idea. Ministers and mandarins should read this tale before
proceeding. In particular, they should attempt to understand the nature
of the beast they want to use.

If you give a firm a thirty-year contract to maintain the railway, as is
being suggested under the PPP for the Tube or even, as was the case at
Hatfield, five-year contracts that were at a fixed price, and therefore without incentives to improve performance, the result will always be highly
unsatisfactory. And, take a deep breath Mr Blair, some public services
simply cannot be commodified and bundled up in such a way as to make
them suitable for the private sector. Railtrack was just such an example.
A monopoly requiring vast amounts of subsidy and needing to be integrated into the rest of the railway, Railtrack was always a bad candidate
for the private sector. It is hardly surprising that broadcasters, seeking an
example of a privatisation gone wrong when interviewing ministers,
always refer to the railways. If this failure leads to an understanding of
the practical limits of privatisation, some of the pain will have been
worthwhile. The only part of rail privatisation that worked was the
rolling stock companies because they had a clear product and there was
competition. Railtrack and many of the outlandish Public Finance Initiative schemes can never fulfil those criteria.

Before looking at possible solutions, it is worth examining mistakes
from the pre-privatisation era. The recurring theme of this book is the
failure of the relationship between government and the railways. It is a
sad history but the only way to avoid despair is to learn from these past
mistakes. And there were lots of them before the recent debacle: the *laissez faire* attitude of the Victorians and their refusal to plan the network;
the obsession with preventing monopolies and stimulating competition;
the failure to invest after the First World War; the lack of direction given
to the Big Four; the complex and unwieldy structure created for the
nationalised railway; the scattergun approach of the Modernisation Plan;
the way the Beeching cuts were allowed to proceed without sufficient

thought; the failure, after Beeching, to recognise the social value of the railway and to establish a coherent funding system; the stop-go investment plans; and, above all, the persistent failure of successive governments to have a vision and purpose for the railways. That last is a permanent theme. British governments have always failed to understand that the railways are a national asset that needs nurturing and that it is up to them to set clear objectives.

The trouble with the railways is that they are not quite important enough. Schools and hospitals could not have been subjected to the treatment that the railways have had to endure. The railways are one of those bizarre concerns which politicians do not regard as that important – witness the absence of discussion of the railways, even though they were in a state of crisis, in the 2001 election campaign – but at the same time can make their presence felt by tinkering with them. The railways are never going to cost an election, but because they occupy an unusually sentimental place in the minds of the people, politicians feel they can earn brownie points both by meddling in them and, now that they are privatised, criticising them.

Since they were nationalised in 1948, the railways have suffered from an almost interminable set of reorganisations. The average life span of each structure is around half a decade. As Gourvish observed, fashions ebbed and waned:

> There is much in the argument that the government's uncertainty about the role and prospects of the railways in the postwar mixed economy with the shift of emphasis from 'coordination', 'integration', public service to competition, commercial freedom and viability has distracted railway managers from the essential tasks of marketing, planning and cost-control.[7]

Given this history and the constant administrative upheavals, can it be possible to justify yet another reorganisation? And if so, how do we get to a rational structure?

The answer to the first question is, unfortunately, yes. And to the second, we must, but, as John Lennon said, 'Christ, it ain't easy'. The new Labour government faces an acute dilemma over restructuring the railways because of the political risks of failure but it must be brave and press ahead. The 'do nothing' muddle through so beloved of British policy makers and advocated by some senior civil servants in the new

Department of Transport, Local Government and the Regions will be, quite literally, disastrous. As we have seen, the present structure is unworkable, expensive and less safe (though it must be stressed time and again that the railways are by far the safest form of transport). The widespread public call for renationalisation is not borne of nostalgia and a desire to return to 1960s Britain, but of genuine fears about safety which, given the three disasters, appear completely justified. Another accident or major breakdown as after Hatfield, and the government will face irresistible pressure for change. Since such an event is highly likely, ministers may as well bite the bullet now.

There are three basic problems with the existing structure, all of which are too serious not to addressed in the search for solutions: first, Railtrack cannot function effectively as a conventional, profit-maximising, private sector company; second, the relationship between government and the railways is too complex and, at times, antagonistic; and, third and most important, there are far too many players in the industry created by the vertical separation of Railtrack, train operators and maintenance contractors.

Dealing with the first is relatively easy, at least intellectually, although, in practice, it will take courage on the part of government, a virtue in seemingly short supply if the past four years is a guide. As we have seen, having Railtrack in the private sector simply does not make sense. Selling off Railtrack was the most crassly stupid part of the whole privatisation process. It has delivered none of the claimed benefits. The only way that a private Railtrack could possibly have been effective was to allow it to make commercial decisions to ensure profitability. The result, which some Third World countries have experienced, would have been the closure of large swathes of lines, the prioritisation of freight traffic on many routes and a complete disregard for any social advantages of the railway.

Fortunately, even the Tories did not dare embark on that path (though there were a few zealots in the Treasury who contemplated it). Instead, Railtrack is, quite rightly, prevented from having such a narrowly commercial approach by regulation. In recompense, it gets oodles of subsidy. As Steven Marshall, the chief executive, put it rather bizarrely when asking for yet more subsidy after the full extent of the Hatfield losses had been revealed: 'We are a special public company because we are delivering a major service to the customer. We have been under-investing in this network for a generation.'[8] What he meant was that since Railtrack has to deliver non-commercial services to its customers – the train operators – then it needs to be remunerated from the public purse.

What then are the possible reasons for keeping Railtrack in the private sector? That it takes its share of the risks? That it brings in investment and can raise capital? That it is better than a nationalised concern at handling big projects? That it is better than a nationalised organisation which would have the dead hand of the Treasury in control? That it is cheaper for the taxpayer? It is impossible to answer 'yes' to any of these questions. Railtrack has essentially become a quasi-nationalised company subject to many of the same strictures as BR. It has not even been able to sanction a few tens of millions of investment on the Chiltern line as part of the refranchising deal because the Treasury insists on having the right of veto. Given such detailed control, Railtrack has effectively become a subsidiary of the SRA. The notion of Railtrack as a profit-maximising company being rewarded for risk-taking with generous rates of return (8 per cent) set by the regulator is clearly a nonsense. In its crippled, post-Hatfield state, the company can no longer raise capital, which was the prime purpose for its creation, and clearly it has no future in its present form.

It is a remarkable fact that renationalisation is now perceived, even by right-wing and City commentators, as perfectly acceptable and straightforward and not a politically radical move. Perhaps they feel Railtrack is a discredit to the private sector that they normally promote so readily. John Kay in the *Financial Times* put the case well, pointing out that Railtrack's capital is costing 8 per cent, which is 6 per cent more than it costs the government to borrow, even though there is virtually no risk: 'The principal uncertainty for shareholders is how much money the government will give the company. It is perverse that the government should let the City earn large amounts from speculating about what it will itself decide.'[9] There is, in other words, no point in having a privatised Railtrack if it simply carrying out work that is all paid for by the taxpayer. It is a jolly expensive way of doing it. Similarly, Anthony Hilton, the city editor of the *Evening Standard* argued that 'Things are reaching the point where the quickest and least painful solution might be renationalisation.'[10] Even Ruth Lea, the extremely right-wing economist at the Institute of Directors, agreed that Railtrack should not have been privatised.[11]

With Left and liberal thinkers also widely in favour of taking the railways back into public ownership, at the time of writing, June 2001, there seemed to be a growing consensus that renationalisation was the solution. Only the government was holding out, presumably because such a move runs counter to the whole thrust of privatising public services that was the little Big Idea of Labour's 2001 election campaign.

There would be two advantages in having Railtrack in the public sector. First, the government would have control over the way that its subsidy is spent and the SRA would then be able to direct investment towards the schemes it decided were a priority. And second, as John Kay has pointed out, the cost of borrowing would plummet, allowing the limited amount of money available to be spread more widely. There is another, more nebulous advantage: renationalisation would enable the railways to regain the public sector ethos which they lost at privatisation, that sense of public duty which is a feature of many foreign railways. One interesting suggestion, by Jon Shaw of Aberdeen's Robert Gordon University,[12] is that Railtrack could be merged in with the Highways Agency to provide a level playing field between the two modes.

An old BR hand reckons that any solution has to be based on a change in Railtrack:

> Railtrack can't remain in its current form, an inefficient monopoly frozen in the headlights of its latest disaster. Aligning the interests of the infrastructure operator with the train operators and with the final customers is the key and I would include the SRA as a customer. It seems to me that Railtrack has to be broken up and logic points to a set of regional bodies which must have more engineering competence than at the moment.[13]

The disadvantages of renationalising Railtrack are mainly in the heads of ministers who have simply refused to engage in a sensible debate on the issue and are terrified of frightening the private sector and of incurring Gordon Brown's wrath. Given the City view, the first is quite wrong and the second merely requires a bit of courage.

They are right in one respect. The renationalisation of Railtrack would, indeed, be a momentous step, as it would begin to define the limits of privatisation. And, yes, there would be risks involved. Ministers would potentially face criticism, and even questioning in the Commons, over every minor setback on the railways. *But they already do.* The railways are a national institution even if they are not a nationalised one, and the speed with which John Prescott turned up at the scene of every accident merely confirms that governments cannot get out of taking responsibility for the railways. Railways are perceived to be a government responsibility by a public which is aware that most of the decisions concerning the industry are effectively taken by politicians, whatever the pattern of ownership. The railways would also be back on the government's balance sheet, but, as we have seen, they never really left it.

The biggest objection to the renationalisation of Railtrack is that the company would remain the inefficient monopoly that it has shown itself to be. How could the owner, the government, drive down its costs so that enhancement projects are no longer exorbitantly expensive? Apart from the fact that it would be impossible to do as badly as Railtrack, the answer is proper project management with clear objectives. Working to one master – rather than as, at present, several – would help. The objection that civil servants are not good at running things can, however, be easily discounted. Given that the SRA is now disbursing massive funds to Railtrack, the civil servants are already *de facto* in charge. They might as well be *de jure* as well. State-run enterprises have been problematic, but Railtrack could be the pointer to a new form of public ownership, with greater freedom, ability to raise capital and flexibility, with a light touch from its political masters.

The initial but interim solution, therefore, is to bring Railtrack back into public ownership quickly. Put it out of its misery. This does not require, as ministers have disingenuously and repeatedly claimed, a huge pot of public cash. Instead, control could effectively be gained merely by insisting that the grants it receives are exchanged for equity. Comparing the level of grants with the relatively low market value of Railtrack suggests that the government's refusal to do this has its roots in ideology rather than finance. As we have seen, over the five years from April 2001 Railtrack will receive in the region of £15bn in grants and through the subsidy for track access, and yet its share price in September 2001 suggests that it is worth £2–2.5bn. Therefore it is not money that is blocking repurchase, or the less radical option of swapping subsidy for equity, but the conservative nature of the Labour government.

Another advantage of the renationalisation of Railtrack is that it begins to address the second problem. The government then becomes a real player, which will stop ministers from barracking from the sidelines. (It only took Stephen Byers three weeks in the job before he issued a document urging the railways to improve their performance.) The government, as the infrastructure owner, would have a vested interest in seeing things improve and this would create a real public-private partnership.

The third principle underpinning any solution must be to address what could be called the railway diaspora – the devolution of much of its activity into a host of different organisations. Many people feel that this is an even greater problem than the ownership of Railtrack, but while that may be true, nothing can be done unless Railtrack first is sorted out. And the quickest way to do that is through public ownership.

The two principal fissures that need urgent repairs are between the train operators and Railtrack, and Railtrack and the maintenance companies. Ideally, the whole railway should be brought back together. Regional Railtracks working with regional maintenance contractors, possibly in-house, and providing services to regional train operators, all with the same boundaries, makes the most sense. While many commentators and senior people in the industry agree this is the obvious solution, getting there is the problem. Should it be a big bang with a massive reorganisation or a slow process working towards that goal? Or should this only happen in certain areas where it is easy – Scotland, the former Southern region, etc – leaving the rest to be run by a rump Railtrack? Many railway executives, battered by past reorganisations, are understandably reluctant to embark on yet another one.

My view is that, while this change need not be immediate, prolonging uncertainty in the industry is deeply damaging. Moreover, the SRA's crazy, headlong plunge into letting twenty-year franchises, now stalled, must be permanently killed off. Perpetuating this terrible structure for another two decades is, quite simply, bonkers. A slow, evolutionary approach will not work for a very simple reason: because the railways are such an inherently integrated industry, once some modifications are made, there are always knock-on effects which lead to further changes. It is clear that, despite the protestations of many rail executives who seek evolution rather than revolution, the latter is preferable. Returning Railtrack to public control is the prerequisite for any sensible solution to the structure of the railways. It may be that parts or all of it will then be merged in with train operators or, as has been suggested by Roger

Ford,[14] broken up to create proper railway companies. A number of ways of restructuring the rail industry have been put forward in the aftermath of the Hatfield disaster. The implementation of part two of the Cullen inquiry will require legislation and this would provide an opportunity for a wider restructuring of the rail industry.

None of the possible solutions is perfect. They all create some new problems as well as solving the old ones, but they are all inherently better than the present system. The simplest is the recreation of the Big Four of 1923–48. A Big Four type of structure with integrated railways is a tempting prospect. It is much like the Japanese model of privatisation, and indeed one railway historian argues that had the Big Four structure been left alone in private hands with a supportive government, there would also have been cutbacks and closures but the private companies 'would also have had a real incentive to attempt economies, adopt new technology and search for radical means of raising finance'.[15] But getting there from here is fraught with a myriad of difficulties. The solution also runs counter to the European Commission's desire to split services from operations, but again this is not an insuperable difficulty. For example, the infrastructure could be leased or vested in a separate subsidiary.

Rail is, according to an inside source, top of the agenda on the Labour government's new delivery unit. It has four priorities – health, education, crime and transport – and the latter includes only the rail network and the Tube. Therefore, Tony Blair will expect some results and Stephen Byers will be ill-advised to try to keep on muddling through with the existing structure. He needs to articulate a vision for the railways and how they will change in the next two or three decades. Governments have always been particularly bad at this 'vision thing' in the past. Should resources be channelled towards commuter routes or the former InterCity lines? How does he ensure that the railways are a factor in reducing social exclusion? And so on. There is, for example, a plan to build a freight-only railway to take lorries from the North West to the Channel Tunnel and beyond. It is a £6bn private sector scheme which needs government support. Maybe it is impossible and the figures put forward by the promoters are just too optimistic. But it is the sort of Big Idea that could make a real difference to the number of vehicles on the roads with all the associated environmental advantages. Or he could put the government's weight behind the plan to have a new north–south high-speed route. There are no end of exciting possibilities which would delight the electorate, as the railways are very popular. Indeed, the railways are a nineteenth-century invention, which have a great future in the twenty-first century, but only if they are nurtured by a sensible government. History, unfortunately, suggests that this is unlikely to happen.

Glossary

ASLEF: Associated Society of Locomotive Engineers and Firemen, the train drivers union.

APT: Advanced Passenger Train, Britain's first tilting train, which was scrapped after problems with the three prototype trains in passenger service.

ATP: Automatic Train Protection which prevents a train from going past a red light by constantly monitoring its speed.

ATOC: Association of Train Operating Companies, the statutorily-based trade association for the train operators which negotiates on their behalf and handles certain common functions such as telephone enquiries and fares allocation

AWS: Automatic Warning System, a device which sounds a horn in the cab to alert the driver when approaching a red light and which has to be cancelled for the train to proceed.

Big Four: The four rail companies created in the 1923 consolidation and which were nationalised in 1948: Great Western Railway; London, Midland and Scottish; London and North Eastern Railway; Southern Railway.

Briscos: British Rail Infrastructure Companies. British Rail's engineering department was packaged up as six renewal and seven maintenance companies, regionally based, for privatisation. These thirteen Briscos were guaranteed long-term contracts with Railtrack and were privatised in 1996.

ECML: East Coast Main Line. The main lines out of King's Cross, linking London with Peterborough, York, Newcastle-upon-Tyne and Edinburgh.

ETCS: European Train Control System. A standard signalling system for European railways. There are three levels which the European Commission hopes will be progressively introduced across the European Union. Level one provides ATP; the second provides signal indications into the cab by radio, but retains some outside signals; the third is a full system of radio control with no lineside signals.

HSE: Health and Safety Executive, of which HMRI has been part since 1990.

HSC: Health and Safety Commission, the board of the HSE.

HMRI: Her Majesty's Railway Inspectorate, part of the Health and Safety Executive.

NAO: National Audit Office, one of the government's financial watchdogs

NMS: Network Management Statement, the document which Railtrack is required by the regulator to produce annually setting out the investment plans for the railways.

OPRAF: Office of Passenger Rail Franchising. Created by the Railways Act 1993 which privatised the railways, OPRAF's task was to franchise out the railway to private operators, a task which it completed just before the 1997 election. OPRAF was subsumed into the Strategic Rail Authority created by the Labour government.

Passenger's charter: The performance tables produced by BR, then by OPRAF and now by the Strategic Rail Authority setting out the punctuality and reliability of each operator. Punctuality refers to the number of trains which arrive less than five minutes (for short journeys) or ten minutes (for former InterCity routes) late. Reliability refers to the percentage of cancellations.

PTEs: Passenger Transport Executives, which provide and fund, with government aid, rail, bus and tram services in six regional conurbations

RMT: The National Union of Rail, Maritime and Transport workers which represents many railway staff, apart from most drivers who belong to ASLEF.

Rail Regulator or the Office of the Rail Regulator: The regulator's principal role is to set the charges which Railtrack levies on the train operators and to ensure that Railtrack does not abuse its monopoly position. The regulator has little to do with the franchises, which are largely regulated by the Strategic Rail Authority. The first rail regulator was John Swift, who was succeeded temporarily by Chris Bolt, and since the summer of 1999 the post has been held by Tom Winsor.

Railway Group Standards: Standards that specify those features which are necessary for the safe operation of the railway. All companies working on the railway must comply with them as a requirement of their safety case.

Railway Safety: A separate, not for profit company owned by Railtrack which was formerly Railtrack's Safety and Standards Directorate, but separated from the main company in the aftermath of the Ladbroke Grove crash. It sets and monitors safety standards for the industry. The HSE is responsible for accepting safety cases after they have been vetted by Railway Safety. In September 2001 the second part of the Cullen report recommended that Railway Safety be replaced by an independent Rail Industry Safety Body.

Railways Act 1993: The Act that broke up British Rail and privatised the railways.

Roscos: the rolling stock companies. The Roscos became the owners of British Rail's 11,260 locomotives and coaches when BR was broken up in 1994 and were privatised in 1996.

Safety Case: A document setting out an assessment of risks and ways of mitigating them which must be prepared by every company seeking to operate in the rail industry.

SPAD: Signal Passed at Danger.

Special Purpose Vehicle: A consortium of companies brought together to bring about a specific investment project on the railway.

SSD: The Safety and Standards Directorate of Railtrack, which later became Railway Safety.

Strategic Rail Authority: The SRA was created by the Labour government to replace OPRAF and to have a wider strategic role in channelling both private and public sector investment into the rail industry. Created in 1999 in shadow form under the chairmanship of Sir Alastair Morton, and eventually assuming permanent status in 2001, the SRA's principal day-to-day task is to let franchises to train operators and to monitor the franchisees' performance. The SRA works to instructions and objectives set by ministers.

TOCs: Train Operating Companies. On privatisation the railway was divided into twenty-five franchises, which were let to train operating companies. Although there are twenty-five, in fact several franchises are owned by the same company and effectively there are only ten different firms involved.

TPWS: Train Protection and Warning System, a more sophisticated version of AWS, currently being fitted across the rail network TPWS will stop a train within the overlap between the signal and the junction it is protecting if it is approaching a red signal at up to 70mph. For faster trains, it will apply the brakes but will probably not stop it before the junction.

WCML: West Coast Main Line. The main lines out of Euston, linking London with Milton Keynes, Crewe, Liverpool, Manchester, Preston, Carlisle and Glasgow.

Notes

CHAPTER ONE

1 Reliable source.
2 Interview with author.
3 House of Commons, Environment, Transport and Regional Affairs Committee, *Recent Events on the Railway*, December 2000.
4 Interview with author.
5 *Modern Railways*, August 2001.
6 Railtrack press release, 27 November 2000.
7 *Modern Railways*, January 2001.
8 *British Railways Track, Design, Construction and Maintenance*, Permanent Way Institution, 1971.
9 *New Civil Engineer*, 15 February 2001.
10 *Financial Times*, 12 May 2001.
11 Several interviews with author.
12 *Sunday Telegraph*, 29 October 2000.
13 *Independent*, 11 April 2001.
14 Interview with author.
15 ITN interview, 1 November 2000.
16 Speech reported in SRA press release, 28 November 2000.
17 Interview with author.
18 According to official statistics, travelling by rail is about six times safer than going by car. However, the figure for deaths on the railways includes anyone with a ticket, even if they fall in front of a train through drunkenness, and if these people are excluded, the true figure is something like 100 times safer.
19 Interview on ITV, 12 December 2000.
20 *Daily Telegraph*, 25 November 2000.
21 *Daily Telegraph*, 14 December 2000.
22 Defined as arriving within ten minutes of schedule for long distance (former InterCity) trains and five minutes for London commuter and other operators.
23 Strategic Rail Authority, *National Rail Trends 3, 2000–1*, March 2001.
24 *Rail Finance Monitor 2001*, p.vii, TAS Publications and Events Ltd, April 2001.

CHAPTER TWO

1 B.R. Mitchell, *Abstract of British Historical Statistics*, p.225, Cambridge University Press, 1962.
2 R.W. Kostal, *Law and English Railway Capitalism, 1825–1875*, p.115, Oxford University Press, 1994.
3 Nick Faith, *The World the Railways Made*, Bodley Head, 1990, gives many further examples.
4 By 1859 ninety-six railway company directors sat in the House of Commons, and forty-four in the House of Lords.
5 Michael Freeman, *Railways and the Victorian Imagination*, p.4, Yale University Press, 1999.

6 T.R. Gourvish, *British Railways 1948–1973, a Business History*, p.13, Cambridge University Press, 1986.

7 Strangely, a version of Parliamentary Trains remains today. Rail companies are obliged by legislation to run at least one train per week on all their lines. There are about a dozen examples of 'ghost-trains' being run once per week along a section of line just to prevent the lengthy closure procedures from kicking in.

8 E.T. MacDermot, *History of the Great Western Railway*, p.436, David & Charles, 1964.

9 T.B. Macaulay, *Speeches, 1854*, quoted in Jack Simmons and Gordon Biddle, eds, *The Oxford Companion to British Railway History*, Oxford University Press, 1997.

10 P.J. Cain, 'Railways 1870–1914' in M.J. Freeman and D.H. Aldcroft, eds, *The Atlas of British Railway History*, David & Charles, 1985.

11 W.M. Ackworth, *The Railways of England*, 1900.

12 Michael Freeman, *Railways and the Victorian Imagination*, p.107, Yale University Press, 1999.

13 See, for example, *Danger Signals* and *Danger on the Line*, both Ian Allan.

14 Jack Simmons and Gordon Biddle, eds, *The Oxford Companion to British Railway History*, p.3, Oxford University Press, 1997.

15 Andrew Dow in *Steel Wheels, Britain's Railways 1825–2000*, Emap Active, 2000.

16 *The Economist*, 9 August 1919.

17 Jon Shaw, Clive Charlton and Richard Gibb, 'The competitive spirit reawakens the ghost of railway monopoly', *Transport Policy* 5, 1998.

18 Jack Simmons and Gordon Biddle, eds, *The Oxford Companion to British Railway History*, p.289, Oxford University Press, 1997.

19 Andrew Dow in *Steel Wheels, Britain's Railways 1825–2000*, Emap Active, 2000.

20 T.R. Gourvish, *British Railways 1948–1973, a Business History*, p.2, Cambridge University Press, 1986.

21 In 1947 the chief inspector of the railways, Sir Alan Mount, in his annual report commented that five serious accidents in which sixty-one people died would probably not have occurred had there not been the maintenance backlog and had the installation of colour light signalling proceeded.

22 T.R. Gourvish, *British Railways 1948–1973, a Business History*, p.14, Cambridge University Press, 1986.

23 David Henshaw, *The Great Railway Conspiracy*, p.37, Leading Edge, 1991.

24 From a staff memo quoted in T.R. Gourvish, *British Railways 1948–1973, a Business History*, p.67, Cambridge University Press, 1986.

25 T.R. Gourvish, *British Railways 1948–1973, a Business History*, p.27, Cambridge University Press, 1986.

26 The Great Western directors managed to retain their free first-class travel passes!

27 Sir Norman Chester, *Nationalisation of British Industry, 1945–1951*, HMSO, 1975.

CHAPTER THREE

1 David Henshaw, *The Great Railway Conspiracy*, p.45, Leading Edge, 1991.

2 T.R. Gourvish, *British Railways 1948–1973, a Business History*, p.67, Cambridge University Press, 1986.

3 Quoted in T.R. Gourvish, *British Railways 1948–1973, a Business History*, p.68, Cambridge University Press, 1986.

4 David Henshaw, *The Great Railway Conspiracy*, p.55, Leading Edge, 1991.

5 Quoted in T.R. Gourvish, *British Railways 1948–1973, a Business History*, p.270, Cambridge University Press, 1986.

6 T.R. Gourvish, *British Railways 1948–1973, a Business History*, p.289, Cambridge University Press, 1986.

7 Gerald Fiennes, *I Tried to Run a Railway*, Ian Allan, 1967.

8 British Railways Board, *The Reshaping of Britain's Railways*, HMSO, 1963.

9 David Henshaw, *The Great Railway Conspiracy*, p.147, Leading Edge, 1991.

10 David Henshaw, *The Great Railway Conspiracy*, p.177, Leading Edge, 1991.

11 British Railways Board, *The Development of the Major Railway Trunk Routes*, BRB, 1965.

12 This was the first of two attempts to undertake such radical cuts to the network – Serpell two decades later was the second – and while such measures seem ludicrous today, it must be noted that several Third World countries, even relatively affluent ones, have suffered equally devastating cuts to their passenger networks or even their total shutdown.

13 David Henshaw, *The Great Railway Conspiracy*, p.234, Leading Edge, 1991.

14 David Henshaw, *The Great Railway Conspiracy*, p.233, Leading Edge, 1991.

15 Actually, that was probably wrong because, as we shall see, InterCity consistently achieved profitability in the late 1980s and early 1990s and even Network SouthEast did so briefly.

16 T.R. Gourvish, *British Railways 1948–1973, a Business History*, p.398, Cambridge University Press, 1986.

17 David Henshaw, *The Great Railway Conspiracy*, p.198, Leading Edge, 1991.

18 Nigel G. Harris and Ernest Godward, *The Privatisation of British Rail*, p.52, The Railway Consultancy Press, 1997.

19 John Welsby and Alan Nichols, 'The Privatisation of Britain's Railways', *Journal of Transport Economics & Policy*, Vol. 33, Part 1, 1999.

20 Jack Simmons and Gordon Biddle, *The Oxford Companion to British Railway History*, p.57, Oxford University Press, 1997.

21 Interview with author.

22 Nigel G. Harris and Ernest Godward, *The Privatisation of British Rail*, p.55, The Railway Consultancy Press, 1997.

23 Reliable source.

24 T.R. Gourvish, *British Railways 1948–1973, a Business History*, p.304, Cambridge University Press, 1986.

CHAPTER FOUR

1   Conservative Research Department, *Report of the policy group on nationalised industries*, 1968.

2   Jon Shaw, *Competition, Regulation and the Privatisation of British Rail*, Ashgate, 2000.

3   Jon Shaw, *Competition, Regulation and the Privatisation of British Rail*, Ashgate, 2000.

4   *Hansard*, 1990, col. 606.

5   Interview with author.

6   This was a misreading of data. While the proportion of journeys undertaken by rail has declined as car use has risen enormously, the number of rail trips has remained largely static since the Second World War, ebbing and flowing according to economic growth but demonstrating remarkable long-term stability.

7   Interview with author.

8   Interview with author.

9   Reliable source.

10 *Financial Times*, 1 May 2001.

11 In fact, by creating twenty-five different train companies, all requiring drivers, the hand of the drivers' union, ASLEF, was greatly strengthened and drivers' wages soared as the union managed to strike lucrative deals for its members. This was an example of the law of unintended consequences that dogged the whole privatisation process.

12 Interview with author.

13 13 April 2001.

14 Christopher Knill and Dirk Lehmkuhl, *An alternative route of legal integration: the community's railway policy*, European integration online papers, Vol. 2 (1998) No. 3; http://eiop.or.at/eiop/texte/1998-003a.htm

15 Interview with author.

16 Interview with author.

17 *Independent*, 18 November 1992.

18 Interview with author.

19 Interview with author, quoted in Freeman and Shaw, eds, *All Change: British Railway Privatisation*, McGraw Hill, 2000.

20 *Independent*, 20 January 1993.

21 Roger Freeman and Jon Shaw, eds, *All Change: British Railway Privatisation*, McGraw Hill, 2000.
22 *Hansard*, cols 156–255, 2 February 1993.
23 *Hansard*, col. 719, 18 Jan 1995.
24 Interview with author, quoted in Freeman and Shaw, eds, *All Change: British Railway Privatisation*, McGraw Hill, 2000.
25 *Evening Standard*, 29 November 1992.
26 Interview with author.
27 *Hansard*, 15 November 1996.
28 *Guardian*, 24 October 1995.
29 *Independent*, 20 November 1995.
30 Interview with author.
31 *Independent*, 1 November 1995.
32 Christian Wolmar, *Stagecoach*, p.136, Orion Business Books, 1999.

CHAPTER FIVE

1 Interview with author.
2 John Edmonds in Roger Freeman and Jon Shaw, eds, *All Change: British Rail Privatisation*, p.59, McGraw Hill, 2000.
3 Interview with author.
4 Interview with author.
5 Interview with author.
6 Interview with author.
7 Shoji Sumita, *Success Story*, p.xvi, Profile Books, 2000.
8 Interview with author.
9 John Edmonds in Roger Freeman and Jon Shaw, eds, *All Change: British Rail Privatisation*, p.75, McGraw Hill, 2000.
10 Interview with author.
11 Interview with author.
12 Interview with author.
13 National Audit Office, *The Flotation of Railtrack*, December 1998, The Stationery Office, HC25 1998/9.
14 NAO report, p.36.
15 NAO report, p.4.
16 NAO report, p.53.
17 Quoted in Christian Wolmar, 'What track is the Labour Party travelling on?', *Independent*, 5 February 1996.
18 *Independent*, 16 April 1996.
19 *Independent on Sunday*, 1 October 1995.
20 *Independent*, 26 September 1995.
21 *Independent*, 9 March 1996.
22 In Roger Freeman and Jon Shaw, eds, *All Change: British Rail Privatisation*, p.225, McGraw Hill, 2000.
23 Interview with author.
24 Railtrack, *Network Management Statement, 1996/7*, May 1996.
25 Railtrack annual report and accounts, 1999/2000, p.9.
26 Interview with *Rail*, 1–14 November 2000 (unused).
27 *Observer*, 2 April 2001.
28 In Roger Freeman and Jon Shaw, eds, *All Change: British Rail Privatisation*, p.64, McGraw Hill, 2000.
29 The structure was expected to be changed again following the publication of the second part of Lord Cullen's inquiry, published in September 2001.
30 *Maintaining a safe railway infrastructure*, HSE, March 1996.

CHAPTER SIX

1　*On the Record*, 2 May 1998, BBC1.
2　*Guardian*, 6 June 1997.
3　*Evening Standard*, 5 June 1997.
4　*Rail Professional*, February 2001.
5　*Daily Mail*, 21 July 1998.
6　*Modern Railways*, January 1999.
7　*Daily Mail*, 'War on the motorist'; *Daily Express*, 'Blair's war on drivers', both front page headlines, 18 November 1999.
8　Although the real cost of motoring has remained unchanged over the past twenty-five years as improved technology has nullified the effect of the rise in fuel prices, there was a widespread perception that motorists were being 'ripped off'.
9　According to a letter from Blair's private office, his last significant mention of public transport before the 4 June election was in a speech on New Year's day.
10　Interview with author.
11　Jon Shaw and William Walton, quoted in *The Times*, 4 January 2001.
12　*Modern Railways*, 'Direction, the political imperative', January 1999.

CHAPTER SEVEN

1　*Maintaining a safe railway infrastructure*, HSE, March 1996.
2　*Railway Safety*, Annual report of HMRI, 1996/7, HSE 1997.
3　Professor John Uff, *The Southall Rail Accident Report*, p.64, HSE Books, 2000.
4　Professor John Uff, *The Southall Rail Accident Report*, p.173, HSE Books, 2000.
5　Professor John Uff, *The Southall Rail Accident Report*, p.68, HSE Books, 2000.
6　Professor John Uff, *The Southall Rail Accident Report*, p.145, HSE Books 2000.
7　Professor John Uff, *The Southall Rail Accident Report*, p.143, HSE Books, 2000.
8　Professor John Uff, *The Southall Rail Accident Report*, p.140, HSE Books, 2000.
9　Professor John Uff, *The Southall Rail Accident Report*, p.87, HSE Books, 2000.
10　Professor John Uff, *The Southall Rail Accident Report*, p.60, HSE Books, 2000.
11　In fact, estimates now suggest that the cost of network wide implementation on 100mph lines will be in the order of £2–3bn.
12　Such cost-benefit analyses of safety schemes are standard practice, although people outside the industry – notably TV interviewers – often find it shocking that such a relatively low figure can be put on a life saved. However, these calculations are essential. Of course, the value of the life of a spouse, sibling or child is virtually infinite, but these calculations are based on the notion of the potential death of an anonymous person at some future date.
13　Reproduced in Annex 26 B in Professor John Uff, The Southall Rail Accident Report, HSE Books, 2000.
14　Reproduced in Annex 26 B in Professor John Uff, The Southall Rail Accident Report, HSE Books, 2000.
15　Interview with author.
16　Professor John Uff, *The Southall Rail Accident Report*, p.154, HSE Books, 2000.
17　Southall inquiry hearings, day 27.
18　Southall inquiry hearings, day 27.
19　Professor John Uff, *The Southall Rail Accident Report*, p.164, HSE Books, 2000.
20　Professor John Uff, *The Southall Rail Accident Report*, p.207, HSE Books, 2000.
21　Southall inquiry hearings, day 25.
22　Professor John Uff, *The Southall Rail Accident Report*, p.207, HSE Books, 2000.
23　Sir David Davies, *Automatic Train Protection for the Railway Network in Britain – a study*, p.18, Royal Academy of Engineering, 2000.
24　Interview with author.
25　Professor John Uff, *The Southall Rail Accident Report*, p.166, HSE Books, 2000.
26　Professor John Uff, *The Southall Rail Accident Report*, p.43, HSE Books, 2000.
27　Professor John Uff, *The Southall Rail Accident Report*, p 87, HSE Books, 2000.

CHAPTER EIGHT

1 The speed of impact in the Great Heck disaster, a head-on crash caused by a Land Rover on the tracks, is thought to have been even faster, at over 140mph, than the Ladbroke Grove crash.

2 Lord Cullen, *The Ladbroke Grove Rail Inquiry, Part 1 report*, HSE, 2001.

3 Lord Cullen, *The Ladbroke Grove Rail Inquiry, Part 1 report*, p.109, HSE, 2001.

4 Lord Cullen, *The Ladbroke Grove Rail Inquiry, Part 1 report*, p.258, HSE, 2001

5 Lord Cullen, *The Ladbroke Grove Rail Inquiry, Part 1 report*, p.3, HSE, 2001.

6 Oddly, one of my contacts, John Fowler, a former railwayman, was on a train stuck as a result of the safety procedures following that SPAD, and spotted the flaw in the track lay-out and regrets not having done anything about it at the time: 'My former signalling bosses at Waterloo would have gone ballistic had they been presented with the design for the interlocking at Paddington,' he says.

7 This would actually have posed major problems for Railtrack, as it would have reduced the capacity of the station and led to reductions in the number of train services and thus less revenue for the company. Indeed, Railtrack HQ made clear that such a scheme was not viable.

8 Lord Cullen, *The Ladbroke Grove Rail Inquiry, Part 1 report*, p.129, HSE, 2001.

9 Lord Cullen, *The Ladbroke Grove Rail Inquiry, Part 1 report*, p.131, HSE, 2001.

10 Lord Cullen, *The Ladbroke Grove Rail Inquiry, Part 1 report*, p.113, HSE, 2001.

11 Lord Cullen, *The Ladbroke Grove Rail Inquiry, Part 1 report*, p 113, HSE, 2001.

12 Lord Cullen, *The Ladbroke Grove Rail Inquiry, Part 1 report*, p.113, HSE, 2001.

13 Lord Cullen, *The Ladbroke Grove Rail Inquiry, Part 1 report*, p.114, HSE, 2001.

14 As an aside, Lord Cullen and, indeed, everyone else who has investigated the accident is at a loss to understand why the gantry was sited there, instead of in front of the bridge where it would have afforded much better visibility. The stated reason was to accommodate fast freight trains which have longer braking distances, but this was a passenger line and therefore this reason does not make sense.

15 Lord Cullen, *The Ladbroke Grove Rail Inquiry, Part 1 report*, p.259, HSE, 2001.

16 Evidence to the inquiry, p.m., 12 June 2000.

17 Evidence to the inquiry, p.m., 12 June 2000.

18 Lord Cullen, *The Ladbroke Grove Rail Inquiry, Part 1 report*, p.108, HSE, 2001.

19 The Great Western was on a different radio system and the Slough signallers would have had to contact Swindon control to communicate with the driver of the HST and that would have taken much too long to prevent the accident. Railtrack had cancelled a plan to install a national system for all trains without explanation in 1999.

20 Lord Cullen, *The Ladbroke Grove Rail Inquiry, Part 1 report*, p.99, HSE, 2001.

21 Lord Cullen, *The Ladbroke Grove Rail Inquiry, Part 1 report*, p.96, HSE, 2001.

22 Lord Cullen, *The Ladbroke Grove Rail Inquiry, Part 1 report*, p.58, HSE, 2001.

23 Lord Cullen, *The Ladbroke Grove Rail Inquiry, Part 1 report*, p.61, HSE, 2001.

24 Lord Cullen, *The Ladbroke Grove Rail Inquiry, Part 1 report*, p.61, HSE, 2001.

25 Professor John Uff *The Southall Rail Accident Report*, Annex 26 D, HSE Books, 2000.

26 *The management of safety in Railtrack*, a review by the Health and Safety Executive, HSE, 2000.

CHAPTER NINE

1 Ian Jack, *The crash that stopped Britain*, Granta, April 2001.

2 *Financial Times*, 7 May 2001.

3 *Guardian*, 16 January 2001.

4 They are not being 'soft'. The force and wind effects generated by the trains are awesome, as anyone who has stood at a station while a High Speed Train thunders past will know.

5 Kevin Sawley and Richard Reiff, *Rail failure assessment for the Office of the Rail Regulator*, p.42, Transportation Technology Center Inc., October 2000.

6 *Financial Times*, 22 February 2001.

7 *Guardian*, 16 January 2001.

8 *Guardian*, 16 January 2001.

9 Interview with John Ware, not broadcast.

10 Demonstrating, incidentally, the amazing improvement in rolling stock over the subsequent thirty-

three years given the very high survival rates at both Hatfield and four months later at Great Heck, where a derailed GNER train smashed head-on into a freight train at a combined speed of around 140mph and only ten out of the one hundred people on board were killed.

11 *Maintaining a safe railway infrastructure*, HSE, March 1996.
12 *Maintaining a safe railway infrastructure*, p.19, HSE, March 1996.
13 Interview with author.
14 *Railway accident at Bexley*, HSE, March 1999.
15 *Railway accident at Bexley*, p.18, HSE, March 1999.
16 *Railway accident at Bexley*, p.17, HSE, March 1999.
17 *Railway accident at Bexley*, p.21, HSE, March 1999.
18 *Railway accident at Bexley*, p.21, HSE, March 1999.
19 BBC Online, 22 March 1999.
20 *Financial Times*, 7 May 2001.
21 Press release accompanying *Railway Safety Statistics Bulletin, 1998–99*, HSE, December 1999.
22 *Railway Safety Statistics Bulletin, 1998–99*, HSE, 1999.
23 Chris Bolt, who was acting rail regulator after John Swift's departure.
24 *Financial Times*, 22 February 2001.
25 Kevin Sawley and Richard Reiff, *Rail failure assessment for the Office of the Rail Regulator*, p.11, Transportation Technology Center Inc., October 2000.
26 Quoted in Ian Jack, *The crash that stopped Britain*, Granta, April 2001.
27 Kevin Sawley and Richard Reiff, *Rail failure assessment for the Office of the Rail Regulator*, p.31, Transportation Technology Center Inc., October 2000.
28 Kevin Sawley and Richard Reiff, *Rail failure assessment for the Office of the Rail Regulator*, p.51, Transportation Technology Center Inc., October 2000.
29 Information on grinding provided to author by Railtrack.
30 Stuart Grassie, 'Preventive Grinding Controls RCF Defects', *International Railway Journal*, January 2001.
31 Interview with author.
32 According to figures supplied by the Association of Train Operating Companies, there were 17,426 trains on a normal weekday in the summer of 1996 and 18,664 four years later.
33 Information supplied by Rail Freight Group.
34 Roger Freeman and Jon Shaw, eds, *All Change: British Railway Privatisation*, p.87, McGraw Hill, 2000.
35 Kevin Sawley and Richard Reiff, *Rail failure assessment for the Office of the Rail Regulator*, p.40, Transportation Technology Center Inc., October 2000.
36 Interview with author.
37 Kevin Sawley and Richard Reiff, *Rail failure assessment for the Office of the Rail Regulator*, p.27, Transportation Technology Center Inc., October 2000.
38 House of Commons Transport Select Committee, Fourth report 1994/5 *Railway Finances Volume 2, minutes of evidence*, Q 141, p.97, House of Commons, July 1995.
39 *Network Management Statement 1995/6*, p.20, Railtrack, 1996.
40 Kevin Sawley and Richard Reiff, *Rail failure assessment for the Office of the Rail Regulator*, p.46, Transportation Technology Center Inc., October 2000.
41 Interview for *Rail*, November 2000.
42 Interview with author.
43 Interview in *Rail* 406, 4–17 April 2001.
44 House of Commons, Environment, Transport and Regional Affairs Committee, *Recent Events on the Railway*, p.7, Q 57, December 2000.
45 House of Commons, Environment, Transport and Regional Affairs Committee, *Recent Events on the Railway*, p.7–8, Q 57/59, December 2000.
46 Interview for *Rail*, November 2001 (unused).
47 *Rail* 398, 13–26 December 2000.

CHAPTER TEN

1 House of Commons, Environment, Transport and Regional Affairs Committee, *Recent Events on the Railway*, December 2000.

2 House of Commons, Environment, Transport and Regional Affairs Committee, *Recent Events on the Railway*, p.18, Q 182, December 2000.
3 Ladbroke Grove Inquiry hearings, 8 December 2000.
4 Ladbroke Grove Inquiry hearings, 8 December 2000.
5 Ladbroke Grove Inquiry, seminar on employee perspectives on safety, 18 October 2000.
6 *RMT News*, p.11, March 1998.
7 Ladbroke Grove Inquiry hearings, 8 December 2000.
8 Ladbroke Grove Inquiry hearings, 8 December 2000.
9 *Mirror*, 12 December 2000.
10 Ladbroke Grove Inquiry, seminar on employee perspectives on safety, 18 October 2000.
11 Ladbroke Grove Inquiry, seminar on employee perspectives on safety, 18 October 2000.
12 *Railway Safety 1999/2000*, p.9, HSE, 2000.
13 *Railway Safety 1999/2000*, p.68, HSE, 2000.
14 These are category 3 (overrun greater than 200 yards with no damage) to category 8 (fatalities to passengers or staff).
15 Ladbroke Grove Inquiry, seminar on employee perspectives on safety, 18 October 2000.
16 The high number of deaths of passengers falling from InterCity trains – around 20 per year – was a scandal in the 1980s and early 1990s which was finally addressed only after a lengthy press campaign, notably in the *Observer*, through the simple and cost effective fitting of central locking devices on all InterCity trains.
17 Interview with author.
18 Why does this not happen in the mostly privately-run aviation industry? Simply because accidents are so rare and the causes can often be traced to matters which clearly have nothing to do with the profit motive, such as the weather or pilot error.
19 For an excellent analysis of road traffic safety schemes, see Andrew Evans, *Economic Evaluation of Road Traffic Safety Measures*, Economic Research Centre.
20 Roger Ford in *Modern Railways*, May 2001, points out that in 1994 BR compiled a list of 250 safety projects by order of Value per Prevented Fatality and there were many in the region of £1m–2m, several of which may well not have been implemented.
21 Professor Andrew Evans, Professor of Transport Safety at the Centre for Transport Studies, University and Imperial College, in fact estimates that it is probable that, on average, only one life per year will be saved.
22 Press statement 29 March 2001 accompanying publication of Professor John Uff and Lord Cullen, *The joint inquiry into train protection systems*, HSE Books, March 2001.
23 Professor John Uff and Lord Cullen, *The joint inquiry into train protection systems*, p.39, HSE Books, March 2001.
24 E-mail to author.
25 E-mail to author.
26 In fact, a senior Railtrack executive told me in June 2001 that the estimate of the cost was already £3.6bn.
27 Letter, *Modern Railways*, June 2001.
28 In fact, getting rid of Mark 1 coaches should have been a requirement during the first franchise round but the opportunity was missed through the feebleness of the Health and Safety Executive which ducked the issue rather than pressing for it.
29 The statistics for the railways include people who have fallen down stairs at stations and even those who are killed 'surfing' on the top of trains (as happened in 1998/9), provided they have a ticket or were expected to buy one; this contrasts with figures for air safety which do not include people killed or injured at airports.
30 E.g. Professor Bill Bradshaw, 'Safe, reliable, resilient and robust – Lord Bradshaw's blueprint', *Modern Railways*, May 2001.
31 Wolmar column, *Rail*, 21 Feb–6 Mar 2001.
32 E-mail to author.
33 British Rail fares increased by 45 per cent above the rate of inflation between 1980 and 1995.
34 *Rail*, 21 Mar–3 Apr 2001, p.29.
35 Correspondence between author and Railtrack.
36 From a table compiled in Roger Freeman and Jon Shaw, eds, *All Change: British Rail Privatisation*, p.174, McGraw Hill, 2000.

37 The Strategic Rail Authority eventually stopped this massaging of the statistics by banning this practice of companies simply discounting their bad days.
38 Booz Allen Hamilton, *Railtrack's Performance in the control period 1995–2001*, Office of the Rail Regulator, March 1999.
39 Booz Allen Hamilton, *Railtrack's Performance in the control period 1995–2001*, Office of the Rail Regulator, p.6, March 1999.
40 Interview with author.
41 Interview with author.
42 Bill Bradshaw in Roger Freeman and Jon Shaw, eds, *All Change: British Rail Privatisation*, p.232, McGraw Hill, 2000.
43 Booz Allen Hamilton, *Railtrack's Performance in the control period 1995–2001*, p.8, Office of the Rail Regulator, March 1999.
44 Roger Ford, 'Customer Service', *Modern Railways*, November 1999.
45 Figures from *Rail Finance Monitor*, TAS Publications and Events Ltd, 2001.
46 Interview with author.
47 *Financial Times*, 3 June 2001.
48 Ladbroke Grove Inquiry, seminar on employee perspectives on safety, 18 October 2000.
49 Nigel G. Harris and Ernest Godward, *The Privatisation of British Rail*, p.139, The Railway Consultancy Press, 1997.
50 According to an analysis by the Railway Development Society.
51 National Audit Office, *The award of the first three passenger franchises*, Stationery Office, 1996
52 *Rail* 398, 13–26 December 2000.
53 Railway Forum, *Financial support to the rail industry before and after privatisation*, April 1998.
54 *Railway Finance Monitor*, TAS Publications and Events Ltd, April 2001.
55 *Railway Finance Monitor*, TAS Publications and Events Ltd, April 2001.
56 Association of Train Operating Companies, press release, 12 April 2001.
57 Letter to commuters from Charles Belcher, Silverlink managing director.
58 Under the Byzantine contractual arrangements between Railtrack and the train operators, compensation payments were restricted to the amount of access charges Railtrack received from each company. For example, GNER pays £2.6m per month access charges but revenue from passengers was around £7m per month before Hatfield. Therefore, since the company lost over half its revenue because of Railtrack's failings, even free access was insufficient compensation to make up the losses. On the other hand, the regional operators, for whom access charges were a huge proportion of their costs, found that the compensation paid by Railtrack more than made up the loss of income from passengers not travelling.
59 *Financial Times*, 18 April 2001.
60 'Insider', *Rail*, 4–17 April 2001.
61 Railtrack *1999/2000 Annual report and accounts*, p.34.
62 Interview with author.
63 Interview with author.
64 Quoted in *Rail*, 24 Jan–6 Feb, p.71.
65 'Insider', *Rail*, 4–17 April 2001.
66 *Daily Telegraph*, 16 January 2001.
67 *Rail*, 7–20 February 2001.
68 The government tried to claim that it could appoint this director but Railtrack's board retains its right under company law to choose who should sit on it.
69 *Evening Standard*, 5 June 2001.
70 Speech to Institution of Electrical Engineers, 12 June 2001.

CHAPTER ELEVEN

1 Interview with author.
2 Analysed in *Modern Railways*, October 1997.
3 Interview with author.
4 John Prideaux, 'Trains: the rolling stock companies' in Roger Freeman and Jon Shaw , eds, *All*

Change: British Railway Privatisation p.107, McGraw Hill 2000. His calculations show that there were 1,043 BR coaches delivered in 1993–7 at a price of £890m compared with 1,952 vehicles at a cost of £2001m ordered in 1996–9 by the privatised rolling stock companies. The higher cost reflects the fact that some maintenance is now usually included as part of the deal.

5 Provided to the author.

6 Railtrack, *Network Management Statement, 1995/6*, 1995.

7 Interview with author.

8 John Swift, 'The role of the rail regulator', in Roger Freeman and Jon Shaw, eds, *All Change: British Railway Privatisation*, p.225, McGraw Hill, 2000.

9 Actually, Railtrack was, in a sense, right. There are no commercially viable investments on the network which can pay for themselves without subsidy. That was a harsh truth which those who privatised the railway failed to understand.

10 Interview with author.

11 *On Track*, the bulletin of the Strategic Rail Authority, No. 2, covering the period 1 April 2000 to 14 October 2000.

12 Interview with author.

13 Booz Allen Hamilton, *Railtrack's Performance in the control period 1995–2001*, p.13, Office of the Rail Regulator, March 1999.

14 Booz Allen Hamilton, *Railtrack's Performance in the control period 1995–2001*, p.22, Office of the Rail Regulator, March 1999.

15 Booz Allen Hamilton, *Railtrack's Performance in the control period 1995–2001*, p.22, Office of the Rail Regulator, March 1999.

16 Interview with author.

17 Interview with author.

18 Interview with author.

19 Interview with author.

20 Interview with author.

21 *Modern Railways*, July 2001.

22 Railfreight Group press release, 6 April 2001.

23 Interview with author.

24 Railtrack press statement, 24 May 2001.

25 How, for example, can the operator make a rate of return on the investment? And who exactly owns the improved section of track or new points?

26 The precise number will not be known until all the franchises have been let as some may be merged during the process.

27 Reliable source.

28 See Wolmar column in *Rail*, 16–29 May 2001, for further details.

29 Interview with author.

30 Press release, 15 February 2001.

31 Interview with author.

32 Department of Environment, Transport and the Regions, *Transport 2010, the 10 year plan*, DETR, 2000.

33 Evidence to the Commons Transport (sub) Committee, 1 May 2001.

34 BBC *Newsnight*, 22 May 2001.

35 Booz Allen Hamilton, *Railtrack's Performance in the control period 1995–2001*, p.21, Office of the Rail Regulator, March 1999.

36 Rana Roy, *A Plan for Growth? An analysis of the 10 Year Plan's perspective for rail*, Railway Forum, March 2001.

CHAPTER TWELVE

1 Memorandum provided to the author.

2 Interview with author.

3 Interview with author.

4 Peter Rayner, *On and Off the Rails*, Novelangle, 1997.

5 Lord Cullen, *The Ladbroke Grove Rail Inquiry, Part 1 report*, p.59, HSE, 2001.
6 *Financial Times*, 7 May 2001.
7 T.R. Gourvish, *British Railways 1948–73: a Business History*, Cambridge University Press, 1986.
8 *The Times*, 25 May 2001.
9 *Financial Times*, 27 June 2001.
10 *Evening Standard*, 5 June 2001.
11 *Independent on Sunday*, 24 June 2001.
12 E-mail to author.
13 Interview with author.
14 *Modern Railways*, August 2001.
15 David Henshaw, *The Great Railway Conspiracy*, p.229, Leading Edge, 1991.

Index